AF395566

COLD WAR II

COLD WAR II

How the War in Ukraine Changed the World

MARC EWERT

FRONTLINE
BOOKS

COLD WAR II
How the War in Ukraine Changed the World

First published in Great Britain in 2026
by Frontline Books
An imprint of
Pen & Sword Books Ltd
Yorkshire - Philadelphia
Copyright © Marc Ewert
ISBN 9781036193638

Typeset by Lapiz Digital
Printed and bound in the UK by CPI Group (UK) Ltd,
Croydon, CR0 4YY.

Printed on paper from a sustainable source by
CPI Group (UK) Ltd, Croydon, CR0 4YY

The Publisher's authorised representative in the EU for product safety is
Authorised Rep Compliance Ltd., Ground Floor, 71 Lower Baggot Street,
Dublin D02 P593, Ireland.
www.arccompliance.com

For a complete list of Pen & Sword titles please contact
PEN & SWORD BOOKS LTD
47 Church Street, Barnsley, South Yorkshire, S70 2AS, England
E-mail: enquiries@pen-and-sword.co.uk
Website: www.pen-and-sword.co.uk
or
PEN & SWORD BOOKS
1950 Lawrence Rd, Havertown, PA 19083, USA
E-mail: uspen-and-sword@casematepublishers.com

"I dedicate this book to my family and loved ones who have been a source of support and ideation. I also extend my gratitude to the staff of Pen and Sword who have helped shape the final product."

CONTENTS

ABBREVIATIONS

AfD	Alternative Für Deutschland Party
AI	Artificial Intelligence
ASEAN	Association of Southeast Asian Nations
ATCAMS	Army Tactical Missile System
BBC	British Broadcasting Corporation
BLM	Black Lives Matter
BRICS	Brazil, Russia, India, China, South Africa
BYPOL	Association of Security of Belarus
CAR	Central African Republic
CIA	Central Intelligence Agency
CSTO	Collective Security Treaty Organization
DPR	Donetsk People's Republic
ECOWAS	Economic Community of West African States
EU	European Union
EUMA	European Union Mission in Armenia
FSB	Federal'naya Sluzhba Bezopasnosti Rossiyskoy Federatsii (Federal Security Service)
GDP	Gross Domestic Product
GPS	Global Positioning System
HIMAS	High Mobility Artillery Rocket System
HMCS	Her/His Majesty's Canadian Ship
HTS	Hayat Tahrir al-Sham
ICC	International Court Case
ICJ	International Court of Justice
IDF	Israel Defense Forces
IED	Improvised Explosive Device
IRGC	Islamic Revolutionary Guard Corps
ISIL	Islamic State of Iraq and the Levant
ISIS	Islamic State
ISW	Institute for the Study of War

LGBTQ	Lesbian, Gay, Bisexual, Transgender or Queer
LPR	Luhansk People's Republic
MSS	Military Support Site
NASA	National Aeronautics and Space Administration
NATO	North Atlantic Treaty Organization
NGO	Non-Governmental Organisation
OSCE	Organization for Security and Co-operation in Europe
PMC	Private Military Company
PKK	Kurdistan Workers' Party
POW	Prisoner of War
RAF	Royal Air Force
RSF	Rapid Support Force
SAF	Sudanese Armed Forces
SDF	Syrian Democratic Forces
SFA	Syrian Free Army
SKS	Samozaryadny karabin Simonova (Simonov self-loading carbine)
SNA	Syrian National Army
THAAD	Terminal High Altitude Area Defense
UAE	United Arab Emirates
UAV	Unmanned Aeriel Vehicle
UFC	Ultimate Fighting Champion
UK	United Kingdom
UN	United Nations
US/USA	United States/United States of America
US Navy SEAL	United States Navy Sea, Air and Land
USAID	United States Agency for International Development
USS	United States Ship
USSR	Union of the Social Soviet Republics
VIP	Very Important Person

INTRODUCTION

The intent of this book is to inform the reader of the current cold war that we all now live under, chronicling each major event that has happened during the Biden administration and the early Trump administration. The aim is to educate the public of the radically changing geopolitics of the globe, caused by Russia's invasion of Ukraine in 2022. The world is now facing the Second Cold War, around thirty years after the end of the First Cold War.

Since the Russian invasion of Ukraine, the world has seen a significant rise in nuclear and military threats between world powers. It has also seen the polarisations of nations, the significant deterioration of foreign relations, economic and food crises, and the rise in countries' aggression towards neighbouring nations territorial integrity.

The invasion in 2022 has led to countries intensifying their pre-existing antagonisms against each other and aligning with others. Relations between Russia, Iran and China have quickly strengthened in this period, due to their opposition towards the US and the West. The world is now separated into three blocs: the West, the Russian bloc, and the neutral benefactors, quite like how the Iron Curtain divided nations into blocs during the First Cold War.

The West consists of NATO countries, and their other allied nations and non-state actors across the globe. The Russia bloc consists of Russia, Iran, North Korea, Syria, and other aligned state and non-state actors across the globe. China would be considered a neutral benefactor, factoring the country's initial hesitancy to provide aid to the Russian war effort. However, due to the rising tensions in the South China Sea and from its neighbours, China is increasingly aligning itself with the Russian bloc against the West. Neutral benefactors, such as Turkey, India and South Africa, play off both blocs with the attempt to accomplish their own interests and economic success. Neutral benefactors, such as India and Turkey, play off the Western and Russian blocs in order to help them establish themselves as global and regional superpower nations respectively. These benefactors appeared neutral during the early years of the Second Cold War. However, as the years have progressed, they have become emerging superpowers that are confronting the Russian bloc, China and the West, with their diplomacy and engagement in proxy wars. The Second Cold War at first was a bipolar conflict between the West and Russia, akin to the First Cold War. However, as the years have progressed, it has steadily become a semi-multipolar conflict, and tensions and proxy wars have steadily become a free for all arena between the superpowers and emerging superpowers of the US, Russia, China, Turkey, India and Iran. As shall be explored in the final chapter, even the US has become an emerging remote superpower, separate from Europe, at the turn of Donald Trump's second presidency, due to Vladimir Putin's exploitation of the West's internal political infighting. The US' growing detachment from Europe adds to the complexity of the Second Cold War's multipolar conflict.

An argument can be made that the Second Cold War started prior to the invasion of Ukraine in 2022 with the Euromaidan revolution and the Russian annexation of Crimea in 2014, where relations between the West and Russia became antagonistic. However, the author argues that the events in 2014 were not to the extreme rivalry and existential gravitas of the events of 2022 between the West and Russia. Russia's actions in Crimea and the Donbas were received with weak condemnation and little international effort was made to stop Putin's advances. However, 2014 was a significant year in which Russian-Western relations started to sour.

The current cold war that we face is not a global wrestle for ideologies like the previous one. It is a competition between the US and Russia for ultimate superpower status by competing for influence over countries and establishing satellite states around the globe. In this competition, up-and-coming countries play the game for superpower status by exploiting the Russo-American rivalries, such as Turkey, Iran and India.

The era of empires and colonial competition came to an end by the mid-twentieth century. We now face a new era of imperialism. Some call the new era neo-colonialism, while others refer to these new forms of empires as superpowers. Countries that are considered as superpowers are nations that have heavy influence over their respective region, and for some, even global supranational influence. This form of imperialism lacks the features of contemporary empires, such as forced occupation over far-off countries. Superpowers spread their neo-colonial grasps over countries by entangling other nations' economy to their own to a point where the said nations are heavily dependent on the superpower. This can be seen with the global superpower nation of China, whose economy and trade are so embedded in various nations that it is near impossible to detach Chinese economic influences away from the global economy.

The nations' attempts to rid themselves of Chinese-embedded economic influence would risk the destabilisation of their economies. Other forms of influence are lethal aid provisions to nations who are wary of a military aggression from another country. This act of military support would increase friendly relations with the said nation and make the nation reliant on their superpower ally. This can be seen with the ultimate global superpower of the US, who's military aid and support towards European nations makes the European military wholly reliant on the US against a possible Russian military aggression. The superpower era of imperial history started in 1945 with the beginning of the First Cold War and seemed to have ended in 1991 when the US won the competition against the Soviet Union, becoming the sole and ultimate global superpower in the world. However, since 2022, the US' reign as the sole and ultimate global superpower has been shaken and tested by various other nations vowing for global influence, hoping to surpass the US' ultimate superpower status.

The rise of democratic-liberalism and authoritarian-communist ideologies hugely impacted the conduct of twentieth century imperialism. Both ideologies detested acts of forceful colonialism. During the cold wars, the American and Russian empires established global influence mostly through indirect control over nations. The world wars saw the sharp decline of contemporary European empires and the emergence of the US and the Soviet Union filling the void. The capitalist American and communist Soviet empires sought to compete for influence over Europe and the world to counter the spread of each other's differing ideology during the First Cold War. Political ideology of capitalist-rightism and communist-leftism was the fuel that drove the First Cold War. With the fall of the Soviet Union in 1991, Russia adhered to capitalism and democracy.

By the mid-2010s, Russia pursued, in earnest, the restoration of its former-global superpower status and aimed to compete over the US' status as the ultimate global superpower. The Second Cold War is, therefore, not a war over ideology like its predecessor, but rather a calculated war between competing superpower nations. Such behaviour is reminiscent of the 1871 to 1914 period in which European empires, such as France, Britain and Russia, were antagonistic towards the Imperial German Empire, but not because of the German's political ideology. Rather Europe was in a state of cold war-esque tensions due to the rise of the Central European nations' growing oversea imperial ambitions, which threatened its neighbouring countries' imperial holdings and colonial trade.

The possession of nuclear weapons also plays into the moulding of superpower empires' imperial conduct as it has forced the superpowers to indirectly engage with their competitors in fear of global nuclear destruction. As shall be seen throughout this book, the nuclear factor has influenced superpowers' foreign policy to indirectly inflict damage or hinderance towards competing superpowers, without risking a world war or nuclear destruction.

There are three categories of superpower status: regional, global and ultimate global. The first two are self-explanatory: regional superpower nations have dominant influence over their respective region, whilst global superpowers have influences on an inter-continental scale. Regional superpowers naturally vie for global superpower status and global superpowers nations thereafter compete for sole ultimate global superpower status. The ultimate global superpower status refers to the superpower nation whose influences over the world are unmatched by other global-superpower competitors.

In the twenty-first century, China has become the US' main superpower competitor, as China's growing global influences are threatening the legitimacy and authority of the US' ultimate global-superpower status.

Russia emerged from the rubble of the collapse of the Soviet Union and became a regional superpower when Putin won the Second Chechen War, and the Georgian War in 2008. Putin attempted to make Russia a global superpower once more with the Russian intervention in the Syrian Civil War, the formation of BRICS and the invasion of Ukraine.

Several may look at this book's title and roll their eyes. They believe that the claims that the world being plunged into the Second Cold War are merely exaggerations derived from hysteria. However, the countless times our leaders have threatened the use of war and nuclear weapons are abundant within the first couple of years since the invasion of Ukraine in 2022. There have been four incidences, in a span of three years in which it appeared that a world war was imminent. The first was on 24 February 2022 with the Russian invasion of Ukraine. We all anticipated a Russian invasion of Ukraine after the Russian build up on the Ukrainian border, but we were all surprised when the invasion actually occurred. The author recalls watching the news intently. The House of Commons was in uproar. However, not against each other like they usually do, but in unison. The once boring and repetitive watch of the House of Commons bared an intense atmosphere, and their anger led to them thirsting for war. An intense wait began for President Joseph 'Joe' Biden's declaration of war against Russia. However, Biden made a speech declaring that the US and NATO would not be going to war.

The second instance in which the world appeared to be on the brink of a third world war was on 2 August 2022, with China's response to the House of Representatives' Speaker Nancy Pelosi's visit to Taiwan. This incident, of course, would not have led to a third world war, but the invasion of Ukraine was fresh in the Western public and press memory. Strange how this incident has been outdone by other incidents that occurred after this event, in terms of severity and causing global tensions. However, the media does not portray successive incidents as nearing to a third world war like they did with the Pelosi visit. Global tensions have become the norm now.

The third time was when Russia accidently bombed a farm in Prezwodów, Poland killing two people on 15 November 2022. NATO's Article 4 was initiated. However, the NATO nations did not retaliate in any noteworthy form against Russia. The cause of the deaths of the two farmers was investigated. However, it was more complex than initially believed, as shall be discussed in Chapter Three.

Both Pelosi's visit to Taiwan and the bombing of the Polish farm are now largely forgotten by today's population.

Biden's eventual decision to permit Ukrainian use of Western long-range missiles against Russian infrastructure and Putin's reactionary threats in November 2024, was a fourth incident in which the world was close to nuclear Armageddon. However, at this point, the author, like most people, with pessimism, dismissed the geopolitical back and forth as yet another exchange of political threats and bluffs. The common exchange of nuclear blackmail became a frequent but mundane feature of the Second Cold War, to which many have grown accustomed.

The world has become more on edge and is nearing militarism with conscription being considered or introduced in Western and other countries. Countries are beginning to choose a side and people's political beliefs are more embedded and intolerable with others. Not only has Western culture shifted following the invasion of Ukraine, but foreign diplomacy has shifted drastically. In the First Cold War, international law was broken numerous times, but not to the frequent and unapologetic extents of the early years of the Second Cold War. International law has been broken numerous times on small and large scales. However, there has been a lack of effective punishment inflicted on the criminal country/leader by the international community.

Chapter One

THE SHAPING OF A NEW COLD WAR

Russia's Fight for Integrity

The immediate dissolution of the Soviet Union sent cheers and celebrations across the Western world. The existential fear hidden behind everyone's mind of a third world war or nuclear holocaust dissipated. The Warsaw Pact crumbled under the revolutions of 1989, the Berlin Wall fell and the Kremlin folded their communist flag in 1991. Capitalism and democracy had won and political scientist Francis Fukuyama declared history to be over.

Russia's 'short twentieth century', as described by historians, came to an end in 1991 and the Russian people struggled in the aftermath. Economic insecurities and disgruntlement ensued. Russian identity was in question. Neighbouring nations in the Caucasus and Eastern Europe fell into regional disputes, causing decades of civil war, ethnic violence and separatist movements. In the eyes of the former Soviet people, their plight was caused by the decisions of Mikhail Gorbachev. Western opinion regarding Gorbachev as 'The good Russian', who had seen the futility of the First Cold War rivalries and sought friendly relations with the West and folded, to ensure peace and avoidance of destruction. This could not be further from the truth when inspecting the domestic and economic turmoil that wrought the Soviet Union in its final years due to Gorbachev's indecisiveness. The death of Gorbachev, in August 2022, was saddening for Western politicians who had worked with him during his presidential years. However, to the Russians a bitter shrug was given, as they had viewed him as the fumbling architecture of Russia's (and former Soviet nations') plight. The failure of the Russian capitalist system under the late Gorbachev rule and under Boris Yeltsin, laid the groundwork for Russian self-victimisation and anti-Western sentiments, which Putin later exploited to rally the Russian people to his cause during the Second Cold War.

The coup attempt to maintain the USSR's integrity in 1991 ended with Yeltsin emerging as the saviour of the situation. This contributed to his success in the first Russian Federation's presidential elections. Yeltsin did well to normalise relations with the NATO and neighbouring countries. Yeltsin sought the Budapest Memorandum in 1994 to defuse Russia's worry that they would lose their nuclear stockpile to former soviet nations. This memorandum ensured Russian, American and British security assurance towards the sovereignty of Belarus, Ukraine and Kazakhstan in exchange for the transfer of soviet nukes to be returned to Russia.

The successor state of the Russian Federation under Boris Yeltsin faced domestic challenges. The Russian shift to a free-market economy was experiencing growing pains, with Russians enduring declining electricity, wages and quality of life. Russia faced a rise in crime rate, food insecurities and political corruption in the immediate post-Soviet Russia. Russia had been relegated to a regional superpower and lost its world-power status during the 1990s, which humiliated the Russian people. The Russian army's failure in the First Chechen War deepened Russian humiliation as it proved that Russia could not even be an effective regional power. In the immediate post-Cold War years, Russia tried to reassert its influence across the former Soviet states with limited success.

Russian relations with the US were relatively friendly until the late 1990s in which NATO membership admissions of former Warsaw Pact nations were highly criticised by Yeltsin. NATO's eastward expansion was perceived as a threat to Russian security and was seen as aggressive despite Russo-American rivalries coming to an end. President Vladimir Putin initially adopted a friendly approach toward the West. However, he too saw NATO's expansionism as a threat to Russia's security and encroaching on Russia's sphere of influence in Europe. Putinist propaganda claims that the West promised Gorbachev not to expand NATO eastwards. However, no such agreements was ever drafted or signed. NATO expansionism never violated any treaty agreement or international law. Despite the end of the First Cold War, Western media and politicians still portrayed Russia as an aggressor state, causing many Russians to fear that the US was still playing the cold war game and that this Western narrative would spread to former Soviet nations, further isolating Russia from its neighbours.

Putin attempted to revitalise Russia from the rump state that it became after the fall of the Soviet Union. Putin reversed the international embarrassment of the First Chechen War with the successful Second Chechen War. Putin attempted to re-establish Russia back to its global superpower status by engaging in foreign diplomacy with the West initially. Thereafter, Russian foreign policy served as a means to counter Western influences against Russia's neighbours, which the Kremlin sees as Russia's 'sphere of influence'. Putin's ideology, motives and intentions behind his diplomacy are highly disputed.

The Cold Peace

Historically, Russian and American relations were at its peak during the 1990s and early 2000s. Western countries would reapproach Moscow to seek friendly political and economic relations. NATO and Russia held cooperative meetings and summits concerning joint nation security (against Islamic fundamentalism). The West's relationship and security summits with Russia subsided somewhat following the Georgian War in 2008 and after a series of Russian assassination attempts of Russian nationals in NATO countries. NATO-Russian collective security programmes ceased in 2014 following Russia's annexation of Crimea.

The colour revolutions throughout the 2000s were a series of revolutions in which protesters from former Soviet republics, demanded that their semi-democratic governments shake off their autocratic constitutional designs, and embrace democracy fully. However, Moscow viewed the revolutions as a ploy by the American government to enlarge its sphere of influence across to Eastern Europe.

The US' increasing oil and gas deals in the former Soviet Central Asian countries and recognition of Kosovo as a separate country from Serbia, undermined Russia's sphere of influence and foreign policy. In 2008, American President George W. Bush publicly vowed to support Georgian and Ukrainian membership into NATO. The combination of American recognition of Kosovo as a sovereign nation and desires to collect Russia's neighbours into NATO, led to Russia invading Georgia, in order to establish a military presence in Georgia's self-proclaimed Republic of South Ossetia and Abkhazia, thwarting Georgian admission into NATO.

The Ukrainian revolution in 2014 took place in response to Ukrainian President Viktor Yanukovych's decision to not allow Ukraine to join the EU. The protests grew in popularity in Kyiv and western Ukraine but were met with violent counter-riot police. The violence that ensued grew to disproportionate levels and the revolution came to an end when Yanukovych fled the country, after the Euromaidans threatened to storm the parliamentary building if Yanukovych did not immediately resign. There was a real risk that Ukraine would fall into a civil war. With the aid of Russian escorts, Yanukovych fled to Crimea and then to Russia. The Euromaidans and western Ukrainians cheered. However, the protests were perceived as a coup by the ethnic Russian Ukrainians residing in the Donetsk and Luhansk regions. The majority of Ukrainians in the eastern Ukrainian regions were against the idea of joining the EU.

Putin exploited the scene by sending his 'Little Green Men' to Crimea in an attempt to annex the region. It was later revealed that these 'Little Green Men' were soldiers of the Russian PMC, the Wagner Group. Crimea has a significant economic value to Russia, as the peninsula due to its geographical position in the Black Sea, has various ports of which can be used for exports of Russian goods. Putin later justified the annexation of Crimea as a means of uniting the Russian Crimean people with Russia proper. Putin claimed that this uniting of Russian peoples was to protect the Crimean Russians from Ukrainian discrimination and prevent Crimea's absorption into the West.

Western countries refused to recognise the Russian annexation of Crimea. Light sanctions were imposed on Russia by the EU, and NATO troops were sent to Eastern European nations that neighboured Ukraine's Western borders to deter further Russian annexation attempts. However, American President Barack Obama's efforts to pressure Putin to reverse the Crimean annexation were a failure, and the West's imposed sanctions were feeble. Obama rejected military intervention as he feared that it would have escalated into a third world war. The world continued on, accepting Crimea as Russian territory.

A separatist civil war ensued in eastern Ukraine following the annexation of Crimea. The disgruntled Ukrainians in the Donetsk and Luhansk oblasts declared themselves as separate republics from Ukraine. Russia backed the separatists and provided diplomatic and lethal aid support. Russian troops were sent to fight the Ukrainian army in Novoazovsk and Ilovaisk during August 2014. The Donbas conflict subsided in 2015 after the Minsk II ceasefire agreements, which resulted in the Ukrainian and separatist military disengaging from the Donbas front lines, the establishment of a demilitarised buffer zone, and the establishment of dialogue between Kyiv and the separatist republics. The Minsk II ceasefire agreements were created by the Ukrainians, Russians Belarusians, Germans and French. Despite several violations of its terms by the Russians, the Minsk II ceasefire agreements rendered the civil war into a frozen conflict. However, minor skirmishes continued, and the Kyiv-Donbas dialogue was steadily deteriorating by 2017/2018. The frozen conflict status of the war, thwarted Ukraine's chances of joining NATO, as countries cannot acquire NATO status if they are currently in a conflict.

NATO-Russian relations, during the years 2014 to 2022, were characterised by sporadic aerial incidents and standoffs, an increase in Russian nationals being poisoned in NATO territories by the Kremlin, an increase in both blocs' nuclear weapons stockpiles, and in an increasingly militarised line of contact between the CSTO and NATO. Historians may mark 2014 as the beginning of the Second Cold War. However, the author argues against this because Obama backed down on antagonising Russia's encroachment onto Ukraine's sovereignty. The subsequent American president, Donald Trump, rarely antagonised Russia during his presidency. The European nations initially condemned Russia in 2014 but then continued to accept Russian gas like a drug addict and the world accepted Crimea as Russian land. It was only in 2022, that the US, under President Joe Biden, staunchly opposed Russia. The Russian invasion of Ukraine in 2014 did not result in nuclear threats being exchanged, unlike the invasion of Ukraine in 2022.

Russia's encroachment of Ukrainian sovereignty caused rising tensions between Russia and the West. During the Syrian Civil War, Putin backed Syrian President Bashar al-Assad, which conflicted with Obama's campaign for the resignation of the Syrian dictator.

Russo-American tensions subsided with the presidency of Trump in 2017. Trump had made many kind remarks towards Putin and had attempted to reapproach Russia and overlook past Russian aggressive foreign diplomacy. Trump tried to bring Putin out of diplomatic isolationism in Europe by attempting to invite him to international summits and inviting him to visit Washington for diplomatic talks. Several intense moments occurred during Trump's presidency, such as the Battle of Khasham in 2018 in which American forces bombed Russia's PMC, the Wagner Group, in Syria, resulting in over 100 Russian casualties. The incident was highly condemned by Russia, but it did not result in serious escalations.

A Russian propaganda narrative, which has gained popularity and attraction in Russian and American discourse is that the West violated an agreement made in 1990 between German and American leaders, and Mikhail Gorbachev that NATO would not expand eastward and accept former communist states accession into NATO. This overblown narrative has led to countless anti-West rhetorics and Russian sympathetic remarks towards Putin amongst Russians and right-wing Westerners. In reality this 'promise' was made in a passive conversation but was never implemented into a written and signed document or treaty. The 'promise' was never fully taken seriously and was forgotten by both the Western and Soviet politicians as Gorbachev had little bargaining power to put this idea into reality. This insignificant exchange between Gorbachev and the Western leaders has become a major propaganda tool by Moscow during the twenty-first century Second Cold War, to fool people into believing that NATO expanded eastward via aggression and by violating international treaties. The reality was that this 'promise' was quickly forgotten by both parties in 1990 and that former communist countries willingly, under no coercion, applied for NATO membership. NATO's eastward expansion was championed by Putin, who wanted Russia to be accepted into NATO during his early presidency, proving the falsehoods of the NATO expansion eastward as an international scandal.

Many Russian narratives claim that NATO expansion eastwards were a series of aggressive actions aimed at threatening Russian sovereignty. However, NATO expansion, in the eyes of Putin, does not hold a serious threat to Russia, rather it undermines Russia's foreign policy and fight to regain global superpower status. Differentiating Moscow's real perception of NATO expansion as an undermining of Russia's path towards global superpower status from the Russian propaganda narratives that NATO expansion aimed to threaten Russian sovereignty is crucial in understanding the causes of the Second Cold War. Russia during the inter-cold war period was trying to regain its regional and global superpower status. The expansion of the uncontested American superpower influences across the globe undermined Russia's goal indirectly. During the inter-cold war period, American antagonism was directed towards Islamic fundamentalism and dictatorships in the Middle East, not towards Russia. Bush and Putin maintained friendly relations until 2008 and European nations were reapproaching Russia for gas imports and geopolitical leverage for their own diplomatic gains. Encroaching on Russian sovereignty was far beyond both the US and Europe's agenda.

The West's wars in the Middle East indirectly caused Russo-American tensions. The US' dismissal of international law and invading Iraq in 2003 and the West's intervention in the Arab spring and winter, was controversial amongst Russian circles. The forceful toppling of dictators and the establishment of successor Western aligned governments in the Middle East made Moscow fear that the West would adopt a similar approach in Eastern Europe. This can be seen in Moscow's reaction to the colour revolutions and the Euromaidan revolution. Washington's recognition of the separatist nation of Kosovo in 2008 was seen as the US disregarding international law yet again following the US' illegal invasion of Iraq in 2003. The US' attempts to legitimise an illegitimate democratic Western orientated state undermined Russian influence in the Balkans. The Western conduct in the Middle East served to undermine prospects of Russia expanding its geopolitical influences in the Middle East, thwarting their global superpower aspirations there. The unchecked streak of the US' ever expanding geopolitical influence across the globe during the 2000s was met with ineffective punitive reinforcement mechanisms from the UN. Prospects of Eastern Europe establishing pro-Western democratic governments served to undermine Russia's foreign policy with its neighbours and its path to regain its regional superpower status. The Russian intervention in Georgia (2008), Ukraine (2014) and Syria (2015) was a means of countering the American superpower spreading American influences in areas of Russian interest. American expansionism did not serve as a threat to Russian sovereignty, rather it served to undermine Russia's desire to regain its global superpower status.

The US' uncontested global superpower projection and NATO expansion was not directed to weaken Russia. Rather their foreign policy, aimed at establishing democratic governments in Eastern Europe and the Middle East, overlooked Russian insecurities and indirectly caused friction between Russia and the West.

The Foot in the Door Doctrine

In 2005, Putin referred to the dissolution of the USSR in 1991 as a catastrophe because '10 million' Russian patriots were left outside of the Russian borders and it was difficult for them to rejoin. There is indeed a large Russian demographic in Eastern European countries. In 1993, it was estimated that 25 million Russians lived in former USSR countries. There were 12.5 million ethnic Russians who found themselves in Belarus and Ukraine.[1]

Just below 1 million Russians lived in the Central Asian countries of Kazakhstan and Kyrgyzstan.[2] Approximately 15 per cent of Moldova's population were ethnic Russians, mostly residing in the eastern Transnistrian provinces.[3] The Russian ethnic groups made up around 30 per cent of the populations of Estonia and Latvia.[4] There is a large Russian demographic in the Baltic countries due to centuries of Russian migration in the years of the tsar and the USSR. Baltic nations fear that Putin will exploit the Russian demography within the Baltic countries for the purposes of fifth-columnist activities and pretexts for Russian expansion. Baltic anxiety has unfortunately led to anti-Russian policies and behaviour.[5] Years of massacres, oppression, wars and suffering, especially during the twentieth century, have made the Baltic peoples staunchly anti-Russian. Many former Soviet nations, such as the Baltic states and Poland, fear that Russia would use their Russian ethnic minority groups for fifth-column activities and as a pretext for invasion. Hence, their ambitions to join NATO during the 1990s and 2000s. The loss of the Baltic states to NATO in 2004 served as a sore to Moscow's supranational goals. Many Russians worried for the Russian diaspora in the former Soviet nations, as it was well known that they faced discrimination from the native populations and did not have civic rights to migrate to Russia.

Putin's calls for a united Russian people and the presence of the oligarchy within Russian society suggests that he is a pan-Russianist. Many analysts describe Putin as a pan-Russianist who wanted to unite the Russian people in neighbouring countries to Russia proper. Although Putin uses this rhetoric in public conferences, he is not genuine in his pan-Russianist remarks. Putin uses these remarks in order to gain domestic and international sympathies for Moscow's invasive foreign policies onto neighbouring countries. Moscow's protectionist rhetoric over certain ethnic groups are used as a pretext to Russian intervention in existing conflicts within the post-Soviet countries. The true aim of Putin's invasive foreign policies are not to come to the aid of ethnic groups, but to forcefully keep neighbouring countries in the Russian sphere of influence against its will. This can be seen with Georgia and Ukraine. In 2008, when Georgia publicly voiced its desires to join NATO and invaded the separatist republic of South Ossetia, Russia utilised protectionist rhetoric over the ethnic Abkhazian and South Ossetian minority and supported their desire for national self-determination. This was used as a pretext for the Russian armed forces' invasion of Georgian sovereignty and indefinite occupation of the northern separatist regions of Georgia.

This occupation thwarted Georgia's entry into NATO as nations are only accepted into NATO if they are not in active or frozen conflicts. Russia used the ethnic Russian Ukrainians in Crimea and Donbas as a pretext to invade Crimea and Donbas as a means of preventing Ukraine joining the EU in 2014 and NATO in 2022. In the case for Crimea, the large Russian ethnic makeup was exploited by Moscow to annex the peninsula, to ensure that Russian naval presence in Crimea and the Black Sea was not undermined in the scenario that the new Ukrainian government joined the EU or NATO. Moscow's foreign policy can be described as a 'foot in the door' doctrine, used to expand

and maintain Russian influence abroad. If Putin was a genuine pan-Russianist as described by analysts and observers, then Moscow would have enforced a similar doctrine onto neighbouring Kazakhstan and Belarus. Putin has not enforced the 'foot in the door' doctrine onto these countries due to Russia's strong influence in these countries and their loyalty to Moscow. Moscow's 'foot in the door' doctrine and its self-portrayal as the protectorate of certain ethnic groups are challenged during the Second Cold War, which shall be explored later in this book.

Ethnic groups, such as Abkhazians, South Ossetians and Russian minority groups, are used by the Kremlin as a foreign-policy tool to negate countries from joining NATO. This foreign-policy instrument is also used as a neo-imperialist tool to establish Russian military bases in the separatist republics, deterring nations from reconquering their land via military means. Once Russian troops are integrated into the separatist republics' defences, the separatists become more prone to Russification due to Russian orientated policies being embedded into separatist institutions. The separatist states become wholly reliant on Moscow (both in defence and economy). International non-recognition and non-engagement with the separatist republics serves to put these separatist republics under geopolitical isolation, limiting their foreign dialogue and cooperation to only Moscow. The 'foot in the door' doctrine serves to negate NATO expansion and to assert and maintain Russian influence in neighbouring countries. International isolation of these separatist republics and Russian imposed social engineering policies play hand in hand with Russia consolidating its control over nations' regions.

The exertive and imperialist nature of the 'foot in the door' doctrine has made many NATO Eastern European nations, such as Poland and the Baltic states, fearful that the Kremlin would use the ethnic Russian minorities in the Baltic states and Poland as a foreign policy tool as a means to expand Russian influence in their country via inciting separatist movements or invasion. Many Westerners scorn this argument by arguing that Russia would not dare to expand into NATO territories as Article 5 acts as a strong deterrent. However, the final chapters of this book analyse how Russia aims to accomplish Russian expansionism in Eastern Europe by disuniting NATO countries via ideological and political discourse, undermining Article 5.

The Perfect Time to Strike

Donald Trump's criticisms towards the US' European allies resulted in a dent in European-American relations, contributing to the disunity of NATO, which played into Russia's interests. NATO's infighting, decreased spending in Western defence and Brexit, undermined the

West's cohesion and undermined NATO's international prestige, prompting Russia's confidence to commit its expansionist policies in Eastern Europe.

Many Western nations were experiencing internal strife and polarisation. As a product of Britain's insecurities in its place in the increasingly globalised world, having to adhere to mass migration and EU obligations, around 52 per cent of Britons voted for Brexit, dismembering the UK from the EU. This caused petty infighting between UK and EU politicians. Many European nations' unstable relationship with the US began to stabilise following Trump's electoral loss in 2020. American disunity and political violence led to the 6 January riots in which disgruntled Trump supporters stormed the American Capitol in protest to Joe Biden's inauguration. Many of the protesters believed that the elections in 2020 were rigged against Trump. The US' disunity, and the humiliating withdrawal from Afghanistan in 2021, indicated to Putin that Russian interests in Ukraine had to be realised within the timeframe of Biden's presidency due to NATO's weak geopolitical posture.

Exploiting NATO's weakness and the rising tensions between Kyiv and the self-declared Donbas republics, Russia sent over 100,000 of its troops to the Ukrainian border, stretching from Ukraine's northern, eastern and southern borders between October 2021 and February 2022. The inauguration of Ukrainian President Volodymyr Zelensky in 2019 raised Putin's eyebrows, as Zelensky publicly campaigned for Ukraine to join the Western bloc. Putin, therefore, believed that Ukraine had to be taken by force in order to coercively sway Ukraine away from Western influences. During Russia's military build-up, pro-Russian forces allegedly attempted to overthrow and assassinate Zelensky, in an attempt to establish a pro-Russian puppet in Ukraine, before invading the country. Several false-flag incidents occurred along the line of contact, and separatist skirmishes escalated in early February 2022. Putin wanted to repeat the Georgian War strategy of 2008 by exploiting Ukraine's separatist republics to insert Russian presence and influence in eastern Ukraine, stopping Ukraine from entering NATO. On 22 February 2022, Putin recognised the DPR and LPR and on 24 February 2022, the Russian army invaded Ukraine. The world nervously waited for Biden to declare war on Russia in response. Russian nuclear sites were on full alert, anticipating an American nuclear response.[6] However, Biden announced that the US would not join the Ukraine War, and thus a third world war was avoided. The 24 February 2022 shall be forever known as the day in which Russia invaded Ukraine and the day in which the Second Cold War had commenced.

Chapter Two

THE UKRAINE WAR

The Invasion of Ukraine
Russia invaded Ukraine on 24 February 2022, via four axis crossings
from Russian occupied Crimea, the Ukrainian-Belarusian border,
and through the Russo-Ukrainian border along the Ukrainian
eastern and northeastern provinces. Russia's objectives were to take
Kyiv and Kharkiv to decapitate Ukraine's political institute. Russian
objectives were to also conquer the Donbas region to prevent Ukraine
joining NATO after the war.

The Russian army also desired to capture the southern oblasts
and rob Ukraine of its naval and shipping capabilities (with future
operations targeting the city of Odessa if Kyiv refused to capitulate).
As many as 6 million Ukrainians fled the country. Zelensky ordered
a general mobilisation and forbade males aged 18 to 60 from leaving
the country. However, over 700,000 Ukrainian males had managed
to flee to European countries in the West via various means, such
as bribery. Russia made significant gains in the south, capturing the
cities of Melitopol, Enerhodar and Kherson in a matter of days. They
even advanced at lightning speed to the city Mykolaiv. However,
the Ukrainians managed to successfully hold the city against the
Russian army in April 2022, marking the first significant victory of the
Ukrainians on the southern front.

Russian forces on the eastern front, established their occupation of
the Donetsk oblast with their separatist ally, the DPR. However, the
most dramatic event in the eastern invasion of Ukraine was the Battle
of Mariupol. The Russian army managed to encircle the city, trapping
the well-trained Azov Battalion and Ukrainian marine brigades. All
roads were cut off by the Russian forces, leaving the Ukrainian forces
no choice but to fight. The fighting was intense and both sides suffered

heavy casualties. Despite the high Russian casualty rates in Mariupol, Russian forces continued to break the besieged Ukrainian defences and on 15 April. The Ukrainian forces withdrew and set up defences in the Azovstal Steel Plant. The siege of the Azovstal Steel Plant raged for around a month. However, by May, the remaining Ukrainian forces surrendered to the Russian army one brigade after the other. On 20 May, Russian forces finally defeated Azov soldiers who had refused to surrender and the steel plant was taken.

The Russian military learned a great deal from this battle and would help create a doctrine of how to conduct military encirclements. This doctrine is used by the Russian army to this day, and the Ukrainian army do not know how to counter it. The Russian encirclement doctrine is to attack the flanks of an urban city and envelope behind the Ukrainian fortified city and slowly closing off corridors of escape. In doing so it pressures the Ukrainian armies to flee the city or face annihilation. The Russian army does not close off the encirclement, rather they allow for the Ukrainian defenders to hastily retreat from the city. Thereafter, Russia enters the city with little resistance as the Ukrainian army has left the city. This is an effective way for the Russian army to take large industrial-urban areas without suffering the expected heavy casualty rates that come from urban warfare. During the Battle of Mariupol, the Russian army fully encircled the city and then entered it, resulting in high Russian casualties. When the enemy force is encircled, it cannot retreat anymore and will perform their utmost to fend off the attackers, but if there is an exit left open, then they are more likely to flee the scene rather than die to the last man. The Russian encirclement doctrine can be seen in the battles of Severodonetsk, Bakhmut and Avdiivka.

Russian forces in the northern front fared less well. Russia managed to establish a foothold in the northern provinces of Luhansk and Kharkiv oblasts with Russia's other separatist ally, the LPR. Russian attempts to capture Kharkiv and Sumy proved to be a failure by early April. Russia attempted to capture the Ukrainian capital city of Kyiv. However, stiff Ukrainian defences prevented the forces from reaching the city. A Russian armoured convoy advanced to Kyiv to reinforce Russia's Kyiv offensive, however, were easily harassed by Ukrainian forces, forcing the armoured convoy to retreat. From 16 March to 4 April, Ukrainian forces managed to push Russian forces out of Kyiv oblast. During the humiliating Russian withdrawal from Kyiv, Russian forces perpetrated a massacre upon Ukrainian civilian residents of Bucha. With the withdrawal of the Russian forces from Kyiv, the Russian siege of Chernihiv was subsequently lifted. The knockout blow that Russia desired to capture the Ukrainian capital to pressure a Ukrainian capitulation failed to come to fruition and Russia sent its troops from the northern front to the eastern front in preparation for the Donbas summer offensive.

The Front Line Changes

Russia's Donbas summer offensive began on 18 April 2022, with the intent of completing Russian occupation of the Donetsk and Luhansk oblasts. Ukraine managed to harass and stall Russia's army, mercenaries and separatist forces advancements. However, Russian forces managed to capture Kremmina a day after the offensive commenced, and the cities of Popasna and Rubizhne, in early May. Severodonetsk and Lysychansk were ferociously fought over during the months of May, June and July. When Russia captured these twin cities, the Ukrainian army was temporarily expelled from the Luhansk oblast. The Donbas summer offensive proved to be a difficult time for Ukraine as they experienced setback after setback. Ukraine managed to successfully defend the cities of Siversk and barely stopped the Russian capture of Marinka. However, Russian forces were beginning to advance to the city of Bakhmut, and Ukrainian morale and manpower were beginning to deplete. It was only the Ukrainian twin offensives that managed to halt further Russian advances.

The Ukrainian forces were mobilised to the southern front to expel the Russian army from the Mykolaiv and northern Kherson oblasts. The Kherson offensive began on 29 August 2022 and raged for around two months. It was an intense offensive with NATO trained Ukrainians fighting battle-sturdy Russian paratroopers. People forget how the Kherson offensive was a slow grinding military endeavour, and it was a matter of who folds first loses. It would be the Russians who folded as Sergey Surovikin, the general in charge of Russian forces during the Kherson offensive, ordered a withdrawal of Russian forces from Mykolaiv and upper Kherson behind the Dnipro River. This was met with much controversy between Russian military and political leaders. People speculated that Russia was not withdrawing, and they were letting the Ukrainians enter a kill zone to be ambushed and encircled. However, when Ukrainian forces entered the city of Kherson on 1 November, it appeared that Russia withdrew its forces to Russian lines past the Dnipro River.

The Ukrainians launched the Kharkiv oblast offensive a week after the beginning of the Kherson offensive, which aimed to remove Russian presence from the Kharkiv oblast. The thinly spread Russian forces across the Kharkiv front were quickly destroyed and encircled by the lightning speed of the Ukrainian advance. The Russians attempted to regroup near the Orskil River to counter further Ukrainian advances. However, the Russian defences did not hold and Russian positions in Lyman were encircled and destroyed. The Kharkiv oblast offensive came to an end on 2 October 2022 and was an outstanding victory.

What was lesser known to the public was the Ukrainian commando landings on the Kinburn Spit and the raid of the Zaporozhe Nuclear Power Plant. Around 20 September 2022, the Ukrainian commandos attempted to establish a foothold in Russian occupied southern Kherson oblast. But by late December 2022, the Ukrainian commandos made no significant gains from this operation and constant Russian harassment led to the Ukrainian forces withdrawing from the Kinburn Spit.[7] On 19 October 2022, the Ukrainians attempted to take the Russian-occupied Zaporozhe Nuclear Power Plant via multiple speedboats crossing the Dnipro River. Some managed to make landing near the nuclear power plant but all the Ukrainian commandos were repulsed. The objective of this operation was to eliminate Russian presence in the nuclear power plant, in order to alleviate Western countries' stress of a second Chernobyl-like incident occurring. This would have won the Ukrainians significant support from its Western allies and Kyiv would have likely been highly rewarded for neutralising the Zaporozhe Nuclear Power Plant crisis for the Western allies. Reports suggest that the October raid on the nuclear power plant was the third Ukrainian attempt to take the plant, with previous raids occurring in August and September 2022.[8] The operations in the Kinburn Spit and Zaporozhe Nuclear Power Plant were not acknowledged by Ukrainian officials until November 2022 and April 2023 respectively.

The Crimean Bridge explosion that occurred on 8 October 2022, served as a significant morale booster after the overwhelming success of the Ukrainian twin offensives. The Ukrainian government highly propagandised the explosion to lift Ukrainian spirits. After the setbacks of the twin offensive, Putin announced the mass mobilisation of Russian men. This resulted in 700,000 Russian citizens fleeing the country to avoid enlistment. Western media highly propagandised this, saying that the mass mobilisation was a complete failure and that the conscripts would not be well trained and that they were subsequently expected to die in Ukraine as a result. However, a lot of Russians did adhere to the call of duty, and many received the adequate training of six months (in comparison most Ukrainians received only weeks of military training). The mass mobilisation in 2022 would later prove Western media outlets and propaganda machines wrong, when the

Russian conscript numbers stabilised the front around mid-2023. The Russian morale was low at this point and serious Russian operational successes were needed to boost the morale of the Russian troops.

On 10 October 2022, Russian bombings intensified in the capital of Kyiv, which hindered the Ukrainian morale. Putin announced the Russian annexation of the Luhansk, Donetsk, Kherson and Zaporozhe oblasts. However, 143 countries did not recognise it and viewed the 'people's referendum' as a sham. In late October 2022, Putin announced joint operations with Belarus, which prompted Ukrainian fears that a second Kyiv offensive would commence, and so Ukrainian troops were subsequently diverted from the south to build fortifications and defences in Kyiv and the Ukrainian-Belarusian border. People feared that this joint operation was another way of saying Belarus was joining the war in Ukraine. In reality, the joint operations entailed the newly Russian conscripts receiving their military training inside Belarus.

The Wagner Group

Whilst the Russian conscripts were being trained, the Russian army intensified their efforts in the cities of Vuhledar, Avdiivka and Marinka. Vuhledar proved to be a failure, but the Avdiivka and Marinka advances proved to make steady advances during the winter season. But it was the city of Bakhmut that was the epicentre of Russia's winter campaign. The head of the Wagner Group, Yevgeny Prigozhin, lead the intensive battle for Bakhmut in November 2022. Prigozhin heavily propagandised the dramatic battle to gain Western media outlets' attention, in order to pressure Ukrainian military commanders to divert brigades from the southern front to Bakhmut, in order to stall Ukraine's spring offensive. The winter battles of 2022 to 2023 were to distract the Ukrainian army from Russia's low manpower status and to apply pressure on Ukrainian positions in order to stall the Ukrainian army launching an immediate offensive in Zaporozhe.

The infantry-based Wagner Group gruellingly advanced around the city of Bakhmut at a slow pace due to the fierce resistance of the Ukrainian army. By late December 2023, Wagner Group soldiers fought for the city of Soledar. Prigozhin needed to capture the city, in order for the Wagner Group to complete the Bakhmut encirclement. By January 2024, Soledar fell to the Wagner Group. One by one, the Wagner Group cut off Ukrainian supply roads to Bakhmut, endangering the encirclement of the Ukrainian forces in the city. Ukrainian forces (including the Azov Battalion) launched the Bakhmut counteroffensive in May 2023 and engaged with Russian paratroopers on the northern and southern flanks of Bakhmut. By May 2023, Wagner Group fighters entered the city of Bakhmut and engaged in urban combat. Ukrainian territorial battalions entered the city in order to replace the withdrawing Ukrainian mechanised brigades. By 20 May 2023, Wagner Group flags were raised in the high commie-block buildings of the last Ukrainian strongholds in Bakhmut. Ukrainian forces continued their Bakhmut counteroffensive after the Wagner Group capture of the city in an attempt to encircle the city and pressure the Russian army to withdraw from the city.

The Wagner Group withdrew from the city after its capture of Bakhmut and the Russian army subsequently occupied the city. During the Wagner Group withdrawal, Prigozhin claimed that Russian mines were deliberately planted on the roads in anticipation to destroy Wagner Group vehicles and personnel. Prigozhin later claimed that the Russian army bombed Wagner Group personnel. This attack resulted in the Wagner Group rebellion. Prigozhin and Russian Minister of Defence Sergei Shoigu had a deep hatred for one another prior to the Wagner Group withdrawal. The most well-known moment in their drama was when Prigozhin complained that Shoigu's withholding of Russian ammunition to the Wagner Group, during the Battle of Bakhmut, resulted in the unnecessarily high death toll of the Wagner Group fighters. Prigozhin claimed that his rebellion was not to overthrow Putin, but to remove Shoigu from power. Prigozhin and his Wagner Group marched from Rostov-on-Don to Moscow on 23 June 2023. Putin left Moscow and the Russian army prepared the defence of Moscow against the coming Wagner Group soldiers, whose march was met with little resistance and even applauds by the Russian civilian population. Prigozhin viewed his 'March of Justice' as a protest against the Russian military rather than a coup. Wagner Group troops and Russian army combat helicopters did engage in minor clashes during the march, resulting in a few fatalities on both sides. Belarusian President Aleksandr Lukashenko made a telephone call to Prigozhin on behalf of Vladimir Putin, claiming that Shogiu will be removed as demanded and the Wagner Group's safety and existence shall be secured if Prigozhin stopped his march. Prigozhin agreed to Lukashenko's offering and the majority of the Wagner Group participating in the march were sent to Belarus. Prigozhin and Wagner Group leader Dmitry Utkin, later died in a plane explosion on 23 August 2023, likely on behalf of Putin's orders, as punishment for Prigozhin's betrayal and to deter other Russian mercenary organisations from committing similar actions in the future.

The Ukrainian Downfall

Summer 2023 was an intense struggle for Ukraine and Russia. All fronts were on the attack. From the east with the Battle of Bakhmut and its subsequent counteroffensive, the Zaporozhe offensive and Dnipro campaigns in the south, the Kupiansk offensive in the north, the intensification of Ukrainian harassment in the Black Sea theatre, the Russian volunteer incursion into Belgorod oblast and the Wagner Group rebellion.

The much-awaited Ukrainian spring/summer offensive was launched against the Russian occupiers in the Zaporozhe oblast on 4 June 2023, spearheaded by the American equipped Ukrainian 47th Mechanized Brigade. However, the offensive was largely thwarted on the first day of operations by the Russian defenders. Ukrainian breakthroughs were extremely tedious and costly, because of the long line of well-fortified Russian defences, pockets of anti-tank personnel scattered around areas to harass advancing Ukrainian armoured columns, lack of Ukrainian air support and fake Russian trenches and defences which tricked the Ukrainian artillery to waste their artillery ammunitions on. The Ukrainians had managed to breakthrough the first Russian line of defence in August. However, they could not pursue it any further due to the high casualty rates and loss of momentum. By September, the Zaporozhe offensive had fizzled out and was deemed a huge operational failure.

In July 2023, a month into the Zaporozhe offensive, the Russian army launched its Kupiansk offensive in the north. This was a huge fright to the Ukrainian high command. However, by November 2023, the Ukrainian front was stabilised in the forested Kupiansk front. A second effort was made by the Russians to take Kupiansk during the Russians' Donbas winter offensive, but this proved to be fruitless. The Ukrainians made minor scouting and raiding missions across the Dnipro River to the Russian occupied Kherson oblast during the final months of 2022. The Russians attempted to stall an anticipated Ukrainian Dnipro River crossing campaign by destroying the Kakhovka Dam, causing massive floodings in southern Ukraine. This proved to be ineffective as the Ukrainians launched their Dnipro crossing campaign in October 2023, after the failure of the Zaporozhe offensive. The Ukrainian forces faced heavy resistance in the city of Krynky. However, they managed to hold their positions across the Dnipro for some months. The Battle of Krynky was criticised for not being launched during the Zaporozhe offensive and for being a waste of human resources.

Russian Successes

In October 2023, Russia launched their winter offensive across the whole of the Donbas fronts. Russia launched its encirclement campaigns in Avdiivka but faced defeat in the first days of the battle. However, Russia would learn from its mistakes and make significant gains in the following months. Avdiivka was nicknamed Bakhmut 2.0 for its ferocity and high casualty rates. The Donbas winter offensive saw the reversal of the long and hard-fought Ukrainian gains of the Bakhmut counteroffensive. The Russians captured Marinka in late December 2023, marking the end of one of the longest battles in the Ukraine War. Russia managed to encircle Avdiivka in February 2024, ending one of the deadliest and longest battles of the Ukraine War. The Ukrainian forces regrouped in the high grounds of Chasiv Yar to prepare for the Russian advances. Analysts have stressed for the need of a Ukrainian defensive victory in Chasiv Yar, because Chasiv Yar would act as a gateway to various other areas of the western Donbas if the Russian army captured the stronghold. The Ukrainian military setbacks of 2023 and 2024, as well as the decline in volunteers and manpower shortages led to Zelensky announcing a conscription law, lowering conscription ages from 27 to 25. Zelensky was hesitant to enact this law as it could endanger the Ukrainian Gen Z male population, which would thwart the rebuilding and stability of post-war Ukraine. The manpower crisis in the Ukrainian army led to Zelensky having to take notes from the Wagner Group and the Russian army and enlist prisoners into the army. Draft dodging activities ensued after the new conscription law was established and the Ukrainian government pressured its male citizens who fled the country in 2022 to return to the country and enlist in the army.

The Ukrainian defences in Chasiv Yar were weak due to the Ukrainian manpower crisis, and so Ukrainian troops were sent from the Kupiansk front to Chasiv Yar to bolster its defences. In doing so the northern front was at risk of another Russian Kupiansk offensive. On 10 May 2024, Russia launched its cross-border offensive into the Kharkiv oblast. The army was launched from the Belgorod region at 5.00 am. The aim of the Russian Kharkiv offensive was to advance into the city of Kupiansk, in parallel with another Kupiansk offensive from the east. This would entail the encirclement of the entire Ukrainian army stationed in the north. The double Kupiansk envelopment would mean the Russian linkup of forces. The Kharkiv offensive bared political goals as well because if it were successful, the offensive would mean the prevention of further Ukrainian Belgorod incursions, winning Russian public praises. The cross-border offensive began to stall by June 2024. The cross-border offensive in 2024 displayed how the Russian army exploited Ukraine's manpower crisis, as it attempted to establish new fronts and multiple concurrent offensives. This in turn caused the Ukrainian forces to be outspread across a huge front in the east and Ukraine's northern borders.

Russia further exploited the Ukrainian manpower shortage crisis and established multiple fronts during summer 2024. In June 2024, they fought in the south, challenging the small foothold that the Ukrainian army managed to establish during the Zaporozhe offensive. In July, the Russians conducted a surprise offensive in the Toretsk-Niu York front and expelled the Ukrainian forces from Krynky. Russia applied considerable pressure around several cities in the Luhansk oblast front, Pokrovsk, Krasnohorivka, Vuhledar and the Siversk axis.

The Kursk Offensive

On 6 August 2024, Ukraine had launched its Kursk offensive. At first, it was believed by Western and Russian media outlets that this offensive was another short-lived Russian incursion attack, perpetrated by anti-Putin Russian volunteer units. However, it became much apparent that official Ukrainian mechanised regiments were participating in the Kursk oblast attack and significant ground was gained within the first couple of days. Zelensky publicly acknowledged the Ukrainian army's invasion of the Kursk oblast, which contrasted with Zelensky's lack of acknowledgement of Ukrainian responsibility during the anti-Putin Russian volunteer incursions into Russia earlier. It is much speculated by analysists as to why Ukraine launched the Kursk offensive. The Kursk offensive serves several strategic benefits for the Ukrainian army. If successful, the Ukrainian army would be able to hold control over the E105 highway and railways, cutting off supplies to the Russian forces participating in the concurrent Kharkiv cross-border offensive. The logistical severing from the rear and even risk of encirclement, pressured the Russian army to halt or even exit the Kharkiv oblast battlefield, in order to avoid annihilation. The success of the Kursk offensive would have also meant that the Ukrainian control over the E38 highway and the R200 road would thwart any chances of a Russian cross-border offensive into the Ukrainian Sumy oblast. It was widely known that Russian forces were amounting near the Sumy oblast borders and it was anticipated that these forces would conduct another cross-border offensive. On 11 August 2024, Ukraine sent forces into the Belgorod oblast, as part of the Kursk offensive, squandering Russia's offensive into the Sumy oblast. By late August, the Ukrainian forces rapid advance began to stiffen with the Russian reinforcements entering the scene and by 10 September, Ukraine faced a firm Russian counteroffensive in the region. In response, the Ukrainian army launched a cross-border offensive in the Kursk region towards the Glushkovo direction to thwart Russia's Kursk counteroffensive on 14 September. This Glushkovo operation was halted shortly after by Russian troops. The Ukrainian gains in Kursk thereafter folded backwards with the Russians making slow advances. A second Russian counteroffensive was launched in the Kursk front, on 11 November 2024, and made tremendous gains.

The Russian army gained significant and rapid ground along the Donbas front during this time. The Russian Pokrovsk offensive coincided with Russian offensive in south Donetsk towards the Velyka Novosilka direction in November 2024. The rapid gains in south Donetsk coincided with Donald Trump's electoral victory for American presidency. The advantageous situation made many observers question if Putin would call for peace. Using Trump as (a favourable) mediator, Putin would lay claim to the Donbas region, in exchange for the end of the war.

The Ukraine War is the most important scene of the Second Cold War, because if Russian were to win the war against the NATO-backed Ukrainian army, it will totally change the dynamics of European security and alignments. Russian occupation of Ukraine would mean a geopolitical shift in Europe and change of global views on American and Russian military strength and superpower status, akin to how the 1989 fall of the Berlin Wall marked global recognition of the US as the sole ultimate global superpower in the world.

Chapter Three

PAX-EUROPA IN PERIL

The outbreak of the Ukraine War almost jeopardised the eighty-year-long Pax-Europa. A war of this magnitude has not occurred since the Second World War. NATO troops increased their presence in Eastern Europe in response to the Russian aggression, as a show of force and to increase NATO's eastern frontiers as a security measure. Russia received international condemnation from 141 countries for its invasion of Ukraine during the UN General Resolution Assembly in March 2022. The 141 countries demanded the immediate withdrawal of Russian forces from Ukraine. Belarus, Syria, North Korea, Eritrea and Russia itself were supportive of Russia's invasion of Ukraine. Thirty-five countries abstained, most notably China, India, Iran and the CSTO countries. Twelve countries were absent in the UN resolution for the immediate Russian withdrawal. The international condemnation of Russia in 2022 greatly isolated the country internationally. However, as the years progressed, more countries reversed their initial condemnation, such as Myanmar and Niger, due to shifting circumstances during the Second Cold War.

NATO's Response

During the Ukrainian crisis from October 2021 to February 2022, NATO troops increased its presence in Eastern European countries that neighboured Ukraine, Russia and Belarus in preparation for a possible Russian incursion into NATO countries and Ukraine. The number of NATO forces have increased during the initial invasion and after the failed Zaporozhe offensive. In Eastern Europe, NATO forces conducted various wargames and military training in preparation for a possible war with Russia. NATO trained Ukrainian troops with certain NATO equipment and war machines inside NATO countries. Unfortunately, these NATO-trained Ukrainian troops would spend no more than six weeks in NATO training before being sent back to the front. This was because the Ukrainian army was starting to face manpower shortages and needed these Ukrainian soldiers to be returned to the front as soon as possible. These newly NATO trained brigades would be rendered temporarily inactive or completely inoperable for further combat, once sent to fight in Bakhmut or in the Zaporozhe region. Some mechanised brigades were so molested by Russian forces, that they would be rendered infantry brigades thereafter.

The most crucial aspect of the West's manoeuvring against Russia is the lend-leasing of lethal aid to Ukraine. Western lend-leasing has remained crucial for Ukraine because the Ukrainian army suffered heavy vehicular and army equipment losses during the initial invasion. If Ukraine had never received lethal aid from the West, Ukraine would have inevitably fallen to the Russian army regardless of Russia's initial failure. The West's lend-leasing is, therefore, the lifeblood to Ukraine's survival. If that is cut, the Ukrainian war effort would be diminished, as the Ukrainian army would no longer have the capabilities for countering the Russian army's advances. Lethal aid to Ukraine initially begun on 27 February 2022. Further aid packages were sent to substantiate the heavy vehicular losses that Ukraine had sustained during the initial Russian invasion of Ukraine (February to April 2022). However, subsequent lethal aid packages were sent to Ukraine with the hopes of modernising the Ukrainian army, to successfully counter Russian forces. Lethal aid packages were initially defensive material, but later, more offensive aid was sent, in anticipation for Ukraine's twin offensives. Ukraine has received such a plethora of aid from the West that it is impossible to list them all. Therefore, the most notable episodes of the West's lend-leasing to Ukraine shall be discussed.

On March 2022, Poland was very staunch in its support to Ukraine and offered to provide them MIG-29 fighter jets. The US, however, successfully urged Poland not to transfer the fighter jets in fear that it would escalate the Ukraine conflict into a wider world war. Biden's hesitancy came at the cost of the Ukrainians as their Soviet-produced air force was dwindling in numbers by Russian jets during the early months of the war. Germany was hesitant also, as they only provided helmets to Ukraine during the initial phase of the war. Western criticism towards Germany's hesitancy pressured Berlin to send more lethal equipment to Ukraine. Most European nations were more than willing to provide Ukraine significant offensive lethal aid whilst the US was hesitant in doing so. It was ultimately Germany that managed to snap Biden out of his reluctance. After the success of Ukraine's twin offensives, NATO countries were increasing their weapon transfers to

Ukraine, in anticipation for Ukraine's spring offensive (the Zaporozhe offensive).

In January 2023, the US displayed signs of hesitancy yet again and contemplated not sending Ukraine their Abrams tanks. As a form of diplomatic pressure, German Chancellor Olaf Scholz refused to send German Leopard 2 tanks to Ukraine unless the US agreed to send their Abrams tanks. This was received with high controversy amongst Western nations, as time was of the essence and both countries needed to send their tanks to Ukraine as soon as possible. Scholz's gamble pulled off, however, as Biden eventually approved sending thirty-one Abrams tanks to Ukraine. Subsequently, Germany sent fourteen Leopard 2 tanks. Germany played a significant role in the Ukraine lend-leasing as it forced the US to realise that they must send more sufficient amounts to Ukraine, in order to provide the Ukrainian army enough capabilities to realistically oust Russia from the occupied oblasts.

On 8 February 2023, Zelensky made a state visit to Britain, appealing for UK modern fighter jets, such as Typhoon jets and F-16s, to be supplied to the Ukrainian air force. Zelensky made a great speech in Parliament, pleading for UK fighter jets and displayed Ukraine's gratitude for Britain's support which touched the hearts of many British politicians and public. In 2023, Ukraine desperately needed a sufficient air force as Russia had air superiority over the Ukrainian skies. The US and other European nations followed suit and approved supplying and training Ukrainians with their F-16s and warplanes in August 2023. The first Western lent F-16s entered the Ukrainian skies in August 2024. Controversially, Biden approved sending cluster munitions to Ukraine in July 2023. Cluster munitions are banned in 120 countries due to the risk of dud bomblets causing battlefields to become dormant minefields in post-war nations. The transfer of American cluster bombs puts the lives of Ukrainian civilians at risk. Zelensky thanked the US for the shipment of cluster munitions regardless, due to the dire circumstances Ukraine was under during this time.

Zelensky's Crisis and Putin's Puppets

The much-anticipated Ukrainian summer offensive came to a sobering failure. This briefly dented the West's confidence in the effectiveness of their lend-leasing programme of lethal aid to Ukraine. During December 2023 and January 2024, Zelensky faced difficulty regaining Western confidence.

Ukrainian relations with its Western neighbours, such as Poland, Hungary, Slovakia and Romania declined during this time, due to the grain issue. Due to the Russian blockade of Ukrainian exports in the Black Sea, the EU ensured that Ukrainian grain was exported through its neighbouring countries to Africa, in order to protect the stability of Ukraine's economy (as grain is Ukraine's biggest export). The EU's assurances of the continuation of the Ukrainian grain exports were also for humanitarian purposes, to ensure that African nations continued to receive Ukrainian grain and not face a food crisis. Because of this, grain produced in NATO Eastern European nations had been devalued and came to the expense of their farming communities. Because of the grain issue, Poland – Ukraine's staunchest ally at the time – stopped transferring modern lethal aid to Ukraine in September 2023. Poland continued to transfer old Soviet weapons from their stockpile. However, the ordeal greatly dented Ukrainian-Polish relations. The grain issue raged on during December 2023 and January 2024, and Zelensky worried that its neighbours would follow Poland's decision to discontinue supply of modern lethal aid to Ukraine. Farming communities in Eastern Europe protested staunchly across West Ukraine's borders, blocking Western transfer of goods to Ukraine. The farming protests seemed to have come to an end by late April 2024.

Zelensky had to deal with the likes of Hungarian Prime Minister Viktor Orban and Slovakian Prime Minister Robert Fico who regularly blocked Western transfer of aid to Ukraine. The rise of right-wing thinking and parties became a concern to Ukraine as these nationalistic and conservative parties wanted to discontinue their country's aid to Ukraine and reverse Western sanctions on Russian goods. Right-wing groups wish to discontinue their obligations to Ukraine, as they believe that they should not intervene in far-away conflicts that do not concern them and should instead redirect their efforts towards their nation's domestic issues. Putin encourages the rise of right-wing parties in the West as they serve as influential anti-lend-leasing lobbyist groups within Western nations, hindering Ukraine's war effort. Putin famously claimed in late 2023, that it was senseless to make further peace-making efforts with the US and the West until the American elections in 2024 when Donald Trump becomes president of the US. Judging by Trump's lenient relations towards Russia during his first presidency, it was assumed that Trump would enforce a peace plan that would favour Russia at the expense of Ukraine. Viktor Orban is infamous for his pro-Moscow leanings and discouraging the West's antagonistic policies towards Russia. In December 2023, Orban was responsible for vetoing and subsequently blocking a four-year-long €5 billion aid package to Ukraine, which led to an open dispute between Zelensky and Orban. Around this time, Senate Republicans blocked

American funding to Ukraine, arguing that the money devoted to Ukraine should be spent on domestic issues and securing the US border against illegal Latin American immigrants. Western public support for Zelensky was at a low during this time also. Russia's online propaganda campaign targeted Western public opinion, which aimed to instil anti-Ukrainian sentiments within Western societies. This aimed to boost the numbers of isolationist right-wing groups, bolstering their leveraging capabilities against their government's pro-Ukraine foreign policies.

Hungarian and Slovakian prime ministers, Viktor Orban and Robert Fico, are widely viewed as puppets of Putin, in the eyes of their NATO and EU peers. Both are right-wing politicians who have voiced their opposition to culture mixing with non-native foreigners and LGBTQ organisations and practices. Both have voiced their desires to end the Ukraine War, in favour of Putin's terms because Russia's oil pipeline exports greatly benefit Central European nations' electricity and economy. Due to Ukraine's decision to stop the Russian oil pipeline to Central Europe via Ukraine in July 2022, power outages and energy prices soared in Hungary and other Central and Eastern European states. This caused a strain in Hungarian-Ukrainian relations and Orban publicly opposed Western sanctions on Russia, arguing that it had real self-inflicting consequences on Western countries' economies.

Orban recovered the poor Hungarian-Russian relations when he entered presidency in 2010. Orban introduced the Eastern Opening Plans. This was a program which saw the Hungarian economy become less reliant towards the West by increasing trade with countries in Central Asia, the Caucasus, Turkey, China and Russia. Putin utilised Orban's Eastern Opening Plans to increase its economic influence on the country, utilising Russia's pipeline exports and establishing the Russian state owned PAKs nuclear power plant in Budapest. Hungarian economy became increasingly more reliant on Russian oil and gas over the years, enforcing Hungary to provide diplomatic support for Russia in times of international controversy. This can be seen in 2014, when Orban opposed EU desires to impose Western sanctions on Russia after the Crimean annexation. It can also be presumed that Orban may be siding with Russia to also expand Hungary's territory and acquire parts of southwestern Transcarpathian Ukraine. Hungary had lost many of its Eastern provinces to its Eastern neighbours after Austria-Hungary's defeat in the First World War and the signing of the Treaty of Trianon in 1920. Putin had mentioned Hungarian 'rights over the Transcarpathian' during the Tucker Carlson interview.[9] Hungarian politicians increasingly claimed that the Treaty of Trianon caused Hungary to be in a state of plight. These claims are a pretext to increase Hungarian sense of victimisation from the Western powers and subsequently increase Hungarian nationality. Many Hungarians wrongly believe that the land that was ceded away in 1920 had a majority Hungarian ethnic population, due to Orban's false statements about the Trianon Treaty. On July 2023, Russia exchanged several Ukrainian PoWs to Hungary, unbeknownst to Zelensky. These PoWs were of Hungarian ethnicity from the Transcarpathian region, and the exchange was likely to stir Hungarian nationalism and opposition to Ukraine.[10] The exchange was to make the Hungarian people question 'why were these Hungarians fighting for Zelensky?'

In May 2025, the Ukrainian Secret Service discovered a Hungarian spy ring in Western Zakarpattia region, located near the Hungarian border. Zakarpattia holds a substantial ethnic Hungarian population. The Hungarian military intelligence network gathered intelligence on Ukrainian defences in the region and tried to forecast the Zakarpattia population's reception to a possible Hungarian incursion into Ukraine.[11] This suggests that Orban was contemplating invading western Ukraine, in an attempt to annex the ethnically populated Hungarian regions of Ukraine, before the conflict came to its resolution. Two alleged Hungarian spies were arrested by Ukrainian authorities and Budapest denied Kyiv's espionage accusations.

Hungary's Eastern Opening Plans towards the Chinese trade were met with mediocre economic results and caused an increase in diplomatic ties with Russia. It should be noted, however, that the Hungarian approach to China and the Eastern Opening Plans are likely to prosper during the Second Cold War, due to China's attempts to create trade routes via Central Asian countries, Azerbaijan, and Russia. Orban frequently spat in the face of his EU and NATO peers by consistently visiting Chinese President Xi Jinping and Putin, for economic talks, such as the trade routes, and gas and oil exports respectively. Orban visited the then standing candidate for the American Republican presidency, Donald Trump, with the intent of making plans to cut aid to Ukraine and ending the war.[12] Orban claimed that Trump would not 'send a penny' to Ukraine. However, Trump made differing statements and actions to Orban's claim after the visit. Hungarian democracy is experiencing a slow decline under Orban, causing EU-Hungarian relations to sour. Hungary consistently thwarted NATO and EU packages to Ukraine, resulting in Hungary being carved out of these decision-making processes in July 2024.

This exclusion also meant that Hungary would not contribute their economy towards the aid packages.

The Long-Range Missile Dispute

In April 2024, the German government sent Patriot air-defence missiles to Ukraine but held off sending long-range Taurus missiles to Ukraine. The decision not to send Taurus missiles was controversial in Germany, in both the political and public spheres, as many Germans wanted Ukraine to be sufficiently supplied to face off against the Russian threat. Whilst many Germans were unhappy, other Germans expressed gratitude for Scholz's restraint. A portion of the German public slowly began to believe that sending more lethal aid to Ukraine was prolonging the conflict and Ukrainian suffering. They believed that by abandoning Ukraine, it would make politicians refocus on domestic German issues. The mindset to neglect Ukrainians began to rise in popularity across the Western hemisphere after the Zaporozhe offensive, due to Russia's effective media-propaganda campaign.

The reasoning for German politicians to deny the Ukrainian request to obtain German Taurus missiles was because Germany did not want Ukraine to use long-range missiles against Russian infrastructure. Many Western nations urged Ukraine to not attack Russian infrastructure in fear that in doing so would escalate the conflict. The US even warned Ukraine that if this were to occur, the lend-leasing would decrease in proportions or cease entirely. However, Ukraine had continuously attacked Russian infrastructure with its non-Western weapons, and the West faced little repercussions for it. Ukraine had been attacking Russian infrastructure in Russia and Crimea since February 2022 and June 2022 respectively. The Ukrainian ground incursions into neighbouring Russian oblasts, perpetrated by the Russian volunteer battalions, began in March 2023 and the Ukrainian sabotage campaign of Russian oil refineries followed from February 2024.

By June 2024, Western nations, such as Britain and France, contemplated approving Ukrainian long-range attacks on Russia. Vladimir This so enraged Vladimir Putin that he threatened these countries with nuclear retaliation. Putin even claimed that if the US was to approve Ukrainian use of Western long-range missile attacks on Russia, then he too would provide his own long-range missiles to the US' enemies abroad. Putin's threats were concurrent with Russian naval military exercises in the Caribbean Sea in cooperation with its Latin allies, Cuba and Venezuela.

The US feared that Russia was spreading its influence further into the Americas and it was reported that nuclear capable submarines were participating in the exercises, which raised American concerns. Despite the farce fearmongering display in the Caribbean, Putin did contemplate sending lethal aid to the Houthis to target Western shipping during the Israel-Gaza War in retaliation, but opted out due to American-Saudi Arabia diplomatic pressure. The Russian naval exercises and display in the Caribbean Sea was a means of deterring Western approval of the Ukrainian use of long-range missiles against Russian infrastructure. The UK's progress into approving Ukrainian use of long-range missiles against Russian territory, under the Conservative Party was temporarily reversed when Sir Keir Starmer and the Labour Party came to power in 2024. By the end of June, Biden considered approving the Ukrainian use of its long-range missiles on Russia if the missiles specifically attacked Russian troops within Russian oblasts that bordered Ukraine. It can be argued that Russia's cross-border offensive into Kharkiv convinced the US to allow Ukraine to shell Russian infrastructure, in order to prevent Russia from conducting similar cross-border offensives into the Sumy or Kyiv oblasts. This limited the Russian army's military tactic of creating multiple concurrent fronts against an outspread and weakened Ukrainian army.

During Ukraine's Kursk offensive, Zelensky also launched a campaign to encourage the West to approve the use of Western long-range missile attacks on Russian territory. In August 2024, Zelensky urged the West that long-range missiles were needed to hinder the Russian war effort and appealed for France, Britain and the US to approve the use of Shadow Storm and ATCAM missiles against Russian territory. During August 2024, Ukraine launched several strikes deep into Russia whilst the shock of the Kursk offensive was still in effect. Ukraine launched successful drone strikes into air bases and oil storage facilities in Volgograd, Rostov-on-Don, Voronezh, Savasleika, Borisoglebsk and Moscow. The Ukrainian's believed that Moscow's weak response to Ukraine's long-range attacks would give the West enough confidence to approve Western long-range weapons against Russian territories, without facing substantial repercussions.

In the wake of news that Iran had sent short-range ballistic missiles to Russia and the Russian violations of Latvian and Romanian airspace, American Secretary of State Antony Blinken and UK Foreign Secretary David Lammy visited Kyiv, to discuss the possibility of Britain approving Ukrainian use of British long-range missiles, in early September 2024. This coincided with Labour Prime Minister Keir Starmer's visit to Washington to discuss the matter. The discussions appeared to have led nowhere substantial, likely because the Democrats wanted to refrain themselves from approving Ukraine's plea due to the forthcoming American presidential elections. The refrainment of the Democrats was likely to shield American voters from fear that Ukrainian use of Western long-range missiles would result in a third world war, as warned by Trump and Putin. Biden's refrainment aimed to reduce scared American voters voting Trump, who promised the de-escalation of the conflict. On 12 September 2024, Putin warned the West that if they were to allow Ukraine to use their long-range missiles against Russia, this would mean a Russo-NATO war. The threat of war and nuclear consequences are a common form of blackmail Putin uses to deter the West from increasing its willingness to help Ukraine.

The Economic Sanctions

Following Russia's invasion of Ukraine, Western countries saw the immediate sanctioning of Russia, resulting in the withdrawal of a plethora of Western companies' services and outlets from the country. In the immediate invasion of Ukraine, the EU launched over 16,500 sanctions against Russia and froze 70 per cent of Russian banks.[13] The EU and the West continued a series of sanctions against Russia, Belarus and Iran as the Second Cold War continued. The sanctions impacted Russian exports, such as its main energy exports to the West, which greatly impacted European nations' economy, as Russia was Europe's main oil and gas supplier. However, by late 2023, analysts and journalists became sceptical of the effectiveness of Western sanctions, as the Russian economy remained stable. This was because Russia found several sanction loopholes by increasing its oil exports to China and India, using countries in the Caucasus and Central Asia as third-party platforms for Western oil purchasing, and continuing to trade with complacent or dependent countries. The sanctions appeared to have inhibited the Western economy. The backfire of Western sanctions contributed to the Western public becoming increasingly disillusioned with their country's support for Ukraine.

Regardless, Russia tried to further thwart Western sanctions by attempting to devalue the American dollar with BRICS expansion. BRICS is an inter-governmental organisation that aims to devalue the dollar in order to thwart American global influence, mutually benefitting the members' economy and influence. Its members include Brazil, Russia, India, China and South Africa. On August 2023, BRICS announced its desires to expand its membership numbers to include Argentina, Egypt, Ethiopia, Iran, Saudi Arabia, and the UAE. The invites were targeted towards nations with strained relations to the US and the West, in the attempt to further thwart the US' economic influence, lessen the impact of sanctions and as a counter to the EU. On 1 January 2024, Egypt, Iran, Ethiopia and the UAE were officially accepted into BRICS. Between 2022 and 2024, twenty-three countries applied to join BRICS, displaying that the West's imposed international isolationism on Russia was dwindling in its effectiveness.

Putin, the War Criminal and Architecture of the Ukrainian Genocide

The West attempted to further isolate Russia by accusing Vladimir Putin of committing genocide in Ukraine. During the early months of the Ukraine War, rumours and reports circulated, claiming that Russian troops were abducting Ukrainian children in the backdrop of the siege of Mariupol. This proved to be true as in June 2022, video images emerged of the FSB forces abducting children in a nursery in Kherson.

During the last days of the siege of Mariupol, Ukrainian civilians caught in the encirclement were offered by the Russian army to be safely escorted out of the crucible. The whereabouts of those that had accepted the deal are currently unknown. Russian politicians reasoned that the motives behind the child abductions were for humanitarian reasons and held no malicious intent. The Russian government claims that the abductions of children were to ensure the children's safety and to get them out of the warzones and battlefields. However, the international community feared that the Russian child abduction operations were part of Russia's goals to pacify and Russify the eastern oblasts of Ukraine. The abducted children were put into Russian homes and schools, to further assimilate them into Russian culture and ideals, before they return back to their homelands with a pro-Moscow mindset. For Russia to counter the inevitable emergence of Ukrainian independence or guerilla movements, after the Ukraine War, Russia has attempted to brainwash the younger Ukrainian generations into being loyal to Moscow. This long-term plan made by Russian authorities supports Moscow in legitimising their claims to the Donbas and helps them gain the newly acquired population to side with them against future Ukrainian rebel independence forces.

Russia's social engineering of the occupied territories of Ukraine are implemented in numerous ways: massacres and torture of Ukrainian civilians, deportation and Russification of Ukrainian children, pressuring occupied Ukrainians to accept Russian citizenship, coercion of occupied Ukrainians to vote in favour of Russian annexation during internationally unrecognised and illegal referendums, encouraging Russian citizens in Russian proper to migrate to occupied regions – increasing Russian ethnic makeup of eastern and southern Ukraine, tearing down Ukrainian signs and cultural heritage, destroying civilian infrastructure to make places of shelter unhabitable – causing displacement and encouraging migration, the Russian seizure of abandoned homes and property, and in some cases genital mutilation of Ukrainian men.

On 17 March 2023, the ICC enacted the Rome Statute, which generated an arrest warrant for Vladimir Putin. As a result, Putin made few state visits and was excluded from many international summits during the Second Cold War. The ICC arrest warrant for Putin has also made many countries face international isolationism whenever they accepted Putin into their country without arresting him. However, by 2024, Putin made a state visit to Mongolia. Although Mongolia was obliged to arrest him, they did not, displaying the declining international adherence to Putin's arrest warrant. Critics have accused the ICC of having double standards. President George W. Bush and British Prime Minister Tony Blair never faced prosecution by the ICC during the initial invasion of Iraq in 2003. The criticisms were mostly voiced by Russia's allies and also South Africa, who contemplated the idea of disregarding the Rome Statute and allowing Putin to make state visits to the country without arresting him. Western countries also gave pro-Ukrainian and anti-Russia gestures by officially recognising genocides that Russia had committed in the past, such as the Holodomor famine between 1932 and 1933 and the Tatar deportations in 1944.

The Nord Stream Pipeline Mystery

The Nord Stream pipelines in the Baltic Sea served to export Russian gas to Germany. The construction of the Nord Stream pipelines was controversial, and Donald Trump rightfully claimed in 2019 that the Nord Stream pipelines would make the European nations' energy heavily reliant on Russian gas and oil exports.[14] On 26 September 2022, Nord Stream pipelines 1 and 2 were sabotaged and rendered inoperable. Who carried out the sabotage and how it was accomplished remains officially unknown. Western media initially accused Russia. However, this appears illogical as Russia needed the Nord Stream pipelines to export gas and hold the EU economy hostage. In terms of motive, the US and Ukraine are the likeliest to have been the perpetrators. An American sabotage of the Nord Stream pipelines would ensure that Russian energy blackmailing over the EU's Russian policy would be thwarted and would encourage the EU to commit to the sanctioning of Russia. A Ukrainian involvement would ensure that the Euro does not fund Russia's war against Ukraine. German investigations into the Nord Stream pipeline sabotage have revealed that a pro-Ukrainian group in Europe was responsible. Six divers in a yacht named *Andromeda* crossed the Baltic Sea to reach the Nord Stream pipelines and sabotaged them.[15]

An investigative journalist from the *Wall Street Journal* found that the Ukrainian special operative Roman Chervinsky was responsible for the coordination of the six-man sabotage of the Nord Stream pipelines under the orders of Ukrainian Chief of Defence Valery Zalzuzhy.[16] Interestingly, the *Wall Street Journal* noted that Chervinsky enacted the Nord Stream pipeline sabotage without the consent of Zelensky. The article claims that Chervinsky was undergoing prosecution for corruption of power in Kyiv, because in July 2022, he attempted to help a defected Russian pilot enter friendly Ukrainian lines, without the knowledge or permission of his Ukrainian superiors. This illegal operation endangered the lives of Ukrainian soldiers and Ukrainian airfield coordinates. The *Wall Street Journal* also noted that the Pentagon leaks of 2023 displayed the CIA's confidence that Zelensky did not approve of the Nord Stream pipeline. The CIA's display of ignorance about who sabotaged the Nord Stream pipeline in official classified documents, therefore, suggested that the US did not intervene in the Nord Stream sabotage in any form and rogue Ukrainian agents were the true perpetrators. Regardless of whether the Ukrainian government or rogue actors carried out the sabotage operation, the success led to a Ukrainian attempted sabotage of the TurkStream pipeline in October 2022, but Russian authorities managed to prevent this from occurring. During the month of February 2024, European authorities' investigations into the Nord Stream pipeline had ceased without discovering who the perpetrators were or enacting any form of prosecution. However, in August 2024, German authorities prosecuted a Ukrainian man residing in Poland for the Nord Stream pipeline sabotage.[17]

The New NATO Members

After the success of Ukraine's twin offensives and the Russian annexation of Ukraine's eastern and southern oblasts, Zelensky announced Ukraine's application for NATO membership. NATO leaders gave mixed reactions. The majority, however, refused Ukraine's submission because if Ukraine were to be accepted into NATO, the Atlantic alliance would have immediately entered a world war. NATO was divided on Ukrainian membership, which angered Zelensky during the G7 press conference in July 2023 and made half-joking remarks about his frustration of Ukraine's process into NATO membership. NATO, however, officially claimed that they were willing to accept Ukrainian membership after the Ukraine War and even claimed to help Ukraine join the EU.[18] Putin claimed to have invaded Ukraine in order to hinder NATO strength and expansionism but inadvertently caused NATO to quickly unite and restrengthen itself against the Russian threat.

In the wake of Russia's invasion of Ukraine, Finland and Sweden realised the dangers of being a non-NATO country bordering Russia and started to consider whether or not to apply for NATO membership. In March 2022, both countries applied for major non-NATO ally status with the US. In May 2022, both Finland and Sweden applied for NATO membership in unison. The majority of NATO countries were adamant for Finnish and Swedish assession to NATO membership. However, Turkish President Recep Tayyip Erdoğan was very much against the idea. Turkey complained that the Scandinavian countries gave asylum to Kurdish militants, especially those that belong to the PKK. Turkey deems these Kurdish political parties as terrorist organisations and as a threat to Turkish sovereignty. This is because these political groups want the southeastern Turkish provinces, which have a significant Kurdish population, to become independent from Turkey. The PKK and other Kurdish parties desire the creation of an independent Kurdistan country, absorbing other ethnically Kurdish regions of neighbouring Syria, Iraq and Iran. This was Turkey's focal concern and demanded for the PKK members residing in Sweden and Finland to be extradited into Turkish custody. Sweden and Finland contemplated Turkey's demand, but were adamant to ensure that the Kurds' human rights were not violated under the custody of the Turks. In late June 2022, Turkey further pushed for the extradition of thirty-three Kurdish militants from Finland and Sweden.

Turkish demands for Kurdish extradition increased over time and Finland eventually accepted Turkey's demands, subsequently resulting in Turkey allowing Finland to join NATO in April 2023. Sweden began to illegalise Kurdish militant parties and began mass arrests of people associated with these Kurdish organisations. This was met with Kurdish protests in the streets of Stockholm in which anti-Erdoğan and anti-NATO slogans were heard. Swedish-Turkish talks continued, and the US proposed to approve a Turkish request to purchase forty American F-16s in return for Turkish approval of Swedish assession into NATO. Sweden followed up on the US' proposal by claiming that they would assist Turkey's bid to be accepted into the EU in return for NATO assession. This ultimately persuaded Erdoğan to accept Swedish assession to NATO on 7 March 2024.

Although Turkey is a NATO ally, Erdoğan's goals of establishing a Turanian sphere of influence in the Middle East and Central Asia, conflicts with NATO interests. This conflict of interests between the West and Turkey has resulted in multiple hostile attitudes between NATO countries, during the early years of the Second Cold War. On 3 September 2022, Erdoğan made warmongering remarks towards NATO ally Greece, regarding the Aegean Islands dispute. Turkey is known for being used as a platform for Russia to circumvent sanctions. No serious effort had been made by Erdoğan to eliminate this Russian loophole. Erdoğan gave diplomatic support to Putin against Prigozhin's 'March of Justice' during the Wagner Group rebellion. Turkey strongly condemned Israel and opposed the US backing during the Gaza conflict. During the Gaza conflict, Turkey had arrested several Mossad affiliated citizens, blocked trade with Israel, cut diplomatic ties with Israel and hospitalised Hamas fighters.[19] On 4 September 2024, Erdoğan announced Turkey's application into BRICS, showing Turkey's disinterest with the Western bloc.[20]

Moldova's Active Neutrality

Akin to most former Soviet nations, Moldova fought in a war against a separatist republic in the early 1990s. Transnistria, a strip of land in the east of Moldova, holds a high Russian and Russian-speaking population who sought independence from the Moldovan government, after the Moldovan government wanted to remove Russian influences and culture from the country. The Transnistrian population are widely Russian speakers, due to Russification programmes of Transnistria during the Soviet period. The Transnistrians believed that their identity and culture was facing existential threat from the Moldovan government. Many Moldovans believed that the country would soon be annexed by Romania in the near future, adding to the Transnistrian existentialism. A Romanian union with Moldova meant the nail in the coffin of Russian identity in the country. Transnistria declared itself as an independent republic from the Moldovan government, entailing the Transnistria War of 1992. The Transnistrians, with the aid of Russian backing, won the war against the Romanian-backed Moldovan army. Russian peacekeeping groups were stationed in the breakaway region after the war, preventing Moldova from attacking the self-declared republic for a second time, in fear of Russian retaliation. The Russian presence in the Transnistria resulted in the Transnistrian dispute becoming a frozen conflict.

Transnistria and even Moldova as a whole has been at risk from Russian influences, since the end of the war in 1992. This risk has severely escalated since the Russian invasion of Ukraine in 2022. Moldovan President Maia Sandu greatly condemned the Russian invasion of Ukraine and on March 2022 applied for EU membership in response to Russian acts of aggression. During the early months of the invasion of Ukraine, many Moldovans feared that if Russia were to successfully capture Odessa and Ukraine's south, the Russian army would subsequently invade Moldova with lightning speed, using Transnistria as a bridgehead. Such fears were not a product of hysteria, as Belarusian President Aleksandr Lukashenko accidentally leaked the Russian war planning of the invasion of Ukraine, which entailed the Russian invasion of Moldova from Odessa and the south.[21] Russian presence in the Transnistria unnerved Kyiv, and on 4 March 2022, the Ukrainian army destroyed the railway over the Kuchurhan River, hindering the possibility of Russian troops stationed in Transnistria entering Ukraine from Moldova. However, Ukrainian and Moldovan fears subsided after the initial failure of the Russian invasion of Ukraine. After the failure of Russia's initial invasion, Russia no longer regarded Transnistria as a military platform for invading Ukraine or Moldova, but instead a platform for espionage and to spread political influences into Ukraine and Moldova.

The Ukraine War rocked Moldova's domestic politics. The invasion curbed Russian oil and gas exports to Transnistria and Moldova. Russian oil and gas companies reduced exports to the country and Russia's bombing campaign of Ukrainian energy infrastructure led to Ukraine cutting its energy exports to Moldova in October 2022. This led to an energy crisis in Moldova, resulting in protests calling for the resignation of the pro-EU Moldovan politicians and calls for the Moldovan government to secure a rapprochement with Russia to reverse the energy crisis. These protests were organised by the pro-Russian Sor Party and raged on until June 2023. The protests were damning and divided the country. It resulted in Moldovan Prime Minister Natalia Gavrilița resigning in February 2023, and widespread counterprotests ensued, demanding for Moldova to stay vigilant and to not bend the knee and continue to be an addict of Russian gas and oil. The Sor Party's campaign was so dangerous to the pro-EU Moldovan government that in June 2023, the Sor Party was banned from any legitimate input in the Moldovan constitution. The Sor Party was subsequently sanctioned by the EU, UK and the US. The protests came to an end after the emancipation of the Sor Party. Sandu feared that the protests were a Russian designed coup against the pro-EU Moldovan government. Security measures were enacted in preparation for the possibility that Russian soldiers would march from Transnistria into Moldova's capital, to complete the coup. Pro-Russian Moldovan news outlets were banned, and Russian nationals were denied from entering the country. In July 2023, the Moldovan government expelled forty-five Russian diplomats for espionage, confirming Russian intent to monitor and exploit the Moldovan infighting.

Russian meddling in Moldovan domestic politics resulted in increasing tensions between Moldova and the Transnistria. The rising tensions were exploited by Ukraine, the West and Russia. Mysterious explosions and attacks occurred in the Transnistria throughout 2022. The attacks targeted Russian depots and airports, undermining Russian peacekeepers' strength in the self-declared republic. These attacks did not result in any casualties, and the perpetrators were unknown, although widely speculated to be Ukrainians. The attacks led to an increase in Moldovan presence near the Transnistria border, in fear that Transnistrian forces would enact retaliatory attacks. Because the perpetrators of these attacks were unknown, the motives behind the attacks were also unidentified. Moldovan and Transnistrian response to these attacks were of caution, as they perceived these attacks as a series of false flag operations to incite Moldova and Transnistria to declare war against each other or to drag them into in the Ukraine War. Moldova's unease with Russian presence in Transnistria led to Ukrainian officials claiming that if asked by the Moldovan government, the Ukrainian army would besiege Transnistria, subsequently removing Russian presence in the region, and returning it to Moldova, ending the Transnistrian dispute. This offer was rejected by Sandu as she feared that this would have drawn Moldova into the Ukraine conflict in which the Moldovan army was too underequipped to partake.[22]

Ukraine has tried to weaken Russian presence in Transnistria, and attempted to assassinate the Transnistrian leader, Vadim Krasnoseslky, in September 2023.[23] Transnistria's economy was also affected by the Moldovan energy crisis and in February 2024, sought Russian economic aid and support against Moldovan antagonism. The supposed Moldovan antagonism was likely in reference to the increasing Moldovan military exercises across the Transnistria border and the West's increasing supply of armoured vehicles to the Moldovan army during late 2023. The rising Transnistrian tensions were complemented by the signing of the French-Moldovan military defence deal on 7 March 2024. On 17 March 2024, a drone strike occurred on a military installation in the Transnistria, of which the Ukrainians were likely behind.

Infighting within Moldova continued during the leadup to the 2024 Moldovan electoral elections. The pro-EU Sandu, head of the Party of Action and Solidarity, stood for election against the Russophile Party of the Socialist Republic of Moldova, headed by Alexandr Stoianoglo. In October 2023, the Moldovan Court allowed certain political figures from the Sor Party to participate in the elections in 2024. During the Russian elections in 2024, electoral polls were established in Transnistria, much to the outrage of Moldovans, inciting anti-Russian rhetorics. In August 2024, a Russian diplomat was expelled from Moldova after inciting Moldovan officials to thwart Moldova's attempts to enter the EU. The elections took place in October 2024, and Sandu claimed that Russian meddling was influencing the electoral results via disinformation and bribery. However, Sandu won the election with 55 per cent of the vote.

The Espionage War

Russian espionage and cyberattacks on NATO countries have increased since the Russian invasion in Ukraine. Russia hacked NATO countries' infrastructure to dismantle NATO cohesion. The most infamous case being the August 2022 Russian cyberattack on Estonian infrastructure. There was even a case in which the smartphones of British soldiers situated in Eastern Europe were hacked in order to gain intel of NATO troop positions in May 2024. Russian hacking increased during the elections in 2024 in an attempt to sway Western votes towards right wing isolationist politicians. The Russians attempted to gather intel on Polish officials' discussions regarding the Ukraine conflict and observing Western lend-leasing procedures by bugging Polish officials meeting rooms and airports. Russia has also disrupted Baltic GPS and sonar capabilities on numerous occasions during the early days of the Second Cold War. Numerous Western diplomats have been revealed to be corresponding to Russian secret intelligence. These diplomats were tasked by their Russian colleagues with intelligence gathering, disrupting parliamentary processes and to stall Western aid to Ukraine.

Russia attempted to thwart the West's hybrid war through a series of infiltration, sabotage and arson attacks across Europe. In May 2024, arson attacks occurred across NATO countries, such as Lithuania, Germany, UK, and Poland, and European authorities discovered that the perpetrators were paid by Russian secret services to commit the arson attacks. The Russian arson attacks coincided with the pro-Palestine protests, which became increasingly more aggressive, causing authorities to broaden their investigation and analyse which attacks were acts of pro-Palestine protesters or Russian espionage. Most of the arson attack perpetrators had dual-Russian nationality and ethnic Russian Ukrainian adolescent men who had been contacted by the Russian intelligence service. The Russian secret services hired Russian sympathisers in the West to do their dirty work, which gave Russia plausible deniability behind the attacks. The target of these arson attacks were military bases and warehouses.

On 18 April 2024, a Polish man, who conducted espionage activities for Russian agents, attempted to assassinate President Volodymyr Zelensky at the Rzeszów-Jasionka Airport in Poland. However, he failed and was arrested. In July 2024, German authorities discovered a Russian plot to assassinate the head of the German Rheinmetall weapons company. In August 2024, an incident occurred in a German military base near the Cologne Bonn Airport in which the tap water was contaminated, risking the lives of the soldiers stationed there.

In June 2024, the Russian secret services exploited the French public's fears over French President Emmanuel Macron's consideration of sending French soldiers into Ukraine and began a terror campaign to sway the French people against Macron. This involved a stunt where the Russian intelligence directly and indirectly made three men of German, Bulgarian and Ukrainian nationality perform a fearmongering stunt at the Eiffel Tower. This involved the hanging of empty coffins on the Eiffel Tower. The coffins wore the French flag, and were inscribed 'French Soldiers of Ukraine'. In June 2024, the French anti-terror wing arrested a Ukrainian-Russian dual national for bombing a hotel situated near the Charles de Gaulle Airport. The failed bomb plot brought the Ukraine War closer to French homes, swaying public opinion to be further against the Macron administration and French involvement in Ukraine.

In 2023, Russian secret services established an espionage unit aimed solely to operate in Europe. Their task was to undermine the West's lend-leasing programme by causing sabotage and local hysteria. The arson attacks were to curb Western lend-leasing logistics and processes to Ukraine. The arson campaign also contributed to Russia's propaganda campaign to encourage people's fears of escalation and a third world war, inciting isolationism and anti-Ukrainian sentiments amongst the European public. Russia's espionage campaign has hindered Western government decision and policy making concerning Ukraine, in fear of disapproval and outrage by the public opinion. The arson attacks coincided with the various European elections in 2024.

The coinciding would help Russia gain new allies inside NATO, as many right-wing nationalist leaders openly desire that their country stop or reduce the amount of lend-leasing to Ukraine.

The Prisoner Exchanges

Prison exchanges between the US and Russia have been a recurring feature during the Second Cold War. Between the months of May 2022 and December 2022, Joe Biden negotiated and finally agreed to exchange the infamous Russian arms seller, Victor Bout (widely known as the 'Merchant of Death') to secure the return of the imprisoned American basketball player, Britney Griner. The basketball player was detained for selling drugs in Russia and was known for her anti-American rhetorics. This prisoner exchange was very controversial as Biden agreed to exchange the 'Merchant of Death' for the cannabis dealer basketball player, instead of the former US Marine Paul Whelan (who was arrested for spy activity in Russia in 2018). The exchange of the 'Merchant of Death' in return of Griner was seen as an unfair trade that served little benefit to American interests in the newly emerging Second Cold War situation.

On February 2024, the US and Germany began talks on how to successfully release the imprisoned opposition leader and Russian politician, Alexei Navalny. These efforts fell flat when Navalny died on 16 February 2024 from a blood clot whilst in Russian custody. The initial talks concerning the release of Navalny naturally changed after Navalny's death, and sought the release of various other Western prisoners under Russian imprisonment. This resulted in a huge prisoner swap between the US and Russia, with Turkey acting as mediator. The prisoner swap was finally agreed on 1 August 2024. The US released eighteen prisoners and two children in exchange for sixteen Western citizens. Amongst the sixteen were political opposition leaders, such as Vladimir Kara-Murza, journalists and Paul Whelan. Russia saw the return of various spies and FSB personnel.

The Spillovers of the Ukraine War

The roaring missiles and hissing drones could be heard in the countries that neighbour Ukraine. Russian missiles roaring across the Ukrainian skies have on several occasions accidentally spilled over to Ukraine's NATO neighbours. The first spillover was on 10 March 2022 in which an unmanned UAV drone crashed in Zagreb in Croatia. The drone flew through Hungarian, Romanian and Croatian airspace without facing interception by any Western power before crashing in Zagreb, causing concerns over NATO defence capabilities. Three days later, a similar incident occurred with a Russian drone crashing in Transylvania. The most significant spillover incident occurred on 15 November 2022 in which a Russian missile struck a Polish farm in Prezwodów, resulting in the death of two Polish farmers. The night of the incident was intense and many NATO officials gathered together to discuss and analyse the situation, questioning if Article 5 of NATO was to be enacted. Zelensky showed his support to Poland and NATO for the Russian attack and called for a collective strike against Russian provocative terror on X (Twitter). However, NATO did not initiate Article 5.

NATO officials approached the situation with cool heads and chose to wait until Western investigations revealed if the Russian attack was deliberate or accidental. Zelensky's offer of Ukrainian investigators to help with the investigation, however, was declined. The investigation concluded that Russia had launched its daily bombardment in the West of Ukraine on the night of 15 November 2022 and the Ukrainian surface-to-air defences launched its missiles to counter the Russian attack. One of the Ukrainian surface-to-air missiles went out of control and strayed towards Poland, subsequently killing the two Polish farmers.

Poland, alongside other nations neighbouring Ukraine, experienced various spillovers and airspace violations during the Ukraine War, involving Russian missiles. The Russian missile airspace violations caused Polish fears that the Prezwodów incident would occur again. In May 2024, Poland alongside other Western nations discussed the prospect of constructing a 'drone wall' to counter Russian drones entering NATO airspace.[24] On various occasions in 2024, Polish jets were scrambled to the southeastern Polish border after Russia launched heavy bombardments on western Ukraine. The repeated spillovers made Poland consider Zelensky's proposal of intercepting any Russian missiles attacking western Ukrainian cities, in July 2024.[25] If the West were to intercept Russian missiles targeting western Ukraine, it would ensure that the Western lethal aid materials were successfully transferred to the Ukrainian front lines free of Russian harassment. It would also ensure the prevention of spillover incidents occurring in the future. NATO opposed this and Poland reversed their consideration, claiming that they would not commit to intercepting Russian missiles without NATO countries contributing also. Putin subsequently intensified the Russian army's missile barrages in western Ukrainian cities as a geopolitical message towards NATO.

It should also be noted that Poland announced the formation of the 'Ukrainian Legion' during this time. This saw the formation of a foreign legion, which recruited Polish Ukrainians and trained them on Polish soil by the Polish military. Poland hoped that the formation of Western formed Ukrainian brigades would encourage their NATO peers to do the same. It has been estimated that 600,000 Ukrainians fled to various Western nations during the initial Russian invasion of Ukraine. Europe was, therefore, a potential recruiting pool for the Ukrainian army. Between the years 2022 and 2024, Ukraine's arms stockpile was increasing due to Western lend-leasing. However, as the years progressed, the Ukrainian army realised that there were too few Ukrainian soldiers to actually man the wealth of weapons, due to high desertion and death rates. Germany and Czechia considered following Poland's lead in forming NATO formed Ukrainian foreign legions in order to counter Ukraine's manpower crisis. The first unit of the Polish Ukrainian Legion was reportedly sent to Ukraine in December 2024.

The Black Sea has been an area of intense episodes between Russia and the West during the Second Cold War. The Pentagon leaks revealed that a Russian jet chased down a RAF reconnaissance jet in Crimea with the intent to shoot it down in September 2022. Had the RAF jet been successfully shot down, Article 5 of NATO would have come into effect. The Pentagon leaks revealed that numerous French and British reconnaissance jets and American drones operated in the Black Sea and Crimea between September 2022 and February 2023.[26]

These reconnaissance missions were likely to aid the Ukrainians in locating and attacking specific Russian infrastructure in Crimea to thwart Russia's war effort in the Black Sea and southern theatres of operations. Western activity in Crimea was well known prior to the Pentagon leaks, as the Black Sea drone incident occurred on 14 March 2023. A Russian jet identified a Western MQ-9 Reaper drone in the international waters of the Black Sea and was ordered to harass the drone. The Russian jet flew close to the drone and released its fuel on the drone, which rendered the drone inoperable and it crashed into the waters of the Black Sea. A race ensued between Russian and Western forces to collect the drone, and the Russians won the race. Russia continued to intercept British and French reconnaissance jets in the Black Sea, well after the Black Sea Drone incident. Russian jets became more aggressive in nature with escorting the jets, likely to deter further Western intelligence gathering to the Ukrainians, especially when Russia was losing ground in the Black Sea theatre.

Since February 2022 (even prior to the 24th) NATO jets have scrambled and intercepted Russian jets violating Western airspace at least once a month. Russian airspace sea violations occur often in the Baltic, Arctic and Black Sea regions, Eastern European countries' airspace (i.e. Poland), and to a lesser extent the Alaskan skies, British and Irish airspace and waters. NATO claimed that Western jets scrambled and intercepted jets around 300 times during 2023.[27] These Russian violations of NATO airspace were likely acts of Russian military preparation in case a war with NATO were to occur. Western jets have also violated Russian airspace on numerous occasions, to which Russian jets similarly intercepted and escorted the planes out of the airspace. Most notably, on 21 July 2024, Russian jets intercepted two American bomber jets in the Russian arctic airspace. Although the back and forth between Western and Russian jets violating each other's airspace and interception occur on a daily and mundane basis, this shook Russian and Western public of fears of an escalation.

On 25 July 2024, Russia conducted retaliatory measures by flying two of their jets, which were capable of carrying nukes, alongside two Chinese jets, in Alaskan airspace, with American and Canadian jets quickly intercepting them. This incident incited fears over previous Russian territorial claims over Alaska, which nobody took seriously during the early days of the Second Cold War. Russia claimed that the Alaskan state should be part of Russia, citing Alaska's former Russian heritage. However, Alaska's former link to Russia is a ploy for Russia to legitimise and justify their claims over the newly found natural riches of Alaska.

Nuclear Blackmail

Akin to the First Cold War, nuclear flexing and threats have been abundant since 2022. Both Russian and American leaders have threatened each other with war and nuclear retaliation when the other made escalatory actions during the Ukraine War. When Russia invaded Ukraine in 2022, Putin made nuclear threats towards NATO, in order to deter NATO from sending troops to Ukraine's aid. Russia flexed their nuclear arms with numerous nuclear exercises and transferred their nuclear warheads to neighbouring Belarus to cause fear and hysteria in the West. Russian nuclear flexing also aimed to recover the 'Russian Bear' reverence after the surprising Russian military failure of the initial invasion of Ukraine. On February 2023, Russia suspended its participation in the New START programme, which was the mutual agreement to decrease the American and Russian nuclear warhead stockpile. These nuclear threats changed from deterring NATO intervention into deterring the Western nations sending further lethal aid to Ukraine. Putin intensified his nuclear blackmail diplomacy in June 2024, when Western nations were contemplating approving Ukrainian use of Western long-range missiles to attack Russian infrastructure in June 2024. The West realised that Russia's nuclear blackmail was feckless as Putin had voiced the same threats over and over without ever acting on it, impoverishing Putin's nuclear warnings.

After the dire situation Russia was under in the aftermath of Ukraine's twin offensives, many Russian politicians considered the use of tactical nukes on Ukraine according to the American intelligence. Biden made a strategically ambiguous warning to Russia in October 2022, claiming that a Russian nuclear attack on Ukraine would be a serious mistake, hinting an American nuclear retaliatory response to Russia. However, Russia again used the nuclear threat towards the West, when news of Macron's consideration of sending French troops to Ukraine became well publicised in the media.

NATO Soldiers in Ukraine?

French-Russian rivalry increased significantly after the humiliating Niger crisis and Macron's attempts to lure Armenia away from the Russian bloc in 2023. Tensions reached a boiling point in February 2024 when French President Emmanuel Macron claimed that the prospects of sending French troops to Ukraine, should not be excluded, after attending a NATO crisis meeting. Macron's statement was supposed to serve as a strategic ambiguity tactic towards Russia. However, the message conveyed by Macron was wrongly interpreted as a blatant message of escalation by both France's allies and enemies. NATO allies, such as Germany, the US, Italy, Spain, Czechia and Poland, opposed Macron's interventionist consideration. The Russian propaganda department exploited Macron's strategic ambiguity against him and misled the Western public's understanding of Macron's strategy to cause public hysteria. However, some NATO allies and political figures backed Macron's consideration, and even entertained the idea of sending NATO personnel to Ukraine, to train Ukrainian soldiers.

As mentioned previously, Russian intelligence services performed the coffin stunt at the Eiffel Tower. Russian propaganda campaigns were made on social media claiming that French and NATO troops were already in Ukraine. Anti-West media outlets claimed that the 3rd Regiment of the French Foreign Legion were already in Ukraine, whilst in reality they were in French Guiana at the time. Russian propaganda portrayed Emmanuel Macron as a satanic figure that spat on the French Christian people and also compared him to Napoleón Bonaparte. Such a comparison with Bonaparte made the common person associate

Macron with the colonial and expansionist nineteenth-century French state, triggering both Progressivist-Left hatred towards Macron for his alleged neo-colonial mindset and intensifying the Western publics' fear of escalation.

Information campaigns were further fuelled in the months of March to May 2024, with several revelations of NATO intervention in Ukraine. On 4 March 2024, the Russian intelligence leaked a telephone call from German Federal Minister of Defence Boris Pistorius. The telephone call revealed German discussions on whether to send long-range German Taurus missiles to Ukraine. The discussion revealed that the long-range missiles could be used to destroy the Kerch Bridge. German counterarguments were made, claiming that the Tauras system were too complex to teach the Ukrainians how to operate them within a short span of time, meaning that German military personnel would have to operate them in Ukraine instead. They compared such a hypothetical situation with British operatives in Ukraine operating British Storm missiles attacking Russian troops and vehicles on Ukraine's behalf.[28] This further intensified mass hysteria of an incoming third world war in Germany and the West.

German Chancellor Olaf Scholz accidently revealed to the public that British personnel were operating in Ukraine, days prior to the telephone leak. Scholz attempted to justify to his NATO peers why Germany was not sending its Taurus missiles to Ukraine. Scholz claimed that the Taurus missiles would have to be manned by German military personnel in Ukraine and explained that he would not authorise German troops being sent to Ukraine to man German war machines on Ukraine's behalf, unlike his British and French peers. Scholz faced backlash for his comment as it revealed that French and British operatives were manning Storm Shadow missile attacks on behalf of Ukraine in the conflict.[29] It has been long speculated by analysts that NATO personnel were active in Ukraine. They point towards the use of M142 HIMARS against Russia and the complex nature of the system, which takes dedicated time to be operated. However, Ukraine obtained and used the HIMARS system within a relatively short period of time, making many speculate that NATO personnel were secretly operating them.

Russian disinformation campaigns exploited Western fears and speculation of NATO covert involvement in Ukraine. In March 2024, Polish Brigadier General Adam Marczak died of natural causes. However, Russian media outlets claim that he had been killed by a missile attack in Chasiv Yar in a bunker amongst other NATO generals. In response to Macron's French intervention into Ukraine, British Prime Minister Rishi Sunak opposed a full-scale intervention into Ukraine. However, he claimed that a small number of British military personnel were in Ukraine with the task of training Ukrainian soldiers and conscripts.[30] Russian media outlets twisted Sunak's words, claiming that Sunak was considering sending British troops to Ukraine and some Russian propaganda outlets claimed that British troops had already been sent.

Despite French protests against sending French troops to Ukraine, accompanied by protests demanding lethal aid to Ukraine be stopped outright, between the months of March to May 2024, Macron still voiced his 'strategic ambiguity' rhetorics. Russia conducted a nuclear exercise in response to 'provocative remarks from the West', further fuelling the Western public's anti-Ukraine sentiments. Macron's strategic ambiguity about sending French troops to Ukraine resulted in a significant backfire. However, it is undeniable that covert NATO intervention is occurring in Ukraine. As mentioned, British and French personnel are gathering satellite intelligence in the Black Sea and Crimea to help Ukraine's Black Sea and Crimea attacks. Western nations, notably the US, have provided a plethora of satellite intel to Kyiv of the whereabouts of Russian forces. Scholz let it be known that both Britain and France military contingents are in Ukraine, operating Storm Shadow missiles to attack the Russian military. The Pentagon leaks revealed that a small number of NATO troops were in Ukraine: fifty British, fifteen French, one Dutch, seventeen Latvian and fourteen American operatives. Western officials claim that these operatives were sent to Ukraine for various reasons: ensuring the safety of VIP officials, the safe transfer of Western lethal aid to the Ukrainian front lines, and to train Ukrainian conscripts and soldiers.

The New York Times correspondent Adam Entous provides a revealing account of the US' direct involvement in the Ukraine War. Entous conducted over 300 interviews with Biden team officials and other Western military and intelligence officers. Entous discovered that during the early days of the Ukraine War, British SAS soldiers extracted several Ukrainian generals from Kyiv to Poland. The Ukrainians were subsequently escorted to Wiesbaden Germany, where they met American General Donohue and a team of American military-intelligence personnel. Wiesbaden became the centre of American intelligence sharing with Kyiv. Entous describes the US as being the dominant partner in the Wiesbaden alliance. Donohue provided Kyiv with satellite images of Russian military targets and subsequently ordered Ukraine to attack the targets. The Biden team wanted to make sure that the joint US-Ukraine coordinated strikes didn't accidentally escalate into Russia declaring war against the US in retaliation. Biden's fear of escalation irritated the Ukrainian partners as they believed that it slowed the Ukrainian's process in swiftly ousting the invaders from their territories. Russian official's nuclear threats in October 2022 following the twin offensives furthered Biden's fears of escalation.

In 2023, Kyiv became more autonomous within the Wiesbaden relationship. Friction between the partners occurred over disagreements on Ukrainian preparations for the Zaporozhe offensive, during which the American partners ordered Kyiv to stop diverting troops away from Zaporozhe to the Bakhmut front and ordered the Zaporozhe offensive only to push towards capturing Melitpol. Kyiv did not listen, much to the protest of the American partners.

In 2024, Ukraine took a defensive posture following the failure of the Zaporozhe offensive but attacked Russian logistics to curb the 2023 to 2024 Winter Donbas offensives, with the Americans providing location intelligence assistance. Kyiv began attacking Russian oil refineries. However, the American partners disapproved due to fears of escalation. Arguably, the American partners' constant fears of escalation resulted in Kyiv not informing Washington of their Kursk offensive plans. During the Russian cross-border Kharkiv offensive, Washington feared that the Russian advances would put the city of Kharkiv in range of Russian missiles, which could have caused a massive humanitarian issue. Two American advisors were sent to the city of Kharkiv and established an 'ops box' in which Ukraine was allowed to fire American ATCAMS and HIMARS missiles against Russian logistics in Belgorod oblast. The American advisers and several CIA officers aided the Ukrainian army in targeting the Russian logistics in Belgorod, which eventually led to the sudden halt in Russian advances on the Kharkiv front.[31]

The North Korean Intervention

North Korea has shown stern allegiance to Russia's war effort against Ukraine by internationally supporting the invasion in 2022. Since November 2022, North Korea has exported its own manufactured ammunition and missiles to Russia sending ammunition and missiles from November 2022 onwards.

In June 2024, Putin visited Pyongyang. The Pyongyang summit was very significant to North Korean-Russian relations as a mutual defence pact was made. The Defence Pact saw the increase in weapons and munitions exports between the two countries. The

Defence Pact was likely sought after by Putin in response to the West's discussions to give the green light for Ukrainian use of long-range missiles on Russian infrastructure. The summit also entailed the agreement for North Korean engineer troops and construction workers to be sent to Russian occupied Crimea. These troops would help Russian maintenance and reconstruction of bombed buildings and infrastructure caused by Ukraine's bombing campaign in the peninsula. Putin's visit to North Korea made South Korea consider sending lethal aid to Ukraine. South Korea sent Ukraine a plethora of non-lethal aid in response to Russia's invasion but did not send lethal aid. During 2023, the US was pressuring South Korea to send munitions and lethal aid to Ukraine and the Pentagon leaks revealed that an American spy within the South Korean political sphere was reporting that Seoul was contemplating a possible transfer of lethal aid to Ukraine.[32]

In mid-October 2024, Ukrainian and eventually South Korean intelligence claimed that 12,000 North Korean troops were being sent to Russia, with the intention of fighting in Ukraine. Dubious Western sources claimed that North Korean troops were already fighting in the Kursk region and a couple of North Korean troops surrendered themselves to Ukrainian soldiers on arrival to the front. Zelensky pleaded to the West to do something to dissuade North Korea from officially entering the war. Western officials remained silent, whilst dubious evidence of North Korean troops arrival into Russia circulated online, as did speculation of North Korea's role in Ukraine circulated in the media. Were they actually going to fight the Ukrainians at the front, to gain combat experience? Or were the North Koreans stationed in Russia or Russian occupied Ukraine to maintain Russian security/logistics, allowing the Russian army to send more of its troops to the Ukraine front?

On 28 October 2024, head of NATO, Mark Rutte, confirmed that North Korean troops were currently fighting in the Kursk Region against the Ukrainians. With the news of North Korea's entry into the Ukraine war, South Korea started to consider sending lethal aid to Ukraine yet again. However, news of North Korean troops in Ukraine was likely to make South Korea more hesitant about sending lethal aid to Ukraine because a South Korean bullet or artillery shell killing a North Korean soldier in Ukraine would cause a serious escalation between the two Korean states. If Ukraine were to be supplied with lethal aid from South Korea, it would mean the Ukraine War would become a North Korea-South Korean proxy war and would escalate tensions at the Korean border.

Ukraine alleged that a clash between Ukrainian and North Korean troops had occurred on 5 November 2024. However, on 11 November 2024, Russia launched a 50,000 manned joint Russian-North Korean counteroffensive in the Kursk region and made significant gains. Keeping track of North Korean troop deployments in the Kursk front had been difficult for journalists and officials, as it has been widely reported that the North Korean troops were supplied with Russian uniforms and equipment. The North Korean troops were integrated into the Russian army and were officially portrayed as a brigade of volunteers and conscripts from Russia's Asian Buryatia region. The reasoning for this decision was to confuse NATO intelligence gathering of North Korean presence in Ukraine and to give North Korea plausible deniability when questioned of their involvement in Ukraine. Videos of Russian forces defacing dead North Koreans and discovered North Korean diaries, which detailed how the North Korean soldiers were ordered to kill themselves with a grenade instead of becoming a Ukrainian POW, added to the argument that Russia and North Korea made extensive efforts to keep North Korean intervention a secret or at least can be rendered as plausibly deniable.

During January 2025, a video was released on the Special Operations Forces of the Armed Forces of Ukraine telegram channel, of a wounded North Korean in the aftermath of a firefight. As the Ukrainian soldier in the video approaches the North Korean to take him prisoner, the North Korean screamed 'Kim Jong Un!' as he detonated a grenade against his skull.[33] As one North Korean POW explained, 'In our People's Corps, being a prisoner of war is the equivalent of defection'.[34] When Ukrainian soldiers retold their experiences of capturing two North Korean soldiers on 11 January 2025, the Ukrainian operatives alleged that heavy Russian artillery were striking their positions in an attempt to prevent the North Koreans being taken alive by killing them.[35]

There has been speculation about what exactly North Korea gains in return for their intervention. Others point to Russian shipment of oil and modern weaponry to North Korea as a reward for their contribution to the Russian war effort. Some argue that it is to give the North Korean army war experience that could be later implemented in a possible war with South Korea. The North Korean army is known for its outdated equipment, due to its self-inflicted and internationally imposed isolationism. North Korean troops have received Russian training with Russian stockpiled weapons and war machines before being deployed in earnest to Kursk. The North Korean troops used these Russian weapons during their time at the Kursk front. Therefore, Kim Jong Un sent the North Korean forces to fight in Russia in exchange for Russian weapon transfers and training which would be utilised to modernise their outdated army.

Minor skirmishes between North Korean and Ukrainian troops were sporadically reported between 4 November and 15 December. On 22 November 2024, the Maryino Estate, which hosted some North Korean forces, was struck by Ukrainian Storm Shadow missiles. The West approved the Ukrainian use of Western missiles against Russian territory. Various disputed reports circulated about the North Korean casualties thereafter. The Maryino Estate strike killed a Russian general and wounded a North Korean general. Zelensky claimed that Putin was using the North Korean troops in earnest on 16 December. Heavy North Korean fatalities and casualties in Kursk were widely reported from 16 December onwards and by 20 December 2024, South Korean intelligence had estimated 100 North Koreans were killed in action in Kursk.

On 11 January 2025, Ukrainian forces successfully managed to capture two North Korean soldiers and subsequently interrogated them. When asked if they wanted to return to North Korea, one of the North Korean soldiers claimed he did not want to return. However, both North Korean PoWs later expressed their desire to seek asylum in South Korea. Zelensky offered Pyongyang to return the North Korean prisoners, but South Korea objected. As part of South Korea's general policy, all North Korean defectors are allowed to gain asylum in South Korea. This brings a dilemma for North Korean soldiers stationed in Kursk, whether to fight for their country or to defect and escape the totalitarian regime. It was widely reported in late January 2025, that North Korean troops were temporarily withdrawn from the Kursk front lines after receiving a casualty rate of over 1,000. During this revelation, it was reported by Western media that Pyongyang was sending more troops and more war vehicles to Russia during the North Korean withdrawal from the Kursk front lines. The North Korean troops that were already stationed in Russia appeared to have returned to the front lines in February 2025.

After the complete ejection of the last remaining Ukrainian forces from Kursk oblast on 26 April 2025, the chief of the General Staff of the Russian armed forces, Valery Gerasimov, thanked the North Koreans for their participation in liberating Kursk. Gerasimov's gratitude to the North Korean troops marked the first official acknowledgment by Moscow of North Korean intervention in the Ukraine War. On the 28th, Putin thanked Kim Jong Un for his assistance to the liberation of Kursk and claimed that Russia was willing to provide similar assistance to North Korea in the future. This put an end to Russian and North Korean officials' denial that North Korean troops were fighting in Kursk. The strengthening of Russian-North Korean ties guarantees Russian support for Korea in the event of a Second Korean War.

Chapter Four

THE SIGNIFICANCE OF THE MEDIA AND PROPAGANDA DURING THE UKRAINE WAR

The Judgement of Measurement

For the Ukrainians, victory is measured in kilometres. If Ukraine is gaining territory, then they are perceived as winning. If they are losing ground, then Ukraine is perceived as losing. This perception of the judgment of measurement is key to understanding the Ukrainian military's 2022-2023 strategy rationale and Zelensky's 'big picture' mindset. Zelensky believes that the West's judgement of measurement is key to gaining Western lethal aid. If Ukraine gained significant territory back from Russian occupation, the West would have confidence in the Ukrainians to continue to push Russia out of the country. With this confidence, Western nations will increase sending lethal aid to Ukraine and even consider transferring to Ukraine deadlier weapons and war machines that were not previously on the table. This can be seen after Ukraine's twin offensives, as the success of the offensives changed Western nations' views (especially American views) on the lend-leasing process from hesitant to confident. After the success of the twin offensives, the US and the West began to provide Ukraine with deadlier war machines, such as F-16s and Abram tanks. If Ukraine was to experience a series of setbacks and loss of territory to the Russians, that would hinder Western confidence in sending lethal aid to Ukraine, as they do not want to waste their military assets to certain destruction or capture. This was seen during the months of December 2023 and January 2024 after the much-anticipated

Zaporozhe offensive, which resulted in a humiliating Ukrainian failure and significant loss in Western lethal aid.

Ukraine has, therefore, put a significant emphasis on their media and propaganda campaign towards the West in order to maintain steady and effective Western support. Media and propaganda, therefore, played an important role in the Ukraine War, significantly more than any war prior. Propaganda has physically influenced the course of the war and altered military commanders reasoning for their military conduct. Russia engaged in the media and propaganda war to thwart Western confidence in the lend-leasing propaganda towards Ukraine and to influence Ukrainian military conduct to Russia's favour. Western media also played a role on the side of Ukraine, as its news channels are an anchor for the Western governments to persuade its public to sympathise with Ukraine and to support Western lend-leasing. Western media repeatedly downplayed the significance of Russian military feats, usually claiming that a city conquered by the Russians was of no strategic value. The BBC infamously claimed that the surrender of Azov soldiers to the Russian forces during the siege of Mariupol was an 'evacuation' which was a deliberate misrepresentation of events, in order to portray the Ukrainian defenders as returning towards their lines.[36] In reality, they were 'evacuating' towards Russian lines.

The judgement of measurement dynamics can be seen played out during Russia's Donbas summer offensive. Ukrainian defence in the Donbas were initially effective in hindering Russian advances. By May 2022, Ukraine could no longer hold back the Russian further advances. However, Ukraine officials publicly claimed that the Ukrainian positions did not move during the Donbas summer offensive and the Ukrainian military continued to halt Russian advances. Western media and news outlets regurgitated Ukrainian officials' false claims without further investigation. When Russia reached the twin cities of Severodonetsk and Lysychansk, many analysts claimed that the soundest move for the Ukrainian army was to withdraw from these cities in order to get to a better defensive position and avoid unnecessary troop losses. However, if the Russian army captured of the twin cities, this would mean the complete explement of the Ukrainian army from the Luhansk oblast, which would be a significant blow to both the Ukrainian morale and its prestige in the eyes of its Western allies. Zelensky refused to withdraw the Ukrainian army from the twin cities and sent a significant number of foreign fighters from Western nations to fight in the twin cities. Zelensky sent foreign legion reinforcements in order to pull on the heartstrings and get the attention of the Western public. Western coverage of the Donbas summer offensive was reduced during this time due to the repeated Ukrainian army's losses and because the public became bored of the initial shock of the invasion in February 2022. They were more interested in other news and dramas, such as the Johnny Depp versus Amber Heard case, and so Western journalism moved away from Ukraine to other stories.

The Battle of Popasna occurred during the Donbas summer offensive, in which Russia's Wagner Group soldiers participated. Ukrainian propagandists circulated tales of Wagner Group troops beheading Ukrainian PoWs and planting the heads on spikes. The Ukrainians compared the supposed Wagner Group war crimes to the actions of the Orcs from J.R.R. Tolkien's *Lord of the Rings* world. This tale was to reinforce Ukrainian hatred towards the Russians and to disgust the Western public's outlook on the Russian military as a gang of war criminals. It was also a propaganda tactic to dehumanise the Russians and to portray them as barbarians. This has caused Ukrainian soldiers to nickname Russian soldiers as 'Orcs' when engaging in a firefight.

Western news outlets refocused their stories back to the Ukraine War, after the successes of Ukraine's twin offensives and the subsequent Russian setbacks that were wrought from it, i.e. the Russian mass mobilisation in 2022. Western media outlets anticipated a follow up Ukrainian offensive in spring 2023, which Zelensky exploited to gain more Western lethal aid. The leader of the Wagner Group, Yevgeny Prigozhin, later realised the significance of the judgement of measurement, and weaponised the West's and Ukraine's Propaganda and Media campaign against them.

Prigozhin's Propaganda War

During the months of September 2022 to May 2023, Russian military personnel was significantly outstretched across the Ukrainian front and was therefore, vulnerable to another Ukrainian offensive. Prigozhin, therefore, applied Wagner Group pressure in the Ukrainian city of Bakhmut. This was to divert Ukrainian troops away from the southern front to Bakhmut, until the Russian troops received their full training and were deployed to Ukraine to fill up the multiple outstretched Russian fronts. Prigozhin wanted to use the infamy of the Wagner Group to gain Western media and news attention to Bakhmut whilst the Russian army silently trained its mobilised troops and fortified its defences in the Zaporozhe oblast in anticipation for the Ukrainian spring offensive. Due to significant Western media coverage of the Battle of Bakhmut, the Ukrainian army could not neglect the media battle surrounding the city or face a decline in Western confidence. Zelensky was, therefore, pressured by the Western media to divert troops from the southern front to Bakhmut in order to maintain Ukrainian prestige and not lose ground to the Russians. It could be argued that the Wagner Group pressure in the Bakhmut sector led to the Zaporozhe offensive being postponed from the spring to summer 2023. Prigozhin made it clear multiple times to journalists and on social media, that the aim of the Battle of Bakhmut was to act as a 'meat grinder' and to reduce the number of Ukrainian personnel. Due to intense Western media coverage of the Battle of Bakhmut, more and more Ukrainian soldiers were diverted from multiple fronts towards the 'meat grinder'. It can be argued that the battle significantly contributed to the Ukrainian army's manpower crisis.

Prigozhin knew that the Battle of Bakhmut was both a physical and propaganda battle. Prigozhin exploited Western media, who indirectly influenced Ukrainian military goals and conduct, in favour of Russia's military objectives. Many analysts argued that Ukraine should have withdrawn its troops from Bakhmut, as the Russian capture of the city was inevitable. They argued for the defence of Bakhmut to be abandoned, in order to save Ukrainian troop numbers. The discussion of Bakhmut flared up in Western media and news outlets, discussing whether Bakhmut was an insignificant city or not. Some Western analysts, such as Michael Clarke, claimed that the city held no strategic value. However, if one were to look at a map, they would realise that he was misleading the Western public, as the city was connected to several roads to multiple surrounding Ukrainian strongholds and logistical hub cities, such as Toretsk, Chasiv Yar and Slovyansk. Bakhmut was indeed of strategic value, as Russia had to take the city in order to make further advances into the Donbas. When the Wagner Group eventually took the city, the Western public believed that a lot of Russians had died for no real strategic goal, due to Western media outlets' manipulation. Discussions were made as to who was winning the battle and who suffered the most casualties. Prigozhin incited more media attention to the Battle of Bakhmut by challenging Zelensky to an aerial dual over Bakhmut, claiming that whoever won would earn the occupancy of the city.

Prigozhin also exploited Russian media outlets to side with him against his rivals in the Russian army and even Putin himself. Throughout the battle, Prigozhin complained online that his men were not being properly supplied by the Russian army and Putin.

This reached a boiling point on 5 May 2023 when Prigozhin filmed himself next to dead Wagner Group troops and shouting that Russian Minister of Defence Sergei Shoigu was not properly supplying the Wagner Group resulting in the unnecessary deaths of fellow Russian Wagner Group soldiers. This aimed to cause public outcry in Russia and pressured the Russian army and Russian officials to adhere to Prigozhin's supply demands. Prigozhin later released a video of a Wagner Group soldier's point of view of the immediate aftermath of a supposed Russian artillery strike on Wagner Group soldiers. The video is rather ambiguous and does not provide clear details as to what happened. This video, alongside claims that the Russian army deliberately placed landmines to attack Wagner Group's withdrawal from Bakhmut, gave Prigozhin sufficient ammunition to launch the Wagner Group's 'March of Justice'. Wagner demanded a reformation of the Russian official army and the resignation of Shoigu. Russian residents did not attempt to thwart Wagner Group's march to Moscow. Instead, they praised the soldiers of Bakhmut. Russian coverage of the Battle of Bakhmut had earned Prigozhin much respect from the Russian public. Even after his death, Prigozhin is viewed with much respect by the Russian society despite his betrayal. To Putin's distain, the prestige of Prigozhin cannot be wiped away from the public mind.

Western media reported that the convict Wagner Group troops attacked Ukrainian positions in Bakhmut in mass hoard-like waves possessing only shovels, which British Secretary of Defence Ben Wallace embarrassingly attempted to convince the British public to be true. Regardless, Wagner Group troops took the city in May 2023, which significantly impacted the Western public's perception of the Ukrainian army. Zelensky initially denied the loss of Bakhmut and then subsequently reiterated Western media arguments – that the city was of no strategic value. Bakhmut can be seen as a turning point in the war, as the battle and the media campaign surrounding it led to the Ukrainian Zaporozhe blunder in summer 2023.

The Spring Offensive Hype

Ukraine had made the Western public anticipate and even be excited for the spring offensive in the southern front on social media and news outlets. This caused discussion as to where and when the offensive would take place across the southern front and speculated what the Ukrainian objectives were online. Ukraine even released a cinematic film-like trailer in anticipation of the spring offensive. Few Western journalists or government officials voiced their concerns of satellite evidence of Russian forces' construction of strong defences across the

Zaporozhe front. It was obvious to everyone that Ukraine would launch its offensive in Zaporozhe. The Kharkiv oblast offensive had warped the West's realistic expectations of the outcome of the Zaporozhe offensive. The Ukrainian army had managed to take swathes of territory and make significant advances into the Kharkiv oblast with ease because the Ukrainian army had exploited Russia's outstretched and vulnerable defences in the region. The West believed that Ukraine would made similar gains in the Zaporozhe oblast. This was impossible because the Russians' strong defences and the deployment of mobilised personnel in Zaporozhe, reinforcing the front. It was, therefore, a sobering experience when the Ukrainian army made little progress in the much-anticipated Zaporozhe offensive.

Brigades that were originally destined for the Zaporozhe offensive, such as the 93rd Mechanized Brigade, were diverted to Bakhmut and then immediately sent back to fight in the Zaporozhe offensive. These highly decorated brigades were demoralised, inefficiently equipped and lacked the professional soldiers that it once had due to their mauling in Bakhmut. Not enough time was given to these brigades to recuperate their losses. It can also be argued that Ukraine's Bakhmut counteroffensive, contributed to the failure of the Zaporozhe offensive, as troops deployments were diverted from the south to the east, in order to take back Bakhmut and reverse the damaging consequences of the loss of Bakhmut on the Western confidence. The territorial gains of the Bakhmut counteroffensive was eventually lost during Russia's Donbas winter offensive, making the effort in vain. In hindsight, the troops participating in the Bakhmut counteroffensive, should have been dedicated to reinforcing the defences of Chasiv Yar and participating in the Zaporozhe offensive, as advised by Kyiv's American partners in Wiesbaden. Again, we see how propaganda and media has influenced Ukrainian military decisions and conduct.

Every month that passed during the Zaporozhe offensive, Western media outlets claimed that Ukraine had successfully breached Russia's first line of defence. Ukraine had passed the Russian first line of defence by the third month of the offensive. Images of destroyed Western tanks burning close together on the field of Zaporozhe became viral online, which significantly skewered Western nations' confidence in Ukraine. The West entrusted these tanks to the Ukrainian army, but they were subsequently destroyed en masse. The burning of the Western tanks symbolised to Western officials that their efforts and money were also burned on the fields of Zaporozhe. The propaganda hype and aftermath of the Zaporozhe offensive resulted in a decline of the Western public's willingness to support

Ukraine. Western media outlets no longer portrayed Ukraine as a winning participant of the Ukraine War. It also reinforced the dent in Zelensky's relations with his Western peers during the months of December 2023 and January 2024.

The Ukrainian Invasion of Russia

Russia attempted to repeat the Bakhmut propaganda strategy during the Battle of Avdiivka which appealed to Western journalists, but not to the significant extent that raged during the Battle of Bakhmut. Avdiivka was dubbed 'Meat Grinder 2.0' or 'Bakhmut 2.0' by Western journalists. However, coverage of the battle subsided as it was obvious that Ukraine was not winning the battle. It should be noted that the anti-Putin Russian volunteer brigades launched incursions in the Russian Belgorod and Kursk oblasts during the battles of Bakhmut and Avdiivka. This was likely to woo the Western public and to divert their attention away from those losing battles. The Russian volunteer incursion in the Belgorod and Kursk oblasts in March 2024 coincided with the Russian elections in 2024. It can be speculated that the incursion was to sway Russian residents there to vote against Putin due to inefficient Russian countermeasures against a Ukrainian incursion. Belgorod residents voiced their concerns of Russia's perceived lack of counter measures after the Belgorod incursions in summer 2023. However, the incursions backfired as residents in these oblasts would vote for Putin, as the incursions increased anti-Ukrainian and pro-war rhetoric in the oblasts. It should be noted, however, that the purpose of these incursions was not solely on propaganda purposes. The incursions provided reconnaissance and intelligence of the neighbouring oblasts defences and strategic areas of interests, for a possible offensive into Russia. This came to fruition in August 2024 with the Kursk oblast offensive.

Many journalists and analysts argued that the Kursk offensive was to strain Russian manpower to alleviate pressure on the Donbas front lines. This is debatable as this offensive actually strained the already struggling Ukrainian defences and manpower in the Donbas front line. Also, the Kursk offensive did not hinder Russia's advance into Pokrovsk. However, the Kursk offensive did result in various Russian battalions being sent from the southern front lines, Kaliningrad oblast, and even Burkina Faso to repel Ukrainian troops in Russia. A possible goal of the Kursk offensive was that in anticipation to Trump's assession to American presidency, Ukraine could use an occupied Kursk oblast as a bargaining chip, during the Russo-Ukrainian peace talks. The main goal of the Ukrainian offensive into Kursk was to capture the Kursk

Nuclear Power Plant. During peace negotiations, Kyiv could have offered to exchange the Kursk Nuclear Power Plant for the Zaporozhe Nuclear Power Plant. This argument appeared to have been confirmed in February 2025, as Zelensky announced his interests to return the occupied parts of Kursk to Russia in exchange for the return of certain Russian occupied lands. This was an ambitious goal, as it would acquire significant Ukrainian presence in the oblast to fend off Russian forces, for a long duration of time. The Kursk offensive was carried out as part of a political campaign to pressure the West to approve of the Ukrainian use of Western long-range missiles against Russian territory. The land offensive into Russia, accompanied by a series of attacks on Russian infrastructure in other oblasts, was to persuade the West that striking Russian territory caused little in the way repercussions, escalation or Russian retaliation as feared by the West. Ukraine's aggressive policy against Russia during this period was to encourage the West to approve the Ukrainian use of Western long-range missiles against Russian infrastructure. Regardless, Western media outlets were sceptical of the success of the Kursk offensive and refrained themselves from outbursts of glee in their headlines, as to avoid outdatedness and tarnishing of the outlet's reputation.

Russia's Disinformation Campaign
During the beginning of the Ukraine War, Ukraine bombarded the internet with anti-Russian propaganda, to which many Western internet users subscribed. The most infamous was a meme that compared Vladimir Putin to Adolf Hitler. This warped Western perception of Putin from the cold, calculated and well-respected figurehead of Russia to a rambling Hitler-esque buffoon. Russia countered this by attacking Western public perception of Volodymyr Zelensky. An effective Russian disinformation campaign raged online, claiming that the Western lend-leasing programme to Ukraine was an elaborate money laundering scheme in between Zelensky and Biden and the American deep state. The claim went viral on social media, and was regurgitated by Russian bots and ill-informed Western social media influencers to influence public perception against the West's lend-leasing programme. The Money Laundering Scheme conspiracy was aimed to make the common Western social media user believe that the cause of their financial hardships was caused by Volodymyr Zelensky's greed. The conspiracy works off repeated news of Zelensky's dissatisfaction with Western lend-leasing. Zelensky consistently demanded more lethal aid, claiming that the amount was insufficient to hold back Russian advances

and criticised Western nations' decision to withhold certain war machines. Zelensky's comments have hindered relations with his Western peers, most embarrassingly British Secretary of Defence Ben Wallace, who once counterargued Zelensky complaints by stating that 'we (the West) are not Amazon'.[37]

Zelensky's dissatisfactions and criticisms were not unfounded and if anyone else were in his position, they would certainly make similar demands. However, this did hinder somewhat Zelensky's image in the West, as they viewed him as wanting more than he could chew. The conspiracy theory also served off the back Joe Biden's son Hunter Biden's scandal in Ukraine. The conspiracy theory was encouraged by the fact that the Ukrainian government was known for its corruption. However, Zelensky passed an anti-corruption bill in summer 2023, which saw the prosecution of politicians and officials for corruption. The bill aimed to deter further corruption scandals, as Ukrainian corruption hindered the Ukrainian war effort and public image.

Social media accounts that circulated the conspiracy theory provided no evidence whatsoever. Those most likely to subscribe to the conspiracy theory were American Republican voters who already believed in countless (anti-government) conspiracy theories. Russian propaganda had even attempted to portray the West's pro-Ukraine stance as being associated with the LGBTQ movement in order to gain sympathy from the far-right niche groups and certain Republican Christian-nationalist groups online. Despite the weak validity of the conspiracy theory, it has proven to be effective, as a significant portion of the Western public view Zelensky with scepticism, which contrasts with Zelensky's image during 2022.

The American population's growing suspicions and disillusionment challenged the White House's support to Ukraine. As shall be further explored in chapter ten, the Russian disinformation operatives' goal is to hinder the West's support towards Ukraine via amassing domestic pressure groups. It also aims to cause social upheaval within Western societies and cause a gulf between Western states. Russian disinformation has also been utilised to interfere in elections and help a desired candidate enter office. This has been most notable during the 2024 Georgian elections, in which the West and Russia engaged in a fierce disinformation and information campaign to persuade Georgian voters to elect their desired candidates into power. The West's interference during the Georgian elections aimed to ensure that pro-EU political figures and parties got into power, assuring that Georgia would continue the country's pursuit for EU candidacy.

However, Russian disinformation bested the Western nations, as the Russian aligned Georgian Dream won the Georgian parliamentary and presidential elections. The Georgian Dream's Russian inspired "foreign agents" law caused major setbacks to the country's progress towards being accepted into the EU, resulting in numerous anti-government protests. Moscow's victory in the disinformation war in Georgia against the Western interventionists prevented the neighboring Caucasian country pivoting to the West and ensured that Georgia remained under Russian influence."

Russia's Justification for Invading its Neighbour

During the Ukrainian crisis and initial invasion, Russian officials and propaganda claimed that Ukraine housed an array of neo-Nazis. The Kremlin cited nationalist paramilitary group the Azov Battalion as evidence to these claims. Russian propogandists referred to the Azov Battalion, to make further claims that the Ukrainian government itself included Nazis in its number. When the initial invasion occurred, Putin justified his invasion by claiming that they are participating in a de-Nazification military operation in Ukraine. Zelensky pointed out Putin's flawed justification by claiming that he was of Jewish descent and his family experienced the Holocaust during the Second World War. Russian Minister of Foreign Affairs Sergey Lavrov responded to Zelensky's counterpoint by claiming that the Jews collaborated with the Nazis during the Second World War, for which even Putin criticised Lavrov's disinformation. Westerners countered Russia's claims that Ukraine is a Nazi nation by pointing out that there were Russian neo-Nazi fighters within the Wagner Group – with its leader, Dmitry Utkin being a prime example. According to the internet, in the twenty-first century, Nazis' speak in Slavic and Hebrew tongues. The de-Nazification propaganda simmered away after the siege of Mariupol, after a significant portion of the Azov Battalion were destroyed in the fighting. Russia altered its motive and justifications for the invasion from being a 'de-Nazification' campaign, to fighting NATO proxies and NATO expansionism. This alteration of motives was widely accepted by right-wing Westerners online.

Russian bots and 'web brigades' (government hired Russians who engage and spread disinformation/propaganda in amongst Westerners) have widely infested social media platforms, such as X (Twitter) and YouTube. Moscow has even paid right-wing social media influencers and news outlets to spread Russian propaganda lies towards their Western audiences.[38] The mass of bots spam disinformation and Russian aligned argumentation points to attempts to convince the common Westerner to follow the perceived majority consensus, which has been falsely created by the Russian propogandists, to be anti-Ukraine and anti-lend-leasing. Republican influencers and certain right-wing voters like to distinguish themselves from their peers and take an anti-American government or anti-Illuminati deep state stance in society by subscribing to Russian propaganda and their baseless claims. Other baseless claims were the supposed Ukrainian chemical weapons factory on the Russo-Ukrainian border and Putin's claim that Poland instigated the Second World War. Russian historians who disputed Putin's claim faced prosecution and all newly published Russian history textbooks redacted the Soviet invasion of Poland in 1939. Russian bots have convinced Westerners to pressure Zelensky to surrender to Russia in order to avoid countless pointless deaths. Little do they demand Putin to end the war for the sake of saving lives, and they do not criticise Putin's consistent refusal to withdraw from Ukraine. After all, it was, Putin who approved the invasion, not Zelensky and it is therefore Putin is in the wrong.

One of Russia's justifications for invading Ukraine was to unite the ethnic Russian people in Ukraine with the motherland. This is not a genuine goal from Moscow, however. The justification has led to widespread sympathy towards Russia from Westerners. Western celebrities, such as Elon Musk, called for Zelensky to consider peace talks with Russia, in exchange for the Donbas region. To give up the Donbas region is an illogical decision as the eastern region is a significant industrial region, which provides mass manufacturing of goods and exports for Ukraine. In a hypothetical scenario, would the American people allow Mexico to partition southern Texas to allow Mexican Americans to reunite with their motherland? Damn no.

However, this logic of allowing ethnic groups to cede Ukrainian territory to Russia as a moral principle has gained prominence in the US. Tucker Carlson has advocated for it and his followers appear to agree to the sentiment. Online users villainise Kyiv for not allowing ethnic Russian regions of Ukraine to be annexed by Russia. People who advocated this sentiment, such as Elon Musk and Steve Witkoff later gained political power in the Republican office following Trump's electoral victory in 2024 and used their position to convince Trump to have similar views. Witkoff used this logic to consider peace terms during the Ukrainian peace discussions. This demonstrates how rapidly Russian disinformation rhetorics have gained momentum from the general American public in the cyberspace to the White House in the real world, much to Moscow's advantage.

Chapter Five

THE CSTO: THE TESTAMENT OF ALLIES

The CSTO is a military alliance between Russia, Belarus, Armenia, Kazakhstan, Tajikistan and Kyrgyzstan and was originally formed in 1992. This military organisation strengthened bilateral ties between the member countries after the collapse of the Soviet Union. For thirty years, the member state countries conducted countless military training drills and operations together. However, the Russian invasion of Ukraine has tested the CSTO alliance, and the Second Cold War dynamics have reshuffled member states' relationship with Moscow. This chapter explores the change in relationships between the CSTO members and Moscow. Belarus' relations with Russia have increased to a point where they are steadfast in supporting Russia's war in Ukraine. The Central Asian countries belonging to the CSTO are reconsidering their alignment with Russia and are looking towards other international players to establish better economic ties with. The ancient Caucasian nation of Armenia has seriously considered aligning itself with the West, due to Russia's consistent failing to protect the country against the provocative Caucasian country of Azerbaijan.

The Lukashenko Regime

Belarus appears to be the only CSTO country that adamantly supports Russia's invasion of Ukraine and operates as an indirect Russian co-belligerent ally during the war. Belarus was used as a platform by the Russian army to launch its Kyiv offensive during the Ukrainian crisis and the invasion in February 2022. Russian missiles and fighter jets were launched into Ukrainian territory via Belarus during the Kyiv offensive. Belarus was the only CSTO country that defended Russia during the international condemnation of the Russian invasion in 2022. Armenia and the CSTO Central Asian countries abstained from condemning Russia, in order to both maintain relations with Russia and to avoid Western criticism. The Belarusian President Aleksandr Lukashenko voiced his staunch support for Russia and the invasion of Ukraine countless times on media and news outlets. Belarus faced sanctions from the West due to Belarus' involvement in Russia's war in Ukraine.

Belarus has participated in Russia's war in numerous ways. Dubious sources claim that certain Belarusians played minor roles in Russia's war in Ukraine, such as medical, logistical and military assistance. Belarus is known to have participated in Putin's systematic child abduction programme by establishing camps in the country to house the Ukrainian children.[39] Belarus has also participated in the Russo-West hybrid war by partaking in numerous nuclear threats and Putin's blackmailing campaign throughout the Second Cold War, the most notable being Putin's approval of Russian transfer of nuclear warheads to Belarus in March 2022. Belarusian troops were deployed alongside Russian troops on the NATO-Russo-Belarusian borders, in case a third world war were to occur. Belarus further contributed to Russia's Hybrid War, by exploiting and weaponizing Europe's Migration Crisis. Lukashenko's weaponisation of illegal migrants against the EU intensified in the summer of 2024, resulting in a series of clashes between the illegal migrants and Polish border soldiers. Moscow, and Belarus observed how the migrant crisis had cause social divide within Western societies. By exporting illegal migrants to the EU, it served complimentary to Russia's disinformation campaign goals.

After the success of the Ukrainian twin offensives and the October bombing of Kyiv, Putin and Lukashenko announced a joint Russo-Belarus military group to dampen the Ukrainian high morale on 10 October. This announcement made many speculate if this meant that Belarus would enter the Ukraine War, but this never occurred. Such dubious threats made Ukraine divert troops from the front lines to the Ukrainian-Belarus border and set up defences in preparation for a possible Russo-Belarus Kyiv offensive. What the announcement actually entailed was strengthening military Russian-Belarusian ties and an increase in Russian deployment and influence in Belarus under the pretext that the deployment was to protect Belarusian sovereignty from Ukrainian aggression. An incident occurred on 30 December 2022 in which Belarusian air defences prevented a Ukrainian missile attacking Belarus' infrastructure.

The Belarusian opposition during the early years of the Second Cold War, called for the removal of Lukashenko from political power. The movement became popular in 2020, when Lukashenko won the presidential elections against his fellow opponent candidate, Sviantlana Tsikhanouskaya, that year. Many believed that Lukashenko's electoral victory was rigged, as the majority of the Belarusian public wanted Tsikhanouskaya to win because of Lukashenko's mishandling in the Belarusian economy and the Covid-19 pandemic. Tsikhanouskaya claimed that Lukashenko stole her electoral victory and rigged the electoral votes, causing mass protests for the removal of Lukashenko.

Lukashenko responded to the protests through violent counterprotests and repressions against the protesters and arrested official figureheads of the opposition movement, such as Tsikhanouskaya's husband. Tsikhanouskaya offered Lukashenko the opportunity to tell the protesters to stop in exchange for her husband's release. However, the proposal was rejected. Tsikhanouskaya told the opposition protests to stop regardless and fled to Lithuania to establish a Belarusian government in exile.

The Belarusian opposition movement participated in the Ukraine War in various direct and indirect ways against Russia and Lukashenko. Tsikhanouskaya and her government in exile voiced their support for Ukraine against Russo-Belarusian aggression. They also produced various anti-war and anti-Lukashenko propaganda campaigns. Oppositionist Belarusians within Belarus attempted to thwart Russia's Kyiv offensive by sabotaging various Belarusian railways heading to northern Ukraine, which hindered Russian military logistics and inhibited Russia's push into Kyiv. On 26 February 2023, the Belarusian opposition partisans attacked the Russian Machulishchy air base in Minsk using drones, which resulted in a Russian A-50 jet being damaged. There were 500 Belarusians associated with the Belarusian opposition movement who volunteered into the Ukrainian Foreign Legion. The majority of these Belarusian fighters joined or established various foreign legion regiments, such as the Kastus Kalinouski Regiment, the Freedom of Russia Legion, Belarusian Volunteer Regiment and others alike. Lukashenko outlawed the regiments and individual volunteers.

Some Belarusians who had participated in the Belarusian opposition protests in 2020 had fled to Poland, in order to avoid prosecutions and Belarusian authorities. These former protesters had established and joined the Belarusian opposition group, BYPOL, who participated in the railway sabotages in Russia and Belarus during the Kyiv offensive and the Machulishchy air base drone attack. In June 2022, members of the BYPOL were trained by former

Polish special forces to commit sabotage, disruption and espionage activities within Lukashenko's Belarus. According to the leader of BYPOL, 200,000 Belarusians had joined the opposite organisation by early 2024. In February 2024, the leader of the organisation, Aliaksandr Azarau, claimed that the BYPOL would launch a coup against Lukashenko, when the time was right. Lukashenko strongly opposed the establishment and activities of the BYPOL and imposed a lengthy twenty-five-year prison sentence on Azarau, to deter Belarusians from joining anti-Lukashenko organisations. On March 2024, Belarusian authorities launched several raids of anti-Lukashenko organisations in Belarus, several weeks after Azarau announced his desires to launch a coup. There were 100 Belarusians who were arrested in the March raids.

Lukashenko played a pivotal role in resolving the Wagner Group rebellion in June 2023. Prigozhin had made numerous attempts to telephone Putin to avoid bloodshed in Moscow, but Putin refused to listen to him. It was Lukashenko who adhered to Prigozhin's demands and successfully reasoned to the Wagner Group leader to stop his 'March of Justice' immediately. The specific agreements and terms that were made during the Lukashenko-Prigozhin telephone call is not entirely clear or well known. Prigozhin and the Wagner Group did not face Russian prosecution for their actions and the Wagner Group was deployed to Belarus thereafter.

Lukashenko utilised the Wagner Group presence in his country to scare the West. The Wagner Group troops were stationed in Belarus to train Belarusian soldiers, but NATO countries, such as Poland, feared a Wagner Group infiltration into the Eastern NATO nations. Many Western politicians remembered how Wagner Group exploited the Serbian War scares and the Russo-West diplomatic back and forth during the northern Kosovo unrest that began on 31 July 2022, to launch a recruitment campaign in Serbia in January 2023. In August 2023, Polish authorities arrested two Russians for participating in a Wagner Group recruitment campaign in Poland. Lukashenko played on Western fears by claiming on State news outlets that the Wagner Group soldiers in Belarus desired to attack Western neighbours.[40]

These scares were accompanied by Wagner Group-Belarusian military drills near the Polish border and on 1 August 2023, two Belarusian helicopters briefly entered Polish airspace. These scares incited Poland and Lithuania to increase its troop presence near the Belarusian-Western borders. During this period, the Parliamentary Assembly of the OSCE designated the Wagner Group as a terrorist group, as a means to deter their infiltration and activities in neighbouring

European nations. NATO fears quickly diminished with the Wagner Group exit from Belarus on 10 August 2023.

The Great Game Retold

Russian relations with its Central Asian allies have declined since the beginning of the Second Cold War. As previously mentioned, all the CSTO Central Asian countries abstained from supporting Russia's invasion during the international condemnation of Russia in 2022. On April 2022, Kazakhstan made it clear that they did not recognise the Donetsk and Luhansk republics. This was likely because they feared that encouraging self-declared separatist Russian minority republics would result in similar behaviour occurring in its northern region, which is populated by Russian minorities. This was such a concern that in 2023 Kazakhstan authorities arrested several pro-Russian Kazakh separatists.[41]

Kazakhstan maintained steady relations with Russia regardless because of Russia's strong economic influence over the country. Kazakhstan's economy was so reliant on the Russian economy that the West's sanctions impacted the Kazakh economy. However, minor conflicting interests between Russia and Kazakhstan occurred during this period, which contributed to the deteriorating relations. Russia launched advertising for military recruiting campaigns in Kazakhstan, which was controversial within the Kazakh government and caused all Central Asian countries to issue a warning to its citizens to not join the Russian army. Kazakhstan even prosecuted a Kazakh citizen for joining the Wagner Group in 2023.

The CSTO experienced further disruption during the twin offensives, as Azerbaijan launched a border attack on Armenia on 12 September 2022. Russian neglect towards Armenia during the Azeri attack had damaging consequences between Russia and Armenia. A similar incident occurred on 14 September 2022 in which the CSTO countries of Tajikistan and Kyrgyzstan engaged in border clashes. The clashes came to an end on 20 September and various regional superpowers, such as Turkey and Iran offered to mediate peace talks.

Due to the changing dynamics that the CSTO Central Asian nations faced with the turn of the Second Cold War, the countries have tried to maintain good relations with Russia whilst beginning to adhere to untraditional foreigner nations diplomatic proposals. The most notable were the West, China and Azerbaijan-Turkey.

On 29 September 2023, Germany held a summit in Berlin with Central Asian countries belonging to the CSTO and Turkmenistan and Uzbekistan. These talks were successful in increasing EU relations with the Central Asian countries, to a point where the Kazakh president claimed that they would clamp down on Western sanctions loopholes in the country by restricted exports to Russia. German businesses subsequently participated in Kazakh infrastructure and ports projects. The Berlin summit also resulted in German proposals for mining, energy and nuclear projects, furthering the EU's influence over the region. On 3-4 April 2025, the first ever EU-Central Asian summit took place in Uzbekistan. During the summit, the EU and Central Asian countries discussed plans to increase trade, investment and security cooperation. It also discussed Central Asia's role in stopping Russia circumventing sanctions and the need to resolve the Ukraine War in a justly manner.

In April 2024, UK Conservative Foreign Secretary (and former Prime Minister) David Cameron made a series of diplomatic trips across all Central Asian countries to propose various economic projects with a £50 million funding investment. The trip was proven successful and undermined Russia's influence in the region. The greatest slap in the face to Russia came in the end of April 2024 when Kazakhstan approved the sale of eighty-one of its Soviet fighter jets (each costing $20,000) to the US, in exchange for American investment in modernising the Kazakh air force.[42] These jets would likely be recycled to help NATO air forces or were transferred to the Ukrainian air force against the Russians.

China has been approaching various Central Asian countries and Azerbaijan with a huge economic proposal, to establish various pipeline, railway and transport trade routes to Europe, via these countries. This ambitious project would greatly boost the region's economy, and most nations had agreed to it. Mutual economic back and forth between China and Kazakhstan increased significantly since the Second Cold War. China increased its purchase of Kazakh grain and China surpassed Russia as Kazakhstan's key trading partner.

China established a military base in Tajikistan, to protect Tajikistan's sovereignty from the neighbouring country of Afghanistan under the Taliban rule. Various Islamic extremist groups reside in Central Asian nations, and there was a fear that Islamic extremist activities would be on the rise as a consequence of the Gaza War. Such fears have substance, as ISIL activities have risen in the Middle East since the Gaza War and in Russia itself since the Crocus City Hall attack in March 2024. It is well known that some of the perpetrators of the attack belonged to Islamic extremist affiliated groups in Central Asia. It was feasible that the Taliban would contact and aid the Tajiki Islamic extremists across the border. It was, therefore, a reasonable concern for Tajikistan to seek Chinese military assistance to suppress Islamic extremist activities in the region.

Since the fall of the Soviet Union, Turkey's Pan-Turanic goals have reawakened and Turkey has attempted to sway the Central Asian countries. The Turkish satellite state of Azerbaijan, acted as an effective bridge for uniting the Turkic nations together and spreading Turkish influence in Central Asia during the Second Cold War. Azeri oil has been the most effective resource to establish economic influence in Kazakhstan and Central Asia. Baku has significantly increased its oil shipping exports and pipeline projects to various CSTO Central Asian countries. Azeri influence in the region was so effective that Kazakhstan partook in a unique military drill with other Central Asian nations and Azerbaijan without the Russian army in July 2024. Turkey has approached Kazakhstan, offering numerous industry and manufacturing projects.

Turkey partook in mediation of peace and border talks between the Turkic nations of Tajikistan and Kyrgyzstan. Turkey's role as mediator displays that they wish to be seen as the father state of the Central Asian nations and to unite the nations under the Turkish-Turanian umbrella. Turkish-Azeri competition with the West, Iran, China and Russia over Central Asia has been the most prominent, as the Turkish-Azeri approach serves both to adhere to the CSTO nations' economic benefits and sense of national belonging.

Azerbaijan's economic seductions towards the CSTO Central Asian allies plays into Turkey's desires to expand its influence into the region. It also plays into Azerbaijan's war effort against the CSTO country of Armenia, as it pressures the Central Asian countries and even Russia, to not interfere in the Nagorno-Karabagh conflict, or else the countries will see a decline in Azeri-Baku oil exports or be excluded from the Pan-Turanic umbrella.

The Thirty-Year Conflict

The drama in the Caucasus region has raged on for decades and has escalated during the Second Cold War. The beautiful land of Artsakh, or Nagorno-Karabagh as referred to by the Azeris, had been fought over by the neighbouring countries of Armenia and Azerbaijan for three decades.[43]

The seeds of the conflict started in 1923, when the then leader of the Soviet Union, Joseph Stalin, proclaimed Nagorno-Karabagh as Azeri sovereignty, even though in 1923, 95 per cent of the inhabitants in the region were Armenian. It has been argued that Stalin ceded Nagorno-Karabagh to Azerbaijan as a means to strengthen relations with Kemalist Turkey.[44] This proved not to be an issue as Armenians and Azeris could travel freely to Nagorno-Karabagh under the USSR. The ethnic tensions between Armenians and Azeris during the years 1905 to 1907 and 1918 to 1920 seemed to be forgotten under USSR. It was in the waning years of the USSR, under Mikhail Gorbachev, when the issue over Nagorno-Karabagh had arisen. Many soviet Armenians took to the streets and protested, demanding Moscow to reintegrate caused an increase in Armenian nationalism which hitherto caused reactionary Azeri nationalism.

De Waal describes Gorbachev's actions towards the Nagorno-Karabagh situation as improvisational at best and at times clueless as to what to do at worst.[45] The situation was difficult for Gorbachev, as to adhere to the Armenians demands would violate Azerbaijan's territorial integrity, and to ignore Armenians demands would cause anger and violence. Gorbachev's choice to ignore the Armenians (or his indecisiveness) led to ethnic violence towards the Azeris which subsequently led to a never-ending cycle of vengeful violence. Russian peacekeeping troops were sent to quell the violence, but to no avail and when the USSR collapsed the Nagorno-Karabagh crisis turned to a full-scale war. The Armenians had won the war and Azerbaijan lost Nagorno-Karabagh.

The Velvet Revolution that occurred in 2018 was a peaceful protest, which held very similar demands to the colour revolutions in the 2000s. Pashinyan was a journalist who criticised the Armenian government for its corruption and its semi-autocracy. Pashinyan heavily criticised Putin for his corruption and for enacting several human rights violations. The Velvet Revolution came in response to Prime Minister Serzh Sargsyan controversial re-election into political power. The revolution was successful and led to the resignation of the corrupt Armenian prime minister. Pashinyan later became the prime minister of Armenia and established a more democratic country. The Velvet Revolution was the beginning of the decline of Russo-Armenian relations. Although Pashinyan's promises to continue the ongoing relations with the CSTO and Russia prevented Putin from outright being against the Armenian Regime change, Putin viewed Pashinyan and the new Armenian government with caution as he saw the Velvet Revolution as another product of Western interventionism.

Although Armenia spent decades with the spoils of the Nagorno-Karabagh War from 1991 to 1994, in recent years their grasp in the region has slipped. Azerbaijan was economically thriving from its oil exports, and its economic surpluses were invested into military spending. Turkey supplied them with arms and training. Azeri forces flexed their new military spoils during border skirmishes against Artsakh forces (Armenian separatist forces in Nagorno-Karabagh) in the Nagorno-Karabagh region in 2016. The Azeris utilised their entire arsenal in September 2020 when they invaded Nagorno-Karabagh. Film clips of Turkish supplied Bayraktar Azeri drones setting Armenian tanks ablaze shook the internet and astounded observers who had never seen tanks be destroyed with such ease.

The modern Azeri army destroyed Soviet armed Armenian forces with ease. A ceasefire between the two opposing forces were agreed on after the Azeri capture of the region's capital, Shusha. Russian mediation intervened and pressured Azerbaijan to stop the war and 75 per cent of internationally recognised Azerbaijani territories would be granted to Baku if they adhered to Russian peace terms. The Republic of Artsakh remained outside of Azerbaijani control.

Azerbaijan agreed to the Russian peace terms. However, Azerbaijan realised that Russia and the threat of CSTO intervention was an obstacle for the 'liberation' of the whole region of the Nagorno-Karabagh. Armenian relations with Russia started to crumble and deteriorate due to Russia's favourable mediation towards Azerbaijan. They were also angered that Russia did not militarily intervene in the war because Russia claimed that Artsakh was not Armenia proper that was invaded, which is why Russia did not adhere to its CSTO obligations. It can be argued that Prime Minister Nikol Pashinyan's past anti-Putin remarks influenced Vladimir Putin to be hesitant in aiding Armenia and that Putin benefited more from Azerbaijani oil than from what Amenia offered economically. Armenia's failure in the war put Pashinyan's presidency on the line as protests erupted in Yerevan calling for his resignation.

The Ukraine War's Impact on the Nagorno-Karabakh Conflict
The course of the Nagorno-Karabagh conflict was heavily impacted by Russia's invasion of Ukraine in February 2022. In August and September 2022, Ukraine launched its twin offensives in the Kherson and Kharkiv regions. Russia was on full alert and committed its military to divert the situation by any means. Azerbaijan exploited the scene and launched an attack on Armenia proper's borders. Armenia activated the CSTO's Article 4 (an attack on one is an attack on all) as Armenia proper was under attack. However, this was dismissed by Russia. Fortunately, the Azeri attack was only a border skirmish. However, it had serious implications. Russia's neglect to aid Armenia during Azerbaijan's attack, proved to Azeri President Ilham Aliyev that Azerbaijan could retake the whole of the Nagorno-Karabagh without fears of Russian

intervention as long as Russia was tied down in Ukraine. Russia could not afford to divert troops from Ukraine to the Caucasus region, especially during Ukraine's alarming twin offensives. Armenia was also greatly aware of their vulnerable position and Pashinyan started to publicly voice his concerns of having Russia as a military partner as they proved to be very neglectful of their obligations over Armenian territorial integrity. Russia's lack of intervention caused Pashinyan to call for French President Emmanuel Macron and Secretary of State Antony Blinken to help Armenia diplomatically. Russia's commitment in Ukraine entailed Moscow's neglect of Armenia. This caused Yerevan to look for dialogue and support outside of the Russian bloc in an attempt to establish strong diplomatic relations with the West. The Armenian prime minister and politicians later argued that Armenia was never a supporter of Russia's war in Ukraine despite being military allies with Moscow, displaying further deterioration of Russo-Armenian relations.[46] Putin made a state visit to Armenia in November 2022 in which he was met with disgruntled Armenian protesters who displayed their dissatisfaction with Russia's lack of intervention during 2020, 2021 and 2022 Armenian-Azeri clashes and even condemned Russia's war in Ukraine.

Azerbaijan launched a blockade on the Armenian populated Nagorno-Karabagh in December 2022 by sending 'climate protesters' to block the Lachlin corridor. The Lachlin corridor was the only connected supply route to Nagorno-Karabagh from Armenia proper. Aliyev's decision to send climate protesters gave him plausible deniability of Azerbaijan's official involvement in the blockade. Because the climate protesters were Azeri civilians, they could not be militarily removed by Armenian and Russian forces. However, from March to April 2023, Azeri forces established military checkpoints across the Lachlin road to block supply trucks to Nagorno-Karabagh. Despite Russian peacekeepers presence in the region to prevent Azeri aggression towards Nagorno-Karabagh Armenians after the war in 2020, they turned a blind eye to the situation, much to the Armenians disappointment. Russia's neglect of this humanitarian issue angered the Armenian politicians to the extent that Armenia began looking to the West for diplomatic aid over the blockade. Armenia refused to attend several CSTO military drills. The most spiteful act from the Armenians was their agreement with the ICC to arrest Putin as a war criminal for his actions in Ukraine if Putin stepped foot in Armenia. This was too much, and Russia threatened to sanction Yerevan if Armenia went through with this, which resulted in Armenia backing down and dropping its ICC obligations.

Armenia's ties with the West increased after Azerbaijani's One-Day War in September 2023, which saw Azeri forces retaking the whole of the Armenian populated Nagorno-Karabagh. Azerbaijan believed that the Republic of Artsakh was internationally isolated after the international condemnation of the 2023 Artsakh elections and subsequently invaded the region. An incident occurred during the One-Day War in which Azeri forces bombed and killed Russian peacekeepers, and the Azeri government compensated the peacekeepers' families. Prior to the invasion, Aliyev telephoned Putin and the Russian peacekeeping troops to inform them that the Azeri army was going to invade the Nagorno-Karabagh. Russian politicians openly denied the telephone exchange and Putin silently enabled the Azeri invasion to occur. Pashinyan was pessimistic towards the Nagorno-Karabagh issue. His CSTO allies were not helping him, and the West had more pressing matters to attend to. Armenia was an afterthought for the two blocs and the UN's efforts towards lifting the blockade were ineffective.

Pashinyan did not send Armenian troops to aid the Artsakh forces under siege by Azeri forces, much to the outcry of the Armenian public. Pashinyan knew that without foreign intervention from Russia or the West, he could not afford to send Armenians to fight a lost war. The Artsakh forces resigned and surrendered to the Azeris as they too knew that they could not win without outside support, at least from Armenia proper. On 20 September, Aliyev publicly announced the reclamation of Nagorno-Karabagh and promised that if Karabagh Armenians chose to stay in Nagorno-Karabagh, they would be treated humanely as Azeri citizens.

A mass exodus of Nagorno-Karabagh Armenians flooded the Lachlin corridor towards Armenia. They did not trust Aliyev's promises, especially after enduring months of the Azeri blockade and the September war. There was a genuine fear that the Nagorno-Karabagh Armenians were facing a Second Armenian genocide during the blockade. The Armenian-American celebrity Kim Kardashian with over 75 million followers on X (Twitter), pleaded to everyone online to support the Armenians in their plight and to spread the news of the Azeri's illegal blockade, as very few media outlets were covering the event. This was successful in bringing media attention to the plight of the Armenians. Despite the moral stance the Armenians had over the Azeris on social media and propaganda, it was too little too late as the Azeris had achieved their goals. Azerbaijan was later confronted with international condemnation and isolation for their aggression. However, they did not face sanctions and their diplomatic isolation faded with time. Out of the 120,000 Armenians that lived in Nagorno-Karabagh, only a handful chose to stay.

During the One-Day War, Armenians in the capital demonstrated for Pashinyan to declare war on Azerbaijan in solidarity for Artsakh. However, Pashinyan refused. The protests continued following Artsakh's surrender. The protesters were distraught by the loss and Pashinyan's refusal to show an ounce of solidarity towards the Artsakh Armenians.

On 24 September 2023, eight members of the Artsakh paramilitary unit, Khachakirner, attempted to overthrow the Pashinyan government and launch an Armenian military operation to take back Artsakh from Azerbaijani control. Armenian authorities managed to foil the coup attempt. The protests appeared to have died down by 25 September 2023.

The International Chessboard

The exodus of the Karabagh Armenians signalled the end of the Nagorno-Karabagh conflict according to Aliyev and Azerbaijan. However, in the eyes of Armenia, the struggle continued. Armenia feared that Azerbaijan would next invade Armenia because Aliyev, on multiple occasions, voiced his commitment to connect the Azeri Nakhichevan enclave to Azerbaijan proper by occupying Syunik region. Armenia, therefore, dedicated itself to gain foreign support, such as France, for arms and economic packages. Armenian desires for Western aid further derailed relations with Russia. Armenia skipped a CSTO meeting in December 2023 and Russia refused to transfer Armenia weapons that Yerevan had purchased for $400 million.[47] Russian peacekeeping forces did nothing to aid the Armenians during the One-Day War and the flight of the Karabagh Armenians. Putin's deliberate neglect further damaged Russo-Armenian relations. The Armenian public who once loved Russia, now detested them. The Armenian public started to believe that Russia conspired with Baku to dissolve the Republic of Artsakh.

Putin's shifting diplomatic relations between Armenia and Azerbaijan are due to Second Cold War dynamics. Azerbaijan is a more valuable ally than Armenia because Azerbaijan holds more benefits, economically and diplomatically speaking. Azerbaijan's oil depots greatly benefit Russia's economy in the wake of the Western sanctions. The easy Russo-Turkish relations may also play a factor in Russia's leniency towards Azerbaijan actions of aggression against their partner Armenia. China is also attempting to establish trade routes to Azerbaijan via Kazakhstan which was met with approval by

Putin after he won the 2024 Russian elections.[48] These factors indicate that Russia was moving away from Armenia in favour of Azerbaijan, as Armenia held less strategic, economic and diplomatic value.

It was in the interests of Iran that Aliyev's desires to occupy the southern region of Armenia did not come to fruition. This was because the Azeri occupation of south Armenia would have meant the severing of the Iranian-Armenian border, which would skewer one of Iran's limited export trade routes. Not only this but the Azeri occupation of south Armenia meant that Azerbaijan had access to new land trade routes to Turkey, creating a corridor for the imports of arms, oil and other economic trade to Western countries, which would go against Iranian interests. Iran held a meeting with Armenia a couple of months after the September 2022 border clashes, which aimed to strengthen Armenian-Iranian relations. It can be argued that Iran realised that Russia could no longer act as Armenia's guardian against Azeri encroachment, due to Moscow's war effort in Ukraine. Iran, therefore, attempted to assert themselves as Armenia's protectorate against Azeri aggression.

On 17 October 2022, Iran deterred Azerbaijan from repeating their border attacks on Armenia by commencing large military drills near the Azeri and Nakhichevan borders. The following month, Azeri officials made public threats towards Iranian sovereignty, by promoting pan-Azeri solidarity towards Azeri-Iranians. In Azerbaijan, Baku supported exiled Iranian Azeri separatist leaders in spreading Azeri separatism ideology online.

This further strained Azeri-Iranian relations as the Azeri stunt could have resulted in civil unrest and even separatist groups advocating for the northern Iran to be annexed by Azerbaijan. It is not known how Putin's favouritism towards Azerbaijan affected Russo-Iranian cooperation. Armenian was, however, hesitant on receiving lethal aid from Iran as they did not want Western countries to be dissuaded from providing foreign aid to Armenia and ruin the West's diplomatic relations with Armenia.

Western nations observed Russia's waning control over its south Caucasian neighbours and attempted to establish their own influence in Moscow's self-perceived 'sphere of influence'. The EU was split on which south Caucasian nation to approach as a bridgehead to establish Western influence in the region. The Ursula von Der Leyen camp was determined to find an alternative energy partnership as a means of reducing the EU's drug-addicted reliance on Russian gas. At any moment Russia could cut Europe's energy and throw Europe into an energy crisis. For security reasons, it was best that the EU established an alternative energy partnership with Azerbaijan to avoid a possible Russian energy blackmailing situation. However, the EU became increasingly sceptical of Azerbaijan due to Baku and Moscow's growing relations and Russian tendencies of using Azerbaijan as an in-between platform to export Russian goods to the West, circumventing Western sanctions. The pro-Yerevan camp within the EU, led by Charles Michel, feared that Baku was also exporting Russian gas to the West – undermining von Der Leyen's efforts against importing Russian energy. While von Der Leyen made apologetic remarks towards Azerbaijani misdeeds, Michel advocated for the EU to pivot to Yerevan's aid as Armenia shared similar values to the EU, unlike Baku who is known for their undemocratic and human rights violation tendencies. Armenia was increasingly perceived as a much more accessible nation to establish a foothold in the Caucasus.

Whilst the EU remained divided, Macron and Biden were set on choosing Armenia as their bridgehead into Russia's 'Caucasian backyard' due to Armenia's democratic values and abstain towards Azeri conduct. Prior to the Artsakh takeover, Paris and Washington gave diplomatic and humanitarian support to Armenia against Azeri aggression, and even condemned Baku at times. A month after the Azeri takeover of Artsakh, Macron began sending military aid to Armenia in earnest and began bilateral cooperation for a security partnership programme. Meanwhile, Biden began sending economic and military assistance to Yerevan. The following sections examine how Russia and the West competed for influence over the two countries.

The Russian Exploit

Peace talks between Armenia and Azerbaijan ensued subsequently after the One-Day War. Armenia refused Russia's offer of acting as mediator as an act of protest against Russia's non-intervention during the One-Day War. The peace talks discussed the sovereignty over Azeri and Armenian enclaves behind the Azeri-Armenian border. Peace discussions were widely reported as being smooth and positive at first, but soured by March 2024 when Pashinyan warned that his country was under imminent danger of Azeri attacks. In February 2024, the Azeri army attacked Armenian soldiers on the Armenian proper border, resulting in four Armenian fatalities. A second and third border attack incidents had occurred in April and June 2024, with both sides accusing the other of opening fire first. The rising tensions between Armenia and Azerbaijan led to Armenia fortifying its defences in anticipation for an Azeri invasion.

After Aliyev's public threats of invading Armenia for the sake of connecting Nakhichevan, Macron increased the French lend-leasing of lethal aid to Armenia and even sent military advisors to the country to further modernise the Armenian army. Aliyev accused France of encouraging Armenia to reignite the Nagorno-Karabakh conflict by arming Armenia. This resulted in Azeri antagonism against France, which began in December 2023, when Aliyev expelled two French Embassy workers from Azerbaijan, as a symbolic gesture against French support for Armenia, which resulted in France doing the same in retaliation.

In December 2023, Azeri authorities arrested a French national for espionage. This was followed by Baku supporting various French colonial independence groups across the globe. In July 2023, Azeri officials helped form the Baku Initiative Group, which saw independence movements from French colonies, such as New Caledonia, Corsica, Martinique, French Guiana and French Polynesia unite and coordinate against French rule. Such efforts led to the increasing Azeri alignment with Russia as both countries conducted a joint propaganda campaign to incite unrest in French colonies, the most effective being in New Caledonia in 2024.

Aliyev later demanded the return of Azeri enclaves in the northeastern parts of Armenia during the Azeri-Armenian peace talks. In April 2024, Armenia returned these villages to Azerbaijan in order to avoid another war with Azerbaijan. These villages held strategic value for the Azeris, as these villages are located near a highway that connects to Georgia. This highway is usually used by Armenians to receive and transfer Russian oil and goods. Disgruntled Armenians blocked the roads to these newly Azeri villages in protest, but were subdued by Armenian authorities.

Following the withdrawal of the Russian peacekeepers stationed in Nagorno-Karabagh in April 2024, Russia announced its withdrawal from the Armenian-Azeri border, Armenia requested this as a step towards normalisation with Azerbaijan during the Azeri-Armenian peace talks in 2023 to 2024. This would leave Armenia more vulnerable to an Azeri invasion and allowed Putin to bolster manpower in the Ukraine War. Pashinyan's constant bending of the knee to Azerbaijan resulted in his rising unpopularity amongst the Armenian public. The transfer of the villages started another protest in Armenia on 26 April 2024, which demanded Pashinyan's resignation. Pashinyan accused former Artsakh officials of encouraging Artsakh Armenians to join the protests. Pashinyan subsequently made anti-Artsakh remarks, increasing public disproval of their president. These protests were rallied behind the Armenian Archbishop Bagrat Galstanyan and resulted in mass counterprotests and arrests in May 2024. The protests seemed to have died down by June 2024.

Armenian officials claim that Russian interference was behind the protests, but no substantial evidence has backed up the claims. Pashinyan's criticisms of Artsakh officials, cession of territories to Azerbaijan, and refusal to grant Artsakh war refugees official Armenian citizenship was exploited by Moscow propagandists to exacerbate the growing anti-Pashinyan discontent. Pashinyan accused Artsakh officials leading the protests in 2024 of being Russian agents. He subsequently arrested several Artsakh officials to behead the leadership of the anti-Pashinyan movement in Armenia. Yerevan continued to accuse Russia of spreading anti-Pashinyan propaganda and intentionally destabilising Armenian authority. Knowing Russian propagandists, they likely spread pro-Artsakh propaganda online to ensure that the protests gained attraction. It is possible that the Russians hoped that these protests would lead to the overthrow of the pro-West Pashinyan and the eventual installation of a pro-Russian Artsakh Armenian leadership. Russian hopes did not come to reality. On 18 September 2024, Armenia accused Russia of attempting to stage a coup against Pashinyan.

The Armenian putschists consisted of members with the Artsakh militia, Sev Hovaz[49], an Artsakh paramilitary group, who were militarily trained by the pro-Russian DPR Arbat Battalion in Russia, to prepare for a military overthrow of the Pashinyan government.

In July 2023, the Armenian military group, the Arbat Battalion, was ceremoniously sent off to fight in Ukraine by the Armenian Cathedral of Moscow (which was greatly condemned by the Ukrainian chapter of the Armenian Apostolic Church).[50] The Arbat Battalion fought alongside Russian forces in Avdiivka and Kursk. The Arbat Battalion, therefore, had strong ties to Moscow and the Arbat Battalion's involvement in the failed 2024 coup was likely known and approved by Moscow. The Arbat Battalion's cooperation with the Artsakh militia of Sev Hovaz suggests that Putin was utilising Artsakh Armenians to forcefully reinsert his influence in Armenia.

Moscow's desires to install a pro-Kremlin government by utilising Artsakh Armenian oppositionists became apparent to Yerevan. Armenian officials from Pashinyan's cabinet feared that Russia would launch a hybrid war against Armenia around the time of the 2026 Armenian parliamentary elections.[51] It was feared that Pashinyan's pro-Russian oppositionists would be backed by Moscow, who would implement the same Russian propaganda tactics that they had used during the 2024 protests. These accusations were dismissed by Moscow officials and condemned by oppositionists.

The EU Intervention

The border clashes across the eastern Armenian border in 2022 had major consequences in the region. The failure of the Russian peacekeeping force led to Yerevan seeking the EU's help. The EU obliged and deployed a forty-man peacekeeping/observation force across the Armenian and Azeri border during the period 20 October 2022 to 19 December 2022. The forty-manned EU monitoring mission was approved by both Yerevan and Baku. However, following the Azeri blockade of Artsakh, Baku rejected an extension of the EU presence in the Azeri side of the border. The EU extended its monitoring mandate on the Armenian side of the border by two more years. At the request of Yerevan, the EU rebranded the observation mission as EUMA and was deployed along the eastern Armenian border and next to the Nakhichevan border in February 2023. The EUMA deployed 209 personnel, including 165 international staff and 44 local staff. The EUMA acted as an unarmed civilian observer mission, consisting of members of the German police and the French national army. The purpose of the EUMA was to observe the border, report on border clashes and to ensure the stability of the border.

Moscow criticised Yerevan's request for the deployment of the EUMU, claiming that it was a tool used by the US and NATO to cause instability in the region. The deployment of the EUMU undermined Russian security influence in the CSTO nation. According to the head of the EUMU, Russian peacekeeping forces obstructed EUMU's entry in the Nerkin Hand, following the Azeri-Armenian border clash in February 2024. This was disputed by Armenia, however. Yerevan did criticise the Russian peacekeeping forces in the Nerkin Hand for failing to prevent the Azeri attack. The Russian peacekeeping force likely blocked the EUMU's entry into Nerkin Hand in order to undermine EU presence in the country and to prevent the Russian personnel being held accountable for the February clash.

Although the original EU observation mission was met with criticisms from local and diaspora Armenians for their lack of input in pressuring Baku to stop the blockade of Artsakh, the EUMU's presence led to a significant decrease in Azeri-Armenian border clashes in both scale and frequency. The presence of the EUMU prevented border clashes as neither side wanted to be held accountable for provocation by the EU. This was a tremendous feat by the EUMU as the decline in border clashes decreased real tensions between the two Caucasus nations. Azerbaijan has used border clashes in the past as a pretext and justification for Azeri aggressive military actions towards Armenia, as can be seen with the July 2020 border clashes – used as a pretext for the Second Nagorno-Karabagh War, the Azeri alleged Armenian attack on 2 - 3 August 2022 – leading to the September 2022 clashes, and the supposed deaths of Azeris via Armenian planted land mines – culminating in the One-Day War against Artsakh. Aliyev was irritated by the EUMA's presence and demanded for their withdrawal in September 2024. Aliyev accused the EUMA of favouritism towards Armenia, purposefully destabilising the region and committing espionage activities across the border. Aliyev's irritancies increased after numerous EUMA's frequent reports of Azeri provocations across the border, the disputed firing at EUMU personnel on 14 August 2023, and the EU condemnation of Azerbaijan following the One-Day War. The presence of the EUMA became a focal point of Azeri-Armenian peace discussions, alongside Aliyev's renewed demands for the Zangezur corridor in January 2025. The EUMA renewed its mandate to a further five years in February 2025. The extension of the EUMA's mandate was met with condemnation by Baku and Moscow, but Tehran did not protest. The EU's effective presence in Armenia likely contributed to Pashinyan's confidence in reducing Russian military presence in the country. The EUMA's effectiveness can also be cited as a major contributing factor as to why Pashinyan was aligning Armenia with the EU and the West.

New Prospects for Armenia

In the wake of 2024, Armenia took drastic steps to unentangle itself from Russia. On January 2024, Armenia formally joined the ICC, despite repeated Russian threats. On February 2024, Armenia froze its membership status within the CSTO and then in March 2024 threatened to withdraw entirely from the CSTO. In March 2024, Armenian politicians asked Russian security guards to withdraw presence in the Yerevan Airport, displaying Yerevan's desires to be more independent from Russia which finally came into effect by August 2024. On March 2024, Pashinyan asked the Armenian people to discuss amongst themselves if Armenia should join the EU. A couple of days later, it was announced that Armenia was attempting to join the EU. Armenian was playing a dangerous line off of various international and neighbouring countries, as Russian exports are deeply integrated into the Armenian economy. Armenia's drastic foreign policy approach infamously led to the Kremlin propagandist

Margarita Simonyan, warning that Armenia would not exist in five years, hinting at a Russian invasion of Armenia in the future. In April 2024, the EU pledged €230 million to Armenia in order to make Armenia's economy less tied to Russian entanglement, which was met with much disgruntlement by the Kremlin.

Russo-Armenian ties were struggling also due to Yerevan's harbouring of Russian conscript dodgers. After the success of the Ukrainian twin Kherson and Kharkiv oblast offensives, Putin called for a mass mobilisation of Russian military-aged men to restrengthen the greatly understrength northern and southern Ukrainian fronts. This resulted in 700,000 Russians fleeing to neighbouring countries and there was a 6-mile traffic queue of Russians migrating to the Caucasus. Kazakhstan saw 200,000 Russian draft dodgers migrating to the country. However, the CSTO countries of Kazakhstan and Kyrgyzstan promised to monitor and share information of the Russian draft dodgers to Moscow. This resulted in incidents in which Kazakh authorities arrested Russian draft dodgers and reporters and extradited them to Moscow.

Over 100,000 Russians fled to Armenia as the country did not enact these discriminatory policies towards Russian draft dodgers, unlike the CSTO Central Asian countries. This was because Armenians welcomed the influx of Russians as it would improve the country's economy and modernisation. Two Russian draft dodgers were arrested and sent to Russia in December 2023 and April 2024 in the Armenian city of Gyumri, where the Russian 102nd military base is located. This breached Armenian law and acted as a message to Armenia that Russia intended to enact their objectives in Armenia, regardless of the Armenian law. Lukashenko voiced his concerns of Pashinyan's Western leanings, resulting in a strain in Armenian-Belarusian relations and causing the Belarusian president to make pro-Azeri comments and statements in June 2024. Russian hostility towards Armenia intensified in June 2024, when Pashinyan announced that Armenia was beginning the process of exiting the CSTO.

Following the announcement, Armenia further appealed to the West in 2024. Rishi Sunak approached Pashinyan with the proposal to send British illegal migrants to Armenia. Pashinyan entertained the idea, as the Armenian economy and modernisation process would benefit from more workers. However, Sunak's failure in the general election in 2024 led to the proposal being scrapped alongside the Rwanda plan.

Between 9 - 11 July 2024, Armenia attended the NATO summit in Washington, to discuss peace processes with Azerbaijan. Moscow displayed its concern over Armenia's attendance at the summit. This was followed by the Second Operation Eagle Partner exercises (which was a follow-up to the September 2023 joint American-Armenian Operation Eagle Partner exercises). The US and Armenia conducted military-peacekeeping exercises on 15 to 24 July 2024.

During the exercise, the US discussed prospects of constructing a nuclear power plant in Armenia with Yerevan. American attempts to entangle the Armenian economy to the dollar plays several factors: to squander the value of the rouble in Armenia, disrupt the trade link between Iran and Russia, establish some form of influence in the Caucasus amid Iranian and Russian influences, and to undermine the Turkic satellite state of Azerbaijan in the region. It is likely that the American end goal of seducing Armenia was to establish an American military base in the country, which borders Iran and Russia. Armenian efforts to appeal to the EU led to successful progress and benefits.

On 17 July 2024, the EU approved visa liberalisation talks with Armenia and a week later, the EU sent a €10 million package to the Armenian army.

As part of Armenia's process of aligning to the West, Armenia attempted to amend its sour relations with Turkey. Armenia attempted to do so when Turkey experienced the devastating earthquake in February 2023 during the backdrop of the Artsakh blockade. Armenia sent humanitarian personnel and aid to Turkey.

Turkey had opened its borders with Armenia for the first time in thirty-five years in order for Armenian aid convoys to arrive at the devastated ruins of south-east Turkey and rescue the earthquake victims. Pashinyan congratulated Erdoğan's re-election in 2023 and attended his inauguration in Ankara in June 2023. This was criticised by fellow Armenian politicians and the public.

Normalisation processes increased in 2024, with Armenia apprehending and sending an American-Armenian to Turkish authorities for assassinating a Turkish official in the US during the 1980s. In June 2024, a rare historical telephone call between Armenian and Turkish officials was made in which they discussed regional and domestic issues as well as emphasis for normalisation of bilateral relations. Pashinyan pursued this latter issue in order to appeal to Turkish President Recep Tayyip Erdoğan in the hope he would agree to the reopening of the Armenian-Turkish border to boost Armenia's trade, modernisation and Westernisation processes. On 30 July 2024, Armenia and Turkey held normalisation talks, and discussed border railway transport of goods, the easing of travel restrictions and the increase in diplomatic talks in the future. On 6 November 2024, Turkish

Minister of Foreign Affairs Hakan Fidan claimed that normalisation of Armenian-Turkish relations would ensue if Armenia completed Azeri peace demands. Fidan's claim was met with scepticism by the Armenian public, however.

Turkish-Armenian relations improved following their coordinated efforts in arresting Turkish criminals Ercan Yilmaz and Ibrahim Yaymak in January 2025. In February 2025, Pashinyan claimed that diplomatic communication with Turkey had significantly improved and saw a significant decline in strain or disagreement between the two countries' viewpoints, showing the progress in relations between Armenia and Turkey. Following the March 2025 Syrian massacres, Turkey briefly opened the Turkish-Armenian border to allow for Armenian humanitarian aid to Syria. Prospects of the opening of the Turkish border plays a factor in Armenia's decision-making during the Azeri-Armenian peace talks. The improvement in relations with Turkey and the perceived persistent bending of the knee to Azeri demands made Pashinyan an unpopular politician amongst the Armenian public and press. Infamously the Armenian press accused Pashinyan of denying the Armenian genocide after Pashinyan publicly questioned why the Armenian genocide is used as a political tool in modern geopolitics in February 2025. The press cited Pashinyan's relationship with Ankara as evidence to indicate his supposed denialism. This further derailed the Armenian public's perception of Pashinyan.

Armenia even made daring forms of appeasement to the West by increasing its ties with Ukraine. Ukraine had taken a pro-Azeri stance during the Nagorno-Karabakh conflict, due to Armenia's alignment to Russia. However, the developments of the Nagorno-Karabakh conflict during the Second Cold War altered Ukrainian relations with Armenia. On October 2023, Zelensky and Pashinyan briefly discussed the security of their nations during the Granada European Political Community summit. Aliyev did not attend the summit due to the international condemnation of Azerbaijan's One-Day War, allowing Pashinyan to reiterate his plans for peace and discussions of aligning to the West, without Aliyev's counterarguments and counterproposals. Rumours circulated that Zelensky was intending to visit Armenia, which further derailed Russian-Armenian relations. On 9 June 2024, Armenian officials visited Bucha to pay their respects to the victims of the Bucha massacres and to show their admiration towards the Ukrainian people fighting the Russians.[52] The visit also saw the transfer of Armenian non-lethal aid, such as medical equipment. Azerbaijani and Russian media outlets reported that Armenia provided missile launcher vehicles to

Ukraine. Such claims were obviously false, as there was no logical sense for Armenia to send lethal aid to Ukraine, due to their current military insecurities. Of course, this Azeri disinformation campaign was to spread anti-Armenian sentiments, especially towards the Russian public. However, Russian disinformation campaign demonstrates Moscow's growing hostility towards Armenia.

Pashinyan's consistent worries of an imminent Azeri attack were not unfounded, as Yerevan's change of allegiances put the nation in near political isolation, rendering the country vulnerable to another Azeri attack. Armenia was in the early stages of establishing Western and EU relations, which had deteriorated Russian and Iranian relations significantly. Armenia's ever deteriorating relations with Russia have led Armenia to be politically isolated from its neighbours, who could provide immediate support unlike the West. At any moment Azerbaijan could have invaded the isolated Armenia as Yerevan lacked allies to back them up sufficiently. Hence why Pashinyan was adhering to Azeri land demands during the peace talk processes, much to the outcry of the Armenian public. Armenia was certainly at risk of repeating the events of the led up to the Georgian War in 2008.

The Point of No Return

Iranian officials made a state visit to Yerevan on 9 January 2025, to talk about the construction of trade routes in the Zangezur corridor. During their visit, the Iranian officials claimed that Iran still maintained its support for Armenian sovereignty from Azeri aggression but insisted Yerevan should keep the Azeri-Armenian tensions at a local level. Yerevan gave its thanks to Tehran but had already passed a law for Armenia to pursue EU assession on that exact same day.

Armenia achieved extraordinary moves towards its Western alignment goals on 14 January 2025 in which Armenia signed a strategic partnership charter with the US. The charter promised for the increase in American investment in Armenia's modernisation efforts towards its infrastructure, economy, trade and military along with other miscellanies, such as improvement of counter-crime and diaspora inclusion. The charter mentions American guarantees over Armenia's sovereignty. This guarantees American support for Armenia in a scenario in which Azerbaijan or Russia were to invade the Caucasian state. The charter was bound to the assurance of Armenian democracy. In other words, if Armenia were to return to its old Russian ally or disregard human rights, the charter would become null and void. The charter of Armenian American strategic partnership is questionable, as Trump was inaugurated only six days later. Many feared that Trump's America First policy would jeopardise American obligations for Armenia in the future. Armenian bid for American strategic partnership challenged Iran's support towards Armenia.

If Armenia were to continue its steady tightrope walk with Iran and the West, friendly relations between the two neighbours could be maintained. However, this is debatable as if the US was to establish more influence in Armenia and set up military bases in Armenia, this could cause a falling out between Armenia and Iran.

The second Trump administration pursued the America First policy. Pashinyan tried to maintain the continuity of the Armenian-American economic and military projects. In early February 2025, Pashinyan tried to accomplish this by visiting Washington and thanking the US for their supportive efforts in the Azeri-Armenian peace processes and Armenia's pursuit for democracy and embracing Christianity (buzzwords that appealed to the Traditionalist-Right American administration). Despite Pashinyan's positive reception in Washington, the continuation of the American-Armenian projects were still undefined. With the American-Armenian projects' continuity in question of the American-Armenian projects, Pashinyan sought to stabilise relations with Moscow, postponing the Russian military withdrawal from Armenia and improving trade relations in March 2025. Mixed reports were made following Yerevan's decision to reapproach the Kremlin, of how Moscow was happy of Armenia's return whilst other reports indicated that Russo-Armenian relations continued to deteriorate. Moscow officials threated to deport Armenian workers in Russia and threatened to impose tariffs on Armenian imports if Armenia continued to pursue its application into the EU.

In February 2025, in an attempt to appease the Azeris during the ongoing peace talks, Pashinyan called for the Armenian constitution to be revised. The revision excluded Armenian obligations over the Nagorno-Karabagh. This was highly controversial within Armenia but was met with delight by the Azeris. This appeared to be the final hurdle of the Azeri-Armenian peace negotiations as on 13 March 2025, it was announced that all peace terms were agreed and the peace treaty would be signed in the near future. All international players of the Nagorno-Karabagh conflict congratulated the development. However, on 16 March 2025, Azerbaijan accused the Armenian army of firing on Azeri positions across the border. Yerevan denied the accusations, and many feared an impending Azeri aggression jeopardising the peace. Ceasefires and peace agreements are a feeble piece of paper.

Without an omnipotent force to willingly enact punitive and deterrent measures, anti-peace forces and actors will find a way of sabotaging the peace to benefit their ideological or monetary motives at the expense of regular people.

The Nagorno-Karabagh conflict has become an increasingly internationalised proxy conflict. Thomas de Waal argues that traditional international players of the Nagorno-Karabagh conflict during the years 1994 to 2019 (Turkey, Russia, Iran and the US) wanted to keep the Nagorno-Karabagh dispute as a frozen conflict, to maintain a stable and comfortable status quo.[53] However, during the Second Cold War, these international players have picked a side in the conflict with the aim of making their proxy nation victorious. New international players have entered the scene, such as France, the EU, India and Israel, who have had a serious impact on the conflict and the geopolitical alignment of the Caucasus nations.

Chapter Six

THE AFRICAN MONOPOLY

The African Stranglehold

When the Ukraine War neared its third year, it was estimated that over 40,000 Ukrainians and 190,000 Russians had died during the conflict.[54] Strangely, however, there has been a rise in the death toll figures across the African continent as a result of the war in Ukraine.

Ukraine and Russia are the greatest grain exporters to Africa and with these two countries warring against each other on Ukrainian soil and the Black Sea, grain exports to Africa have decreased, causing continent-wide food insecurity. Food insecurity was an anticipated issue by African leaders at the beginning of the war, but by late 2023, famine and food insecurities began to take full effect. If the African grain issue is not resolved, Africans will become a significant percentage of the Ukraine War's death toll figures.

For humanitarian reasons, Ukraine and Russia made a brokered agreement in July 2022, to allow Ukrainian grain exports to reach Africa. However, after signing the Black Sea Grain Initiative, Moscow had struck a Ukrainian port in Odessa with a missile. Regardless, Ukrainian and Russian grain exports sailed to the African continent unmolested thereafter. This was until July 2023, when Russia suspended its agreement obligations because of supposed Ukrainian violations of the rules of the agreement.

During the Ukraine War, Russia blockaded and seized Ukrainian grain ships in the Black Sea. The Russian blockade of Ukrainian ports served two purposes. The first and primary reason was that by blockading the Ukrainian ports, Ukraine would not receive money it would have earned from grain exports. By doing this, it hindered the Ukrainian economy and defence spending. The second reason why the Russian navy blockaded Ukrainian grain exports was because in doing so, Russian exports of grain have become the lifeblood of African nations. Therefore, Russian grain exports receive a higher demand. This can be used as a tool to spread Russian influence across the African continent, as African nations look to Russian trade as the best provider of grain. African dependence on Moscow was more a by-product of the Russian Black Sea blockade than a premeditated decision, however.

This can be seen in Egypt, who received a significant increase of Russian grain exports in November 2022 in comparison to the exports received in November 2021 – more than double. After the Russian suspension of its Black Sea Grain Initiative obligations, Putin offered to Eritrea, CAR, Mali, Burkina Faso, Zimbabwe and Somalia, 25,000 to 30,000 tonnes of grain for free. The Black Sea blockade made Russia confident that they were the number one African grain exporter and so gave these countries free grain as a display to other African nations that they should subscribe to Russian grain exports. Half of these countries were diplomatically aligned with Russia (and defended Putin against African nations' criticisms of Moscow during the Russia-Africa summit in 2023) while the other half were suffering from severe levels of food insecurity. Moscow's transfer of free grain to these African nations served as a symbolic message to African countries, to align themselves with Russia, and be rewarded handsomely. This encouraged African nations to seek Russian grain exports, as they wanted to avoid famine and the societal instability that flows from food insecurity.

This aggressive Russian tactic to pressure African nations to subscribe solely to Russian exports was on full display during South African President Cyril Ramaphosa's state visit to Kyiv in June 2023. During the visit, Russian missiles struck the capital, serving as a symbolic pressure point to all African nations to drop their grain negotiations with Ukraine.[55]

Egypt was one of the greatest victims of Russia's stranglehold over Africa as they must trade with Russia to keep its economy and food security aloft. Egypt had urged Russia to continue the grain trade deal after Russia withdrew from the Black Sea Grain Initiative. Ukrainian grain exports to Egypt were destroyed by Russian naval forces a month after the Russian withdrawal, further pressuring the Egyptians to give in to Russian pressure.[56] Egypt was invited to join BRICS around the same time, and Russia exploited Egypt's weak economy and food insecurity to lure the country into joining.

South Africa has played a leading role in the non-aligned peacekeeping African coalition organisation which seeks to establish peace and grain export guarantees between Ukraine and Russia. South Africa's decision to play a leading role serves several purposes: guarantee of Russian and Ukrainian exports of grain to the African continent, and to boost the African continent input on global affairs and in the UN. South Africa led a neutral African peacekeeping coalition in order to appeal to Washington who had become increasingly critical of South Africa's diplomatic alignment with Russia. South Africa's apologetic attitude towards Putin's actions in Ukraine, their BRICS membership status and the US' condemnation of South African shipment of lethal aid to Russia strained South African-American relations. Many African nations within this coalition have taken a neutral stance towards the Ukraine conflict. This is because if they were to pick a side, it would undermine their efforts to re-establish pre-Ukraine War rate of grain imports from Europe.

The African nations have taken a neutral stance of the conflict because they fear that the hostilities of the Second Cold War may spread to the African continent. The Niger crisis and the subsequent coup hysteria served as cautious proof that the Second Cold War was spreading to their continent. Ukrainian officials have tried to woo the non-aligned African mediation coalition out of their neutral stance by accusing Russia of blockading and sabotaging Ukrainian shipment of grain destined for Africa in the Black Sea. During the July 2023 Russia-Africa summit, members of the African Union pleaded with Moscow to renew the grain initiative programme and criticised Putin for unleashing air strikes on Kyiv during African officials' visit to the Ukrainian capital. Both points of African concern were dismissed by Putin during the summit.

The low grain imports and rise in food prices caused by the Ukraine War, as well as the impacts of Covid-19 and climate change causing drought and killing African crops had left various African nations suffering from food insecurity by 2024. This can be seen in Zimbabwe and the Horn of Africa. Countries in the Horn of Africa region have experienced a rise in food insecurity levels as a result of the declining grain imports from the Black Sea affecting tens of millions of Africans there.

The Secret Wars in Sudan

The African country most at risk of mass famine as a result of the invasion of Ukraine in 2022 was Sudan. The Sudanese Civil War, which started in April 2023, had caused the world's largest hunger crisis in which 25 million people were at risk of starvation in Sudan, South Sudan and Chad. The Sudanese Civil War that began on 15 April 2023 was a complex conflict. The Sudanese armed government forces, led by President Abdel Fattah al-Burhan, were fighting the Sudanese paramilitary group, the RSF led by Mohamed Hamdan Dagalo. Both al-Burhan and Dagalo ousted Sudanese Prime Minister Abdallah Hamdok al-Kinani during the Sudanese coup in 2021. Sudan was then ministered by al-Burhan and official heads of the Sudanese military. The RSF held a joint political position with the SAF in the Sudanese government. However, a power struggle between Dagalo's RSF and al-Burhan's SAF naturally resulted in Dagalo's daring war against the SAF in April 2023. RSF forces were stationed in Khartoum and the southern and western regions of Sudan months prior to the war. It was in these areas where the RSF launched their surprise attack on the SAF and hitherto established the front lines of the Sudan Civil War. Khartoum became both the centerpiece and the bloodiest battle of the war.

Sudan is a strange, overlooked and multifront battlefield between many neighbouring and international nations. Prior to the war, Iran was in talks with al-Burhan to establish an Iranian port in the Sudanese Red Sea coast. When the civil war occurred, Iran backed al-Burhan with drones in order to prevent the disruption of Iranian desires over the Sudanese coast; by backing the Sudanese government, it would quicken the pace of establishment of an Iranian port in Sudan as a reward for backing the Sudanese government. To counter Iran's desires over the Red Sea and Saudi Arabia's hegemony in the Gulf region, the UAE backed the RSF with arms via Chad and Cameroon. Chad's continued shipping of UAE weapons to the RSF led to the SAF threatening to bomb Chadian airports to put an end to the UAE interference in African affairs. This led to mounting tensions between Chad and the SAF in March 2025, but it did not amount to serious escalation. Certain reports claim that the UAE sometimes transferred arms to the RSF via Wagner Group troops stationed in CAR and Sudan (until April 2024).[57]

The most interesting proxy war revolving around Sudan is the one between Russia and Ukraine. In April 2023, Ukraine partook in the international evacuation operations of foreign nationals in Sudan. Ukraine had evacuated 138 Ukrainian, Georgian and Peruvian citizens.[58] This appears to be the first (official) Ukrainian intervention in the Sudan Civil War. According to the *Kyiv Post* and *The Washington Post*, Ukrainian forces were used to escort President al-Burhan out of the battlefield of Khartoum during summer 2023.[59]

Prigozhin claimed that the Wagner Group had not been operating in Sudan since 2020. However, the Wagner Group never left Sudan, allying itself with RSF forces and obtaining natural mineral resources in the RSF occupied Sudanese lands during the chaos of the civil war. Evidence emerged proving that Wagner Group was backing RSF forces with weapons.[60] It appears that Russia had taken a liking to the RSF throughout the coups of 2019 and 2021, and the war in 2023, believing that they were the strongest candidate to maintain Sudanese power, prompting Russia's position in Sudan and obtaining the country's natural resources. Another reason why Moscow backed the RSF in Sudan was because Sudan, the country which has the largest stockpile of weapons in Africa, had been supplying Ukraine with weapons since the Russian invasion in 2022.[61]

The official Sudanese government was, therefore, an enemy of Russia and the transfer of Sudanese arms to Ukraine had to be thwarted. Thus, the Sudan Civil War was beneficial for Russia, as the Sudanese army had to reconsider limiting arms for Ukraine, as they would be needed for the SAF's war effort against the RSF. The purpose of Wagner Group's stay in Sudan was to obtain the Sudanese gold mines, which could be used to fund the war effort in Ukraine and for the Russian oligarchs to gain more wealth. Agreements had been made between Wagner Group and African countries, such as CAR, that if Wagner Group forces protected the African nations' mineral deposits from rival militias, the company would be rewarded with a transfer of a percentage of the guarded resources. Russian interests in supplying the RSF can also be linked to Sudanese hesitancy in allowing Russian access to Port Sudan, which Dagalo displayed no objections to. The port would allow Russia to have access to the Red Sea and establish a logistical chain in which natural resources are cross the Red Sea to Syria and Crimea.

It was, therefore, in the interests of Khartoum to rid Sudan of the Wagner Group presence, who were pouring fuel to the fire of the civil war in 2023. In September 2023, video evidence emerged of Ukrainian drones attacking RSF forces on the Shambat Bridge, north of Khartoum.[62] Analysts concluded that Ukrainian forces were behind the six drone attacks on the bridge. However, the Ukrainian government remained silent on the matter. If Ukrainian forces intervened in the Sudanese Civil War in September 2023, then the Ukrainian and Sudanese governments had long prepared for a Ukrainian intervention in the conflict, prior to the September 2023 meeting between Zelensky and al-Burhan. The president of Sudan had a security meeting with the Ukrainian president in the Republic of Ireland on 23 September 2023.[63] Zelensky and al-Burhan discussed the transfer of Ukrainian grain to Sudan and Sudanese arms to Ukraine. Judging by the series of Ukrainian intervention videos, of which will be discussed later, it is likely that Zelensky offered to send commando special forces to Sudan to harass Russian-backed troops and Wagner Group forces. Both parties would benefit from this. The transfer of African natural resources to Russia would be thwarted and the supplier of the RSF would be harassed.

In October 2023, another video circulated on social media of an unidentified white skinned sniper and several white soldiers attacking Wagner Group forces in the Sudanese desert and urban areas. *Clash Report*, who posted the video on X (Twitter), claimed that these white soldiers were Ukrainian special forces.[64] On 4 January 2024, the *Kyiv Post* posted another video of a Ukrainian drone bombing Wagner Group vehicles (which were clearly long abandoned Sudanese cars).[65] On 5 February 2024, the *Kyiv Post* published a less ambiguous video of Ukrainian soldiers in Sudan, interrogating a white Russian soldier kneeling alongside two other POW RSF soldiers.[66] The Russian POW claimed that there were 100 Wagner Group troops in Sudan who entered the country via the CAR-Sudan border.

On 7 March 2024, *The Washington Post* published an article that had exclusive interviews with supposed Ukrainian Intelligence Service operators that operated in Sudan, confirming that Ukrainian operatives were present in Sudan. Al-Burhan was evacuated out of Khartoum in August 2023 by 100 Ukrainian soldiers from the Timur Special Unit. The president of Sudan then travelled to the Republic of Ireland from Port Sudan. There he met Zelensky. After the meeting, various Ukrainian groups from the Ukrainian Main Directorate of Intelligence were sent to Sudan to harass RSF-Wagner Group logistics and attack RSF forces. It was also mentioned that the Wagner Group recruited local Sudanese people into the PMC.[67]

Ukrainian intervention is much more than harassing Wagner Group bases in Sudan. The Ukrainian intervention ensured that the Russian-backed RSF did not take over Sudan's governmental processes, as if the RSF succeeded in doing that, Ukraine would no longer be supplied by Sudan – the country with the highest weapons stockpile in the African continent.

Misinformation and disinformation circulate on the internet all the time. Russian, Western and Ukrainian propaganda is used to trick people's understanding of troop positioning. All of the above may later prove to be false propaganda. However, if proven to be correct, then the Ukraine War has extended outside of Europe. As revealed in the Pentagon leaks in 2023, Zelensky did plan to intervene in the Syrian Civil War and harass Russian troops stationed there, in the hopes that it would divert Russian troops from Ukraine to Syria.

However, due to a series of issues that the Ukrainian Main Directorate of Intelligence faced, Zelensky cancelled the Ukrainian intervention in the Syrian Civil War in December 2022. If the Ukrainians were willing to intervene in the Syrian Civil War, it is reasonable that they would do so in Sudan also.

Further information about Ukrainian intervention in Sudan was revealed by the French *TFI Info* journalists, who interviewed two supposed Ukrainian operators fighting in Sudan. The operators claim that their purpose in Sudan was to harass the Wagner Group's extract of Sudan's natural resources and curb Russian influence in Sudan and neighbouring African countries. This was accomplished by directly engaging with the Wagner Group or by attacking the Russian-backed RSF group transferring materials to Wagner Group bases and their logistical routes. Ukrainian operators launched an amphibious raid on RSF bases in the River Nile State. *TFI Info*'s exclusive video footage showed NATO-equipped soldiers fighting in an African town alongside Sudanese men and soldiers. They conducted various amphibious assault practices with the Timur Special Unit, as well as other brigades under the Ukrainian Main Directorate of Intelligence, which later participated in various amphibious assaults in Crimea and the Dnipro campaigns. Ukraine has been training loyalist Sudanese troops with arms and drones to further restabilise al-Burhan's country against RSF assaults and Russian influences. They had supposedly been operating in Sudan since August 2023 according to the interviewed Ukrainians.[68]

News reports of Ukrainian operations in Sudan began to subdue significantly after March 2024. However, it appears that in mid-2024 (approximately April to May 2024), Russia shifted its allegiance away from the RSF and towards the SAF. In June 2024, Russia offered the SAF weapons in exchange for building a naval base in Sudan. Russian foreign diplomats began to openly support the SAF and Sudan offered to provide Moscow access to Sudanese minerals in exchange for Russian shipment of weapons to the SAF.[69] Sudan started to increasingly expand its ties with Moscow, likely in response to the RSF's series of victories in the battlefield in 2024 and offered to establish a Russian naval base in Port Sudan in exchange for more weapons in April 2024. Russia swiftly accepted the deal and the construction of the Russian naval base began in February 2025. In September 2024, The *Financial Times* reported that Ukrainian service personnel were sent to Sudan as air force instructors to the SAF. Simultaneously with Kyiv's continued support of the SAF, the *Financial Times* claimed that Russian shipment of arms to the SAF became more apparent, and it was even alleged that Russian snipers were operating alongside the SAF.[70]

It is unknown how Kyiv reacted to Moscow's switch in allegiance in Sudan. Washington's sanctions and war crime accusations towards al-Burhan in January 2025 served to pivot the SAF further into the Russian camp. Fresh from the SAF's offensive victories in Khartoum and south-west Sudan in February 2025, Sudan voted against condemning Russia's invasion of Ukraine in the 24 February 2025 UN General Assembly resolution.

Russia's Backyard

Wagner Group presence and exploitation in Africa came following the straining relations between France and Sahel African countries. *FrancaAfrique* or 'France's Backyard' refers to France's strong relations with African countries after their colonial independence from their French imperial rule. France and these African countries had a symbiotic relationship in which the economy of these African countries was closely tied to France. French politicians used money gained from investments in Africa to fund their political electoral campaigns.

By 2012, African economists began to criticise France's ties to their countries, claiming that France's economic exploitation was an act of 'French Colonial Era Tax'. This further caused discontent between African citizens and their governments, who financially benefited from France's exploitation and were, therefore, seen as corrupt politicians. African citizens and newly established governments, formed via coup and public disgruntlement with France, pressured France to withdraw from their countries. Russian disinformation and propaganda campaigns in Africa played a huge role in influencing the African population to turn against French and American presence.

French troops were originally stationed in these African countries to counter Islamic insurgencies. However, their stay became increasingly unwelcome as time progressed. This resulted in the French withdrawal from CAR in 2016, which Wagner Group later exploited and took their place in 2018. Anti-French sentiments increased significantly in Mali after the coup in 2021 and the newly formed government pressured French withdrawal from the country, which commenced in August 2022. Putin immediately affirmed his relations with the newly established Mali government by offering to send Russian military advisers to come and replace the French ones, which Mali accepted. Mali-Russian ties were so strong that the Mali government refused UN troops to operate in the country to counter extremist insurgencies, as they were satisfied with the Russian forces.

The African people's history of colonialism under Western imperialism has been the underlying cause for their disdain of Europeans. The deep political-ties with France, the exploitation of their economy and the presence of French military troops affirmed their beliefs that France was continuing their colonial rule over their countries, albeit unofficially. In their eyes, Russia is their liberator and their presence is, therefore, welcomed by these people even though Russia's operations in African countries are conducted in a similar way to how the French army had conducted itself. In actuality, Wagner Group's presence has made these countries much more dangerous and hostile under their supervision than under French supervision. This can be seen in the list of atrocities committed by Wagner Group troops against African civilians. The most infamous occurred in Mali in March 2023 with the Moura massacre. During the Moura massacre, Wagner Group troops alongside Malian troops massacred Malian civilians in Mali's northern region in retaliation of repeated Islamic extremist insurgency attacks on Malian positions. In CAR, the Wagner Group were known for their perpetration of the Bongboto and Aigbado civilian massacres in 2021 and 2022 respectively, and for their acts of robbery and sexual assault towards civilians.

Similar to the fallout of the Mali coup in 2021, Burkina Faso demanded French withdrawal after the coup in January 2022. However, in September 2022, Lieutenant Colonel Paul-Henri Dambia, who was anti-French, and had led the January coup and subsequently the country, was ousted from power by Captain Ibrahim Traore. Dambia was ousted from power due to the army's dissatisfaction with Dambia's handling of the rising Islamic extremist insurgency in the country. The alarming fact that 40 per cent of Burkina Faso remained under rebel control, coupled with the public's dissatisfaction with Dambia's handling of the siege of Djibo, which began a month after the January coup, provided ammunition for Traore to oust and succeed Dambia. Traore, however, also had anti-French and pro-Russian sentiments, and invited the Wagner Group to help them counter the Islamic insurgents in exchange for natural resources. An attempt was made to overthrow Traore in December 2022. However, Traore defeated the putschists, further solidifying his position as leader of Burkina Faso. Macron claimed that France had to reduce military presence in Africa in response to the threat from Russia after the invasion of Ukraine. This demonstrated that outside factors led to France losing grip over their 'back garden'.

The Coup in Niger

On 26 July 2023, a coup occurred in Niger in which President Mohamed Bazoum was ousted and succeeded by General Abdourahamane Tchiani. Like Traore, Tchiani's reasoning for taking control over Niger was due to Bazoum's mishandling of the Niger economy and dissatisfaction with the country's security against Islamic extremist terror and Western influences. However, there might be an ethnic dimension behind the coup. Tchiani was of Hausa ethnic background, which is the majority demographic (55 per cent) in Niger. Bazoum belongs to the Ouled Slimane Arab ethnicity and Tchiani may have been disgruntled with the idea that an Arab was leading a majority Hausa African populated country.

ECOWAS countries, including Gambia, Cape Verde, Guinea-Bissau and Senegal, were furious of the Niger coup as they feared that this would spark a series of coups across the Sahel region. ECOWAS knew that they had to act to reverse the Niger coup in order to deter bad-faith characters from committing coups against ECOWAS members' leaders.

On 30 June 2023, ECOWAS sanctioned Niger and declared an ultimatum to Tchiani to restore Bazoum into power within a seven-day deadline. If not, then ECOWAS countries would reverse the Niger coup by military force. However, when the ultimatum was not met, Nigeria and its ECOWAS allies refrained from invading Niger. It is likely that Nigeria did not want to go to war and so bluffed Niger into pressuring the country to accept a ECOWAS' ultimatum. This proved to be a failure.

ECOWAS also feared that Burkina Faso and Mali would intervene if ECOWAS invaded Niger. Burkina Faso and Mali, suspended members of ECOWAS, voiced their support for Tchiani as they shared an anti-Western sentiment and perceived ECOWAS as being antagonistic towards African independence from the Western neo-colonial powers. On September 2023, the countries formed a military alliance, which saw that an ECOWAS (and Islamic extremist) attack on one country would be viewed as an attack on all. Burkina Faso sent troops to Niger immediately after the signing of the defence treaty, further deterring ECOWAS from invading Niger.

Prigozhin celebrated the Niger coup as a Wagner Group victory on social media. He claimed that the coup was a result of Wagner Group meddling. However, he may have claimed the Niger coup to be a Wagner feat, to maintain Wagner Group relevance after the Wagner Group rebellion and Prigozhin's loss of prestige. Wagner Group disinformation campaigns further fuelled people to believe the Niger coup to be the work of the Wagner Group. Misinformation had circulated, claiming that France was preparing an air attack on Niger in support of ECOWAS, which further fuelled Niger's anti-French sentiments.[71]

Regardless of whether Wagner Group was responsible for the coup taking place, Russia exploited the subsequent crisis to their advantage. Immediately after Bazoum's removal, thousands of Niger demonstrators in the capital of Niamey took to the streets with celebrations. Niger, North Korean and Russian flags were hoisted in the air and chants for the removal of French troops and pro-Russian sentiments could be heard in the streets. In a frenzy of excitement, the Niger demonstrators attacked the French Embassy and attempted to set fire to it. Niger soldiers successfully urged the crowd to disperse, and Macron warned that any harm inflicted on French citizens would result in retaliation. The pro-Tchiani Niger demonstrators protested outside the French military base in Niamey.

For a second time in the year, the international community evacuated its citizens from an African country, although the evacuation from Niger was a less dangerous endeavour compared to the evacuation of citizens from the war-torn country of Sudan. Tchiani tried to play off French, ECOWAS, American and Russian interests in order to maintain power. Tchiani held successful diplomatic talks with Macron and pressured him to withdraw French troops from Niger. In December 2023, France withdrew its 1,500 troops from Niger. Pro-coup Niger demonstrators attempted to block entryway for international evacuee forces to airfields, demanding that the French troops should withdraw first before any more international citizens were to be evacuated. This likely played a significant pressuring point to force Macron to call for the withdrawal of French presence in Niger.

The Aftermath of the Crisis

By 13 March 2024, Nigeria began to drop its sanctions and opened its borders with Niger due to 'humanitarian reasons'. These humanitarian reasons were to continue trade relations between the two countries. The real rationale behind the reopening of trade routes was to avoid a Nigerian economic downfall. If Nigeria was to suffer economic insecurity, the country would fall into social and political instability which would result in a possible coup attempt.

Biden did not officially recognise the military takeover as a coup. This was likely a diplomatic move to appease Tchiani in order to keep the 1,000 American troops in the country. This came to the detriment of the American citizens in Niger, who had to wait a couple more days until Biden changed his mind. Tchiani entertained the idea of American presence in Niger, but he favoured a Russian presence instead, in order to appeal to the Niger public. In March 2024, Niger pressured the Americans to withdraw its presence and in April 2024, 100 Russian military trainers arrived in Niger to help combat local Islamic extremists. The arriving Russians were accommodated in the American military air base in Niamey. The Americans and Russians awkwardly coexisted on the two opposite ends of the camp with minimum contact in May 2024. Whilst Tchiani faced pressures from the West and ECOWAS, Moscow provided diplomatic support to Niger. In December 2023, Moscow sought to strengthen Russo-Niger security cooperation against local Islamic extremist groups. Tchiani later accepted Russian military presence in the country to further pressure Biden to withdraw US presence from Niger. The presence of Russian military personnel made the population of Niger more fervent and eager to remove the Americans and protests intensified in April 2024. The Russian military personnel sent to Niger was identified as the Africa Corps (Wagner Group). By mid-September 2024, American, German and British troops were completely withdrawn from Niger.

On 29 November 2022, a mysterious explosion struck a Wagner Group base in Bossangoa in the CAR. It was speculated by the CAR government that the Chadian air force was behind the attack as the plane flew northwards after the attack, indicating it was returning to Chad.

Chad had engaged in the ongoing CAR civil war sporadically through the years against the CAR government forces. The CAR also previously accused Chad of harbouring opposition militia fighters, making it difficult for the CAR forces to crush rebel forces in the CAR's northern region. Chad was also dealing with a refugee crisis from neighbouring Sudan which has seen a rapid influx of over 550,000 war refugees as of April 2024. The Sudan Civil War not only served as an economic hinderance but a source of political polarisation. The Chadian Zaghawa political elite were pressuring Chadian President Mahamat Deby to support the RSF against the Sudanese Arabs. The Zaghawa elites' demands were derived from ethnic rivalries between Arabs and native Africans in that region. Deby contemplated adhering to the demands to secure the Chadian military's loyalty, as the Chadian military mostly consists of Zaghawa tribesmen. By solidifying the military's loyalty, it would ensure that the military would be on the side of Deby in case a coup or civil war were to occur in the future. If the Zaghawa's demands were not met, that would risk military disgruntlement and prospects of a military coup against Deby.

Deby was fearful of possible coup plots against him. This can be seen during October 2022, where Chadian protesters marched in the capital of N'Djamena demanding democratic rights. This had been met with government authorities firing at the protesters, killing 200. In February 2024, during the wake of the Chadian presidential elections, Chadian security forces attacked and killed opposition leader Yaya Dillo, ensuring that Deby's success in the presidential elections. The death of Dillo was a product of Deby's anxiety of losing power, which had increased after the Niger coup.

Even before the Niger coup, Deby was riven with anxiety over his rule from Russian interference. In February 2023, *The Washington Post* reported that American intelligence informed the Chadian president that the Chaden rebels, in support of the Wagner Group, were attempting to destabilise the country and even plotted his assassination.[72] American intelligence later informed Chad that the Wagner Group was attempting to amass Chadian rebels from within the country and within Russian aligned African nations and paramilitaries in neighbouring countries, such as CAR, Libya and Sudan, in preparation for a violent coup against Deby. Fears of Russian desires to topple Deby led to instances in which Wagner Group affiliated Russian citizens in Chad were detained in September 2024 for suspicion of assisting political oppositionists and rebels. It also led to Deby feeling pressured to align with the Sahel Alliance in order to thwart Moscow's intentions of removing Deby from power.

On 19 April 2024, a letter was sent to the American air base Adji Kossei in N'Djamena to cease its aerial operations. An American spokesperson claimed that the letter did not necessarily mean the total withdrawal of American presence in Chad. Several days later, the US announced the withdrawal of the American military presence in Niger and Chad. The reasoning behind Chad's decision to remove Western military presence was not necessarily because Deby was anti-West. On the contrary, the West provided arms, training and fighter jets to the Chadian government to eliminate Islamic extremist presence in the northern region of Chad. The US too saw Chad as a valuable ally in the continent. The removal of American presence was to establish normalisation with Niger, which ensured the resumption of Chad-Niger trade and political ties. The Sahel became a little cold war between ECOWAS and the Sahel Alliance in which Deby believed that he had to side with the Sahel Alliance, in order to maintain his rule. Deby believed that the American withdrawal was necessary to cement Chad's alignment with the Sahel Alliance.

On 24 January 2024, Deby visited Putin to discuss the matter, to which Putin offered Russian soldiers to replace the Western forces.[73] Russian grain may also have played a factor in Chad aligning itself with the Sahel Alliance. In the backdrop of the US' gradual withdrawal from Chad, Chad terminated its military cooperation with France in November 2024. Deby claimed this move would not sour Chadian-French relations. However, the ceasing of military cooperation entailed the removal of French troops from the country. Moscow had, therefore, successfully pressured Deby into aligning with the Russian bloc and to expel Western presence during a period in which Deby was facing several other crises such as the Sudanese refugee crisis, the Niger crisis and increasing unrest from pro-democratic Chadian civilians.

Russian presence in Libya and Mali increased after the partial Russian withdrawal of Syria in December 2024 following the fall of al-Assad. In November 2024, Equatorial Guinea received 200 Russian military instructors to improve the country's army. Internal insecurities and external pressures led to the Ivory Coast and Senegal demanding the withdrawal of the French military from their countries in December 2024.

The African Loophole

The Russian foothold in the Sahel region served as a significant advantage to Russia, not just because it diminished Western influences, but because it undermined the West's sanctions. In May 2023, it was discovered that Russia received weapons and goods from foreign suppliers, and Russia-aligned Mali was used as a transit hub for these illegal trades. This greatly undermined Western sanctions and although the West responded with further sanctions on the Wagner Group operating in Mali, Russia's influence in Mali led to an increase in Russian purchases of war materials to be invested in Russia's war efforts in Ukraine. Secret trade between Russia and foreign nations is known to have occurred. The Pentagon leaks of 2023 revealed that Egypt traded gunpowder and artillery to Russia in secrecy to avoid Western condemnation and international isolation. It was revealed that Turkey was in talks with the Wagner Group to purchase lethal aid. The increase of Russian influence spreading across Africa would be exploited to undermine Western sanctions and to continue Russian trade.

However, it should be noted that by summer 2023, Ukraine was winning the war in the Black Sea. Russian hold over the Black Sea loosened due to consistent harassment by Ukrainian air attacks and naval drones, resulting in Russian naval vessels withdrawing from Crimea to Abkhazia in 2024, loosening Russia's Black Sea and African strangleholds. Russia attempted to circumvent these shortcomings by intensifying its air strikes on Ukrainian port facilities to hinder Ukraine's grain exports and maintain the value of Russian grain.

Despite Ukraine's success against the Russian blockade, Ukraine and their Western partners were playing an asymmetrical game of influence in Africa against Russia. Moscow had strong historical ties with various African nations during the First Cold War and performed an excellent anti-West propaganda campaign across the continent, as has been explored in this chapter. When Malian troops and Wagner Group troops were ambushed by Tuareg and Islamic extremist fighters during the July 2024 battle of Tinzaouaten, the Ukrainian Main Directorate of Intelligence claimed that they provided intelligence to the Mali rebels of the Wagner Group-Mali advances towards the city, contributing to the success of the ambush. *BBC Verify* found the Ukrainian Main Directorate's photo evidence to be a fake.[74] However, the Main Directorate of Intelligence's claims had an explosive backfire on Ukraine's charm diplomacy in Africa, as both the Alliance of the Sahel States and several ECOWAS countries condemned Kyiv for aiding the Tuareg-Islamic extremist forces and intervening in African affairs. Ukrainian representatives denied Ukraine's involvement in the battle of Tinzaouten, but with little success. Russia exploited Ukraine's blunder to enhance their consolidations over the newly Russian aligned African nations.

Chapter Seven

SYRIA: THE LAND OF PROXY WARS

The Arab spring of 2011 was a series of protests calling for the removal of authoritarian regimes in favour of democracy across the Middle East. Some of the Arab spring protests were successful in putting down various authoritarian governments. But for some, such as Libya, Yemen and Syria, it would destabilise the nation states and leave a power vacuum for various factions and nations to fight over. Syrian President Bashar al-Assad's brutal repression of the protesters in 2011 resulted in the formation of the Syrian opposition army, who vowed to oust the al-Assad family from power. Syrian Kurds exploited the civil struggle and attempted to incite Kurdish independence from the Syrian government in the northeastern region of Rojava. The US and the West contemplated intervening in the Syrian Civil War against al-Assad but decided not to. ISIS later exploited the power struggle in 2014 and by 2015 brutally occupied the eastern half of Syria.

When ISIS entered the frame, the US intervened by air striking ISIS positions and armed Kurdish militias, such as the SDF, to eliminate the ISIS threat. Turkey backed the northern Syrian opposition forces against ISIS and the Kurdish militias. Russia intervened also to fight ISIS on behalf of al-Assad and engaged in combat against the Syrian opposition, as a counter to American influence over Syria. Russian support for the al-Assad regime came in exchange for the Russian control over naval ports and air bases in the Taurus and Latakia regions. This gave Russia access to the Mediterranean Sea, which would boost Russian trade. Iran unofficially intervened in the conflict in support of al-Assad against ISIS and rebel forces, with the use of Iranian-backed Shia paramilitary groups, such as Hezbollah. This served Iranian interests as if the Syrian opposition succeeded to power, it would mean the disruption of Iranian transfers of lethal aid to their allied paramilitary group, Hezbollah, in Lebanon to harass Israel. The Iranian involvement subsequently led to Israeli intervention, aimed at countering Iranian presence and influence.

The ISIS threat was eliminated by 2019, at the hands of American-backed Kurdish and rebel forces. The American bombing campaign of ISIS oil installations rendered ISIS ineffective, as their main source of war revenue was destroyed. It was discovered that Turkey was buying ISIS oil which was funding ISIS war effort and occupational needs. However, ISIS cells were still present in the country and American troops stationed in Syria conducted commando raids to eliminate them from 2019 onwards to the early years of the Second Cold War. The American military's continued presence in Syria was not solely to destroy ISIS cells, despite what American officials may claim.

After the March 2020 Idlib ceasefire, the Syrian Civil War started to die down and began to slowly evolve into a chess board between various international nations pitted against each other over who influences the country. By 2022, it appeared al-Assad had won the civil war as he had gained control over the Western half of Syria and remained in power. However, pockets of opposition rebels' presence remained in the Idlib province, and under the Turkish co-occupied northern regions of both the Aleppo and Raqqah provinces. The Kurdish militias managed to establish a large autonomy in the Rojava region to the east and co-occupied a portion of the al-Tanf region with American forces. The immediate 'freezing' of the conflict created a much divided but static landscape of war-torn Syria, which served as a quiet proxy war between the US and Israel against Russia, Iran and even Turkey during the Second Cold War.

Rebuilding From Ashes

It was now al-Assad's goal to reunite the lands of Syria under his rule to re-legitimise his government, in order to establish control over the Syrian people and to be accepted by the international community. This could have only been accomplished by expelling rival international players from Syria, such as the American presence in the southern and eastern provinces as well as Turkish occupation of the northern regions. The only way al-Assad could have accomplished this task, was by relying on his much dependable Russian and Iranian allies' ambitions during the Second Cold War, in exchange for their diplomatic and military support against further Western presence in the country.

Bashar al-Assad was one of few leaders to have supported Russia's invasion of Ukraine during the international condemnation of Russia in 2022. Al-Assad was supportive of the US war against the Taliban after the 9/11 terrorist attacks. However, Syrian-American relations were skewered after President George W. Bush accused al-Assad of supporting the Taliban in a speech in 2002. Thereafter, al-Assad took an anti-American stance, which intensified during the 2003 American invasion of Iraq. Russian support and American antagonism towards Syria in the twenty-first century naturally led to al-Assad's alignment with Russia during the immediate Second Cold War years. The Russian army began scaling back its forces from Syria in March 2022, due to the unforeseen stiff Ukrainian resistance during the Russian invasion of Ukraine. Regardless, Russian forces still maintained their presence in Syria, conducting aerial bombing campaigns against Syrian opposition and ISIS holdings. Although al-Assad understood Moscow's circumstances, this served against his interests as Russian presence was needed to counter the West's presence in the East. Al-Assad voiced his wishes to make Russian presence in the country permanent and tried to increase Russian military bases in the country in March 2023. Al-Assad allowed Russian recruitment of Syrian soldiers to volunteer into the Russian army to fight against Ukraine. In March 2022, Putin claimed that al-Assad sent 16,000 Syrian troops to Russia for the Ukrainian war front. This number was met with scepticism, as the number of Syrian forces was too high and it was later believed that a mere 100 Syrians volunteered to fight in Ukraine.

In May 2023, al-Assad's government was accepted to return to the Arab League, ensuring al-Assad's legitimacy at least to the eyes of Middle Eastern countries. Turkish President Recep Tayyip Erdoğan even held a diplomatic meeting with al-Assad in July 2023. However, Turkey displayed adamance that it would not be withdrawing from Syria. Turkey proved to be the most difficult obstacle for al-Assad's reunification due to Ankara's fervent desires to eliminate Kurdish nationalist forces in the east. In July 2023, Russia repeatedly bombed the opposition holdings in the north-west Syrian regions and demanded Turkey decrease its troop presence in Syria. Turkey did not budge and the Russian bombings in July were in response to Syrian opposition forces (backed by Turkey) harassing al-Assad-Russian troops there weeks prior. On 5 October 2023, the city of Homs was struck by drones, killing eighty-nine. The strike was suspected to be perpetrated by the Syrian opposition in the north-west region of Idlib, resulting in an intensification of Russo-Syrian bombarding of the region in October 2023.

Despite al-Assad's welcoming to the Arab League, Jordan was against Syria's reintegration. This was because of al-Assad's Captagon drug production and trade. Due to years of economic turmoil and international sanctions, during the Syrian Civil War, al-Assad turned to drug production and exports to maintain the country's economic stability. In August 2023, al-Assad faced protests from his citizens in the southern regions of Syria over domestic and economic hardships and demanded al-Assad stop economic mismanagement and fix Syria's hyperinflation problem. Syrian opposition flags were waved during the protests and chants for the removal of al-Assad were echoed in the streets, which caused al-Assad to be fearful that these protests would renew the Syrian Civil War. It was, therefore, in the interests of al-Assad to revive the economy in order to prevent a new phase of the Syrian Civil War.

The Russo-American Conflict in Syria

Russian presence in Syria partially decreased as a result of the Russian army's defeats in Ukraine in 2022. Moscow and Damascus feared that the partial withdrawal would be exploited by the Americans and weaken the Russian bloc's posture in Syria. According to the Pentagon leaks, in November 2022, high official Russian, Iranian and Syrian intelligence-military officers agreed to establish a coordination centre that aimed to coordinate the American presence's expulsion from Syria. It can be presumed that the Iranian piracy campaign in the Strait of Hormuz, the Hezbollah intervention in the SDF-Arab Tribal clashes in Deir ez-Zor in September 2023, the Iranian backed militant groups' drone and IED attacks on American-SDF military bases and logistics in Eastern Syria (pre-Gaza War) as well as Russia's aerial harassment campaign were all part of the Russian-Iranian-Syrian coordinated effort to expel American presence from Syria.

Syria proved to be an overlooked flashpoint between Russo-American tensions. The Pentagon leaks revealed that in November 2022, Russian air defence missiles failed in an attempt to shoot down an American MQ-9 Reaper drone. However, the following year saw an intense Russian aerial harassment campaign against the Americans stationed in Syria. During summer 2023, American and Russian fighter jets and drones made dangerous manoeuvres and interceptions against each other, risking the lives of American and Russian military personnel stationed in Syria. The series of aerial manoeuvres could have risked a third world war if the manoeuvres had resulted in an American or Russian fatality. Such Russian aerial provocations were believed to be inspired by Russia's successful downing of an American drone in the Black Sea on 13 March 2023. However, this is a misconception, as Russian aerial provocative behaviour in Syria predates the Black Sea drone incident.

Beginning on 1 March 2023, Russian jets in Syria performed 'dangerous manoeuvres' by flying their jets above American military bases in Syria. The motives for Russian aerial harassment in Syria were unknown at this point, with many Western officials claiming that they were to incite an international crisis. However, this seems to be a weak reasoning, as an international crisis would serve as a detriment to Russian interests. This Russian aerial incident proved to be very provocative against the US, as it displayed Moscow's firm support for the legitimisation of al-Assad's regime over the country as al-Assad gave the Russian air force permission to fly in its airspace. The Russian aerial action was a symbolic gesture to the American troops stationed in Syria that their stay did not have the consent of the Syrian government and so was illegal. The Russian tactic of aerial harassment was to make the Americans as uncomfortable as possible and to incite Syrian unrest over the American presence. Russian backing of the Syrians against American presence in the south-east pressured the Americans to exit the country, akin to the events of the Niger crisis.

Well into the following month, Russian fighter jets intensified its provocative tactic of flying over American bases in Syria and on several occasions attempting to incite dogfights with American fighter jets. Between 1 March and 29 April, eighty-five Russian aerial harassments were documented. In April 2023, Russian jets flew over the American military base al-Tanf. The American al-Tanf base is a very strategic point, as it serves as a roadblock for Iranian lethal supplies to the Iranian-backed paramilitary group Hezbollah in Lebanon. It can be speculated that the Russian harassment campaign was requested by Iran.

Jeff Schogol, an analyst from Task and Purpose, speculated that the reasoning behind the Russian harassment campaign in Syria, was to disrupt American air operations from attacking al-Assad forces and Iranian-backed militias.[75] American flight schedules were altered and reviewed as a result of the Russian harassment. As a precaution to the intensification of Russian aerial harassment, Washington sent F-22s fighter jets to Syria in June 2023. In the beginning of July 2023, Russian fighter jets began to harass American drones operating in northeastern Syria by firing flares at them. Russian jets also conducted dangerous manoeuvres around a French fighter jet in the Iraq-Syria border. American officials speculated that the Russian fighter jet pilots harassed American drones and jets to get war medals, referring to how the Russian pilot who successfully downed the American reaper drone in the Black Sea in March 2023 earned a war medal as a result of his actions. According to American officials, the Russian harassment tactics became more aggressive and prolonging in nature, which put the lives of American pilots at risk.

On July 2023, the Syrian situation escalated to a near fatal extent, when it was reported that a Russian jet successfully evaded American F-16 guidance missiles.[76] The Russian deputy head of Reconciliation Centre for Syria publicly announced the incident and claimed that American jets were operating illegally in al-Assad-Russian airspace prior that month. These American manoeuvres likely occurred to deter Russian jets from their dangerous behaviour, but proved unsuccessful as Russian jets continued to harass American drones and fighter jets days later.

In mid-July, more American fighter jets were sent to Syria to protect American commercial shipping traversal through the Strait of Hormuz, in the wake of Iran's growing seizure operations which targeted Western commercial ships, during the summer of 2023.[77] Iran's seizure operations in the Strait of Hormuz may have also played a factor in Russia's aerial harassment campaign in Syria. The Russian air force's curbing of American fighter jets' operations in Syria served complementary to their Iranian ally's anti-West campaign in the Gulf region.

On 14 August, an American jet confronted and escorted a Russian jet away from the al-Tanf air base. August saw a sharp decline in Russian aerial harassments, with only seven recorded incidents occurring that month. It appeared the Russian aerial harassment campaign fizzled out by September 2023. There could be several reasons behind this. Putin saw the escalating severity of the Syrian situation and reasoned that the aerial harassment campaigns were not worth the risk. Although the Russian campaign and American counter campaign in Syria came to an end in September 2023, an incident occurred on 19 August 2024 in which a Western fighter jet committed dangerous manoeuvres around a Russian fighter jet in the skies of Homs, meaning that the Russo-American provocative measures in Syria had not ceased, despite the escalatory dangers.

Ukrainian Forces in Syria?

The Pentagon leaks in 2023 revealed that Zelensky considered sending a Ukrainian commando force into Syria to harass stationed Russian troops, pressuring Putin to alleviate his forces from the Ukrainian front lines to the Syrian front.

The Pentagon leaks revealed the American assessment of an aborted Ukrainian plan to intervene in the Syrian Civil War. According to the leaks, during the period October to December 2022, the Ukrainian Main Directorate of Intelligence held secret talks with anti-al-Assad aligned Syrian groups, such as the Kurdish SDF, over the possibility of providing them with UAV drones in exchange for these groups attacking Russian positions in Syria. It appears that Turkey was aware of the Ukrainian intervention in Syria and on 8 December 2022, had suggested to Kyiv to not provide aid to the Turkish- backed oppositionist Syrian forces in the rebel held Idlib province and recommended sending aid to the SDF insert. *The Washington Post* reasoned that Turkey suggested Ukraine send lethal aid to their rival Syrian SDF to provoke a Russian retaliatory strike against the SDF.[78] Turkey promoted an SDF-Ukrainian alliance as a means to counter the Russian-SDF alliance and ignite a Russian retaliatory response unto SDF positions.

The Ukrainians adhered to the Turkish command but faced obstacles. The Pentagon assessed that the SDF refused to strike Russian positions in Syria but was willing to attack Russian allied forces instead. The SDF wished for the Ukrainian aid and training to be of utmost secrecy as they did not want to jeopardise their alliance with Russia. The SDF's willingness to commit to the Ukrainian deal was, therefore, questionable to Kyiv. In November 2022, the Ukrainian Main Directorate of Intelligence found logistical problems in supplying lethal aid to the SDF. On 29 December 2022, Zelensky cancelled the Syrian adventure, and the Pentagon assumed that Kyiv would not resume the Syrian project without American and Turkish approval. It appears the Pentagon were sceptical to the idea of approving Ukraine's Syria adventure in fear that American bases would be at risk of a Russian retaliatory response to the Ukrainian-backed SDF attacks on Russian bases. Zelensky redirected the planned Ukrainian military activities in Sudan. However, in 2024 the Ukrainian Syrian adventure was revived.

On 6 June 2024, *Kyiv Post* published a video claiming that Ukrainian forces, belonging to the Khimik group (under the umbrella of the Ukrainian Main Directorate of Intelligence) were operating alongside

Syrian opposition forces against al-Assad and Russian forces in the eastern Golan Heights. After Syria's failure in the Yom Kippur War, Western and central Golan Heights were occupied and later illegally annexed by Israel. As part of the Golan Heights Agreement in 1974, the east of the Golan Heights remained under Damascus control. Since November 2023, Russian forces were sent to the Syrian controlled eastern territories of the Golan Heights and began to increase in presence as the months progressed.[79] Middle Eastern journalists questioned why Russian presence increased in the Golan Heights. Most analysts speculated that it was to deter Israeli forces from attacking the Golan Heights during the Gaza War.

The *Kyiv Post* claimed that the video took place in March 2024, in the Quneitra and Daara areas, but stated the Khimik operators had been operating in the area since the beginning of 2024.[80] The video showed Ukrainian and Syrian opposition forces harassing ongoing vehicles, patrols and checkpoints. It can be speculated that the assaults depicted in the video were early Ukrainian operations in Syria, who were harassing Russian checkpoints with the aim of penetrating further into Russian occupied Syria to harass Russian extraction of Syrian natural resources. It could also be possible that Israel was concerned with Russia's growing influence in the Golan Heights and Israel issued the Directorate of Ukrainian Intelligence a deal. Israel-Ukrainian relations were rather strained during the beginning of the Second Cold War. Israel took a fence-sitting stance during the invasion of Ukraine. Israeli politicians claimed to support Ukrainian sovereignty whilst avoiding vocal condemnation of Russia. Zelensky consistently attempted to obtain Israeli lethal aid packages, especially the anti-missile system: the Iron Dome.

However, Zelensky's pleas were in vain. Both the US and Ukraine attempted to pressure Israel to transfer the anti-missile systems and lethal aid to Ukraine, but Israel was hesitant in doing so. This was because Israel feared that if their military hardware or materials were captured by the Russians, they would be handed over to the Iranians to be examined and replicated against Israel. However, as the Second Cold War progressed, Israel became concerned with the ever-increasing relations between Iran and Russia, when it was confirmed that Iranian missiles were being sent to the Russians. Israel provided military intelligence to Kyiv, concerning Iranian involvement in Russia's war effort in Ukraine in October 2023.[81] It is, therefore, feasible that during the multifront war Israel was facing in 2023, Israel proposed Ukraine transfer its lethal aid in exchange for harassing Russian troops in the border. This is all, however, speculation and the Ukrainian intervention in Syria may be a product of Ukrainian disinformation propaganda.

In September 2024, the *Kyiv Post* released an exclusive video, showing the Ukrainian Main Directorate of Intelligence commandos attacking the Kuweires Military Aviation Institute base in the southeast outskirts of Aleppo.[82] The supposed attack took place towards the end of July 2024. The Russian government denied any attack on the Kuweires base, claiming that the video produced by the *Kyiv Post* was a fake to distract the West from the Russian successes at the Ukraine front. If the video is not a product of Ukrainian disinformation, then that would mean that the Khimik group was stationed in northern Turkish occupied Aleppo province or in the HTS-held Idlib province, before they attacked Kuweires Military Aviation Institute. In November 2024, *Kyiv Post* claimed that the Khimik group provided military training to Syrian oppositionist factions in Idlib, prior to the November Hayat Tahrir al-Sham's offensive into Aleppo and western Syria.[83]

It appears that Ankara had reversed its plea to Kyiv to not arm the oppositionist forces, such as the HTS, in Idlib. This was likely so, both in preparation for the HTS offensive in November 2024 and in response to the Syrian-Russian air forces' consistent air-striking campaign against oppositionist forces in Idlib that had intensified from October 2023 to November 2024. After the fall of al-Assad, Western news outlets claimed that Ukrainian operatives provided the HTS with 150 drones and 20 drone operators in October 2024, to harass the Russian military in Syria in order to divert Russian troops from Ukraine to Syria.[84] The Ukrainian drone provisions to HTS served modest contributions to the HTS' successful offensive in November and December 2024. The Ukrainians were operating with Syrian opposition forces instead of Kurdish forces as previously planned in order to maintain appeasement to the Turkish government. Ukrainian operatives' support of Syrian oppositionist in the north against al-Assad forces serves Ankara's interests. Perhaps the Ukrainians were aiding the oppositionists in exchange for certain Turkish weapons and war machines.

Turkey later backed Kyiv's bid for NATO membership and return of territory during the Ukrainian peace discussions in early 2025. It was in Turkey's best interest for Ukraine to retain its southern territories as a counterbalance towards the prospect of Russia annexing the land and, thereafter, having a stronger presence in the Black Sea. Russia is trying to become the number one grain exporter to the African continent. If Russia annexes the southern parts of Ukraine, it greatly boosts their grain exports and subsequently their influence in the African continent. Turkish pressure for the return of Ukrainian territory serves to negate Russian influence in African regions of Turkish interest (i.e. North Africa and the Horn of Africa). If the rumours are true, then the Ukrainian intervention in Syria served to strengthen Turkish-Ukrainian relations, contributing to Turkey's firm stance in supporting Ukrainian sovereignty during the Ukrainian peace discussions in 2025.

The Turkish-American Rivalry

With the elimination of ISIS in Syria, American President Donald Trump believed that American presence in Syria was no longer needed. This meant the abandonment of their Kurdish ally to Turkish aggression in 2019. The Kurdish SDF struck a deal with the Russians and al-Assad to allow the regime's troop presence in the autonomous Kurdish region of Rojava, as it meant protection from Turkish invasion. Putin and al-Assad agreed to the SDF's truce, as it was a step closer to al-Assad reunifying his country and curbing Turkish encroachment in the north-east.

It is likely that this covenant truce led to Trump changing his mind and announced that the 900 American soldiers and undisclosed number of American contractors were to remain in the al-Tanf region of Syria. Trump changed his mind because the truce severely undermined American global influence. This was a significant American foreign diplomatic blunder. However, with the Russian invasion of Ukraine in 2022, Russian presence decreased in Rojava inciting Erdoğan to take advantage of the vulnerable Kurdish autonomous region. It was feared that following the partial withdrawal of Russian troops in Syria, Turkey exploited the scene and committed further landgrabs in the north-east Kurdish provinces. During the years 2022 and 2023, Ankara increased their threatening rhetoric towards the SDF and conducted various anti-Kurdish operations across the Iraqi and Syrian territories bordering Turkey.

The American backing of Kurdish militias served two purposes: to counter ISIS and Turkish influence. American backing of Kurdish militias, such as the SDF, served as a tool to invoke Kurdish nationalism and independence movements across the whole of the Syrian Kurdistan region, undermining the Russian-backed al-Assad regime. The American backing of Kurdish forces was designed to counter Turkish encroachment and influence into Syria. American backing of the Syrian Kurdish groups served as a security threat to Turkish southeastern territorial integrity, as it threatened to encourage Kurdish separatism within Turkey. Although a NATO ally, Turkey does not view itself as a diplomatic ally to the US and the West, as evidenced by Turkish

President Recep Tayyip Erdoğan's somewhat friendly relations with Putin. Ankara wishes to spread Turkish influence with neighbouring countries, establishing numerous military bases across the Western nations of the Middle East and the Mediterranean Sea, such as Libya, Azerbaijan, northern Cyprus, Somali, Iraq, various Balkan countries and northern Syria. The spread of Turkish influence undermines US influence. Turkey's friendly ties towards Russia and initial resistance to Finnish and Swedish NATO membership made the West cautious of Turkey's allegiance. In January 2021, Antony Blinken complained '(Turkey) is not acting as an ally should and this is a very, very significant challenge for us and we are very cleared eyed about it.'[85] Turkish desires towards superpower status have begun since the presidency of Erdoğan in 2014, which has resulted in the souring of Turkish-American relations. The Turkish threat to Syrian tranquillity resulted in Washington pleading with the Kurdish militias and al-Assad to form a more concrete alliance against the foreseeable Turkish threat.[86]

The War of Resistance: The Syrian Front

Iran, an ally of Russia, is a key international player in the multifront proxy wars in Syria.

Syria became part of a new multifront proxy battlefield during the Gaza War. On 17 October 2023, the Iranian-backed proxy groups, under the umbrella of the Islamic Resistance in Iraq, attempted to carry out a drone strike on the American military base, al-Asad in western Iraq. Iraqi militia groups, sponsored by Iran, launched eighteen more drone and air strike attacks on American bases in Iraq and Syria by the end of the month, which resulted in American casualties, but no deaths. The Iraqi militias and Katib Hezbollah (an Iraqi offshoot of Hezbollah) continued their aerial attacks on American and Kurdish military bases and oil fields until late January 2024.

The US retaliated on 26 October 2023 by carrying out a drone strike and aerial bombing the militia groups in Syria. Iranian militia groups' military bases and weapons depots were destroyed by American forces. In November 2023, Khatib Hezbollah drone bases were destroyed in American air strikes in Iraq. In mid-January 2024, an American drone strike was conducted in Baghdad, killing a Khatib Hezbollah leader, Mushtaq Talib Al-Saeedi.

On January 2024, Iran claimed to have bombed several Kurdish, Israeli and ISIS positions across various locations in Iraq and Syria. Iranian officials claimed that the Iranian bombing campaigns across Syria were in response to the ISIS suicide bombings that occurred on 3 January 2024 in Kerman. American Secretary of Defense Lloyd Austin described the American air strikes as a means to protect American soldiers' presence in the region from Iranian-backed proxies. Whilst he is correct in these statements, it should be noted that the American air strikes on Iranian militia groups in Iraq and Syria were tit for tat in nature as these strikes came days after one of their bases was attacked.

The US' tit-for-tat strategy withstood and won the standoff between them and the Iranian proxies by February 2024. On 28 January 2024, Islamic Resistance in Iraq carried out a drone strike on an American military base, Tower 22, in Jordan. This strike injured forty-seven American soldiers and killed three. America responded firmly and conducted a series of intense aerial bombardments in Iranian-proxy groups' locations in Iraq and Syria between 2 and 7 February 2024. The US-Middle East air-strike campaign came to an end on 7 February 2024. On the advice of Tehran, the Islamic Resistance of Iraq stopped their campaign against American bases. The Islamic Resistance stopped their campaign against American military bases however, did conduct several one-off attacks against American and Israeli troops following Iran's Operation True Promise.

American presence in Syria and Iraq had been a controversial topic in American society as they were falsely informed by state news outlets that the US Army withdrew from Syria and Iraq in 2019 and 2021 respectively. The American general public wished to discontinue their presence in the Middle East after the controversies that came from the War on Terror. Both the Iraqi government and the Iraqi public wished for the Americans to leave Iraq due to anti-American sentiments and because the American troops no longer served Iraqi interests (American presence was no longer needed as ISIL was no longer as prevalent as they once were following their defeat in 2017).

Iraqi demands for American withdrawal intensified during the American bombing campaigns in Iraq and Syria. The US claimed that there were no civilian casualties during American attack on Katib Hezbollah sites during November 2023. However, the Iraqi government claimed this to be false and said that there were eighteen wounded and one killed during this bombing. The Iraqi government argued that the American bombing campaign was unjustified and inflicted on Iraqi sovereignty. This led to an intensification of American-Iraqi negotiations concerning the removal of American presence in the country.

In January 2024, the US agreed to withdraw from Iraq, but an intended date for American extraction was not confirmed. Iraqi demands intensified after Operation True Promise, as Iranian drones and missiles heading towards Israel, could be heard and seen in Iraqi and Syrian skies, bringing the Gaza War closer to Iraq. Iraqi rhetoric of American presence being a source of Iraqi endangerment intensified further. Iraqis were tired of outside (American) influence dragging Iraq into wars which the Iraqi people or government did not provoke or wanted to participate in. Iraqi pressure led to Washington and Baghdad signing a deal in September 2024 guaranteeing the complete withdrawal of American troops from Iraq by the year 2026.

Al-Monitor revealed that the US had negotiated a deal between the Kurds and al-Assad to fight ISIL cells together, if the US was to withdraw from Syria. The Kurds were much disgruntled about the deal and prospects of America abandoning them for a third time.[87] If the US was to withdraw from Iraq this also entailed the withdrawal of American forces from Syria. If the US failed to maintain their presence in Syria, this deal acted as precautionary measures to ensure that ISIL cells continued to be suppressed.

Israel bombed Damascus, Aleppo Airport and Syrian controlled Golan Heights on 10 October 2023. These Israeli bombings targeted Iranian-proxy groups, to prevent Iranian arms reaching the Iranian-backed Hezbollah group in southern Lebanon. It can be reasoned that the Israeli decision to bomb Iranian-proxy militias in Syria was to prevent Iran from exploiting the Gaza War and creating a strong second front. If a second front was established during the Gaza War, the IDF would have to divert its brigades away from the Gaza front, negatively impacting Israel's campaign against Hamas. Al-Assad's forces mortar shelled Israeli positions in northern Israel in retaliation which was then met with Israeli bombing retaliation.[88]

Sporadic Israeli bombings of Iranian proxy forces in Syria continued and intensified to weaken the Lebanese front. Notable bombings were the Syrian missile attack on Israeli occupied Golan Heights in mid-January 2024 and Israeli bombing of Aleppo, which killed approximately thirty-five al-Assad soldiers and eight Hezbollah fighters. Israeli fighter jets killed Hezbollah fighters in Homs on 7 February 2024. In December 2023, January 2024 and March 2024, Israeli missiles killed several Iranian Islamic Revolutionary Guard leaders and soldiers in Damascus and Baniyas, which provoked fear that Iran would be dragged into a regional war against Israel. On 1 April 2024, Israel struck the Iranian Embassy in Damascus, killing a mix of Iranian Islamic Revolutionary Guard Corps, Iranian-proxy soldiers and Syrian civilians. Although this was a breach of international law, most European countries did not comment or condemn Israel's strike on the Embassy. Iran was enraged by the Israeli bombing of the Embassy and Tehran declared they would inflict revenge on Israel for their crime. Twelve days later Iran launched Operation True Promise.

The Fall of Bashar al-Assad

On 27 November 2024, the Syrian opposition faction, which renounced its former Islamic extremist affiliations HTS, led by Ahemd al-Sharaa, launched a rapid offensive from the oppositionist-held Idlib province into the al-Assad controlled Aleppo province. During this offensive, the oppositionists inflicted casualties on Iranian and Russian troops stationed there, resulting in the deaths of a Russian and Iranian soldier. Joint Russian-Syrian air bombing campaigns of the rebel occupied areas ensued. The Ukrainian Main Directorate of Intelligence claimed that Moscow ordered its PMCs in Africa to be sent to Syria to hold off the HTS advances.[89] These supposed Russian mercenaries never arrived in time to save al-Assad. By the third day of the shock offensive, the oppositionists had entered Aleppo. SDF forces occupied the northern districts of Aleppo to secure the safety of the Kurdish civilians that resided there. The following day, the fortress Citadel of Aleppo was taken, and the Syrian army withdrew from Aleppo completely. During the withdrawal, the SDF expanded its presence from northern Aleppo to the eastern districts.

Without halt, the HTS advanced southwards towards Hama. By 30 November, HTS forces entered the northern outskirts of Hama, where they met stiff resistance from al-Assad's forces. Despite slowing down the HTS' rapid offensives, al-Assad could not hold on to Hama and began withdrawing his troops from the city on 5 December. The situation worsened for al-Assad, as the Syrian National Army, from the Turkish-oppositionist co-occupied provinces of northern Aleppo, launched Operation Dawn of Freedom. The operation saw the Turkish-backed SNA advancing from northern Aleppo towards the Kuweires Military Aviation Institute, east of the city of Aleppo. The SNA's advance from the north was met with little resistance, as al-Assad's forces were too busy fighting the HTS in the west of Aleppo. The double offensives led to al-Assad forces being ordered to abandon their posts in the north and flee to the south, in anticipation for al-Assad's counteroffensives. Russian forces withdrew alongside al-Assad troops from the Aleppo and Kurdish provinces. Russian officials greatly condemned the attack and voiced their support for the al-Assad regime. Between 30 November and 3 December, Russian navy vessels stationed off the Syrian coast were evacuated to avoid the ships being damaged from possible oppositionist attacks. As the Russian army and navy were withdrawing from their positions in Syria, the Russian air force continued to attack the HTS as they advanced towards Damascus.

Operation Dawn of Freedom led to the SDF forces being encircled in north-east Aleppo and cut off from Kurdish forces in the east.

A destroyed Russian tank during the siege of Mariupol. The 2022 Russian Invasion of Ukraine had shaken the global status quo and the 80-year long pax-Europa. The West's intolerance of the illegal invasion entailed the return of the Cold War. Source: Ministry of Internal Affairs of Ukraine

The 2022 illegal Russian Annexation of the Donetsk, Luhansk, Zaporozhe and Kherson Oblasts. Russia has utilised the ethnic and Russian speaking population of Ukraine's eastern oblasts as justification for Russia's invasion of Ukraine. Putin has utilised minority ethnic groups to negate countries from entering NATO, as can be seen in Georgia (2008) and Crimea (2014). Moscow has conducted a Russification campaign in occupied Ukraine to solidify their holdings over these territories. Source: The Kremlin Official Website

A Ukrainian soldier replacing the Russian flag with the Yellow and Blue Ukrainian flag during the Kurk Offensive. Zelensky wanted to occupy the Russian Kursk region in order to utilise it as a bargaining chip to exchange Ukrainian territory back during the foreseeable Russo–Ukrainian peace talks. Source: Naval Forces of the Armed Forces of Ukraine's Telegram

The head of the Ukrainian Main Directorate of Intelligence visiting Bakhmut. Prigozhin had waged a military and propaganda battle around the city in order to pressure Zelensky to divert divisions away from the much-anticipated Summer Offensive in order to save face towards his Western allies. This bided time for the Russian army to increase their defences and manpower in the Zaporozhe front in anticipation for the expected Ukrainian offensive. Source: The Ukrainian Main Directorate of Intelligence Website

Biden with Zelensky during state visit to Ukraine on 20 February 2023. US President Biden was a firm ally of his Ukrainian and European allies. However, many American voters believed that Biden prioritised foreign affairs over American domestic issues, exacerbating his domestic unpopularity. Source: US Embassy in Ukraine

The Armenian Prime Minister Pashinyan has increasingly pivoted Armenia towards the EU following Russia's failure to fulfil its obligation to ensure Armenian security against Azeri aggression. Armenia and the Nagorno-Karabagh Conflict has become a sight of international competition between the West and Russia during the Second Cold War. Source: European Parliament

South African President Cyril Ramaphosa has led the African Union's mediation between Ukraine and Russia concerning grain exports. During the Ukraine War, Putin attempted to blockade the Black Sea, in order to prevent Ukrainian grain exports to the African continent. By curbing Ukrainian grain exports, African demands for Russian grain exports have grown substantially. The African continent is heavily reliant on Russian and Ukrainian grain imports. Without them, various regions of Africa would fall into political instability and famine. Source: The Kremlin Official Website

Wagner mercenaries in Central African Republic. During the Second Cold War, clever Russian diplomacy and anti-Western propaganda has led to African nations kicking out French and American presence in Northern Africa , allowing for Moscow to send its mercenaries to replace them. Moscow has utilised Wagner and other Russian PMC's to monopolise on African insecurities and natural resources. Source: Corbeaunews Central African Republic

Russian fighter jet harassing an American MQ-9 Reaper Drone over the skies of Syria, July 2023. Due to Second Cold War dynamics, the frozen status of the Syrian Civil War was in jeopardy as America, Russia-Iran and Turkey intensified their three-way proxy war. Source: US Air Forces Central

US airmen guarding the American shipment of arms to the Israelis days after the October 7th Attack. The massacres and hostage taking of Israeli citizens at the hands of the terrorist Palestinian group, Hamas, cascaded the Middle East into a region wide War of Resistance. Western participation in the Gaza War has led to international uproar. Source: Department of War

An American Naval Vessel bombarding Houthi controlled Yemen. The Houthi's piracy campaign against international shipping in the Red Sea has been a serious strain on international trade. Russia has shaped The Red Sea front of the War of Resistance into a Russo–American proxy warzone by providing the Houthis with aid and satellite intel sharing. Source: US Air Forces Central

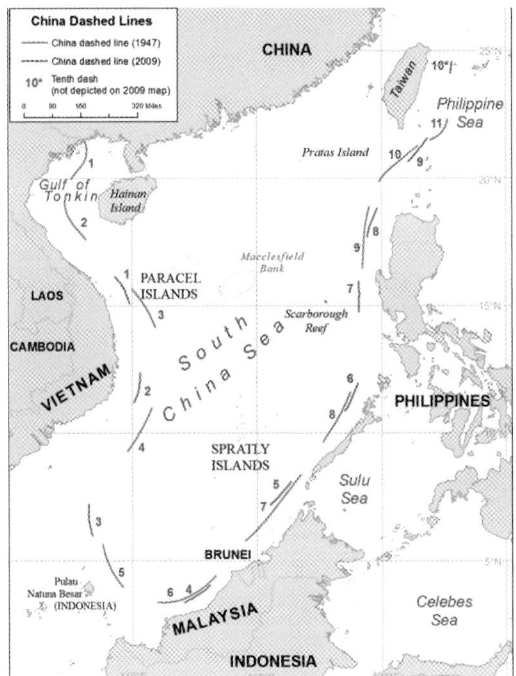

Territorial disputes over the Chinese Sea between China and the other smaller Far Eastern Asian nations. America has exploited the territorial dispute to establish more influence in the Far East. Perceiving themselves as increasingly isolated amongst aggressive pro–American nations, China has pivoted themselves closer to the Russian bloc. Source: United States Department of State

China's Change 6 lunar lander located in the southern pole of the Moon. During the Second Cold War, international players, such as America, China, Russia and India are racing each other to be the first to land astronauts on the far side of the moon and extract natural resources there. These international players are competing in the Second Space Race to ensure that their civilisations are more technologically advanced than their Cold War rivals. Source: NASA

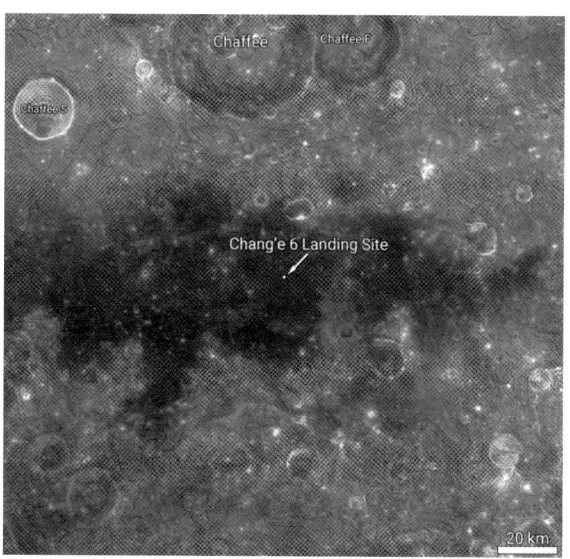

In July 2024, Trump miraculously survived an assassination attempt during his electoral campaign rally in Butler, Pennsylvania. The assassination attempt was a by-product of America's Populist Divide, which is the current incarnation of the "Culture War" between the political Left and Right. Moscow's propaganda campaign has exploited America's domestic upheaval and divide to negatively warp the American public's support towards Ukraine. Source: Photographer, Tim Kennedy

American President Donald Trump arguing with Ukrainian President Volodymyr Zelensky in the Oval Office (February 2025). Trump's televised humiliation of Zelenskyy made many American allies question the stability of their security alliance with America. The televised exchange between the two presidents contributed to the emerging American-European Split. Source: The White House

United Nations General Assembly resolution ES-11-7 vote. Europe was very concerned by the Trump's administration's refusal to condemn Russia for their invasion of Ukraine in 2022. America's U-turn away from condemning Russia is part of Trump's questionable policy of appeasement towards Russia during the 2025 Ukrainian peace negotiations. Source: United Nations

The SDF's alliance with al-Assad complicated SDF's relationship with the oppositionists. On 1 December, the HTS demanded the SDF stationed in Aleppo surrender their weapons and withdraw from the city, claiming that they did not want to fight. The Kurdish commander in Aleppo agreed to these demands and evacuated Kurdish militias and civilians from Aleppo, the following day. The SNA had captured the city of Tell Rifaat, where they committed several atrocities towards the Kurdish fighters and minorities. The SNA established their forces in Raqqa and Manbij, in response to SNA advances. Skirmishes and casualties ensued along the SNA and the SDF frontiers in the north-east.

The oppositionists' rapid offensives worried the Kurdish militia forces, as many feared that the SDF's overstretch in Aleppo and the oppositionists' increasing control in the north-west, would be exploited by the Turkish army, who could attack the SDF's weak posture. For these reasons, the Kurds voiced their opposition to the HTS' decision to reignite the war, and claimed that the Turks helped plan it, in order to compromise the Kurds.

The reigniting of the Syrian Civil War undermined Russian and Iranian influences, bolstered Turkey's position in Syria, and left the US silent and hesitant to react to the rapid unfolding of events. Iran expressed full support for al-Assad and the Iranian Minister of Foreign Affairs Abbas Araghchi visited Damascus in late November. During this time, it was reported that 200 Iranian backed Iraqi militias crossed the Syrian-Iraq border to fight for the al-Assad regime. Once the Iraqi militias crossed into the Syrian border, they were harassed by American air strikes.

Araghchi, alongside Secretary of State Antony Blinken, visited Ankara to discuss de-escalating the Syrian conflict with Turkey. Although publicly endorsing immediate de-escalation of the conflict, Turkey participated in the oppositionist's offensives by air striking Kurdish positions across the northern Syrian border. The unfolding events prompted the Syrian Civil War to become a much more confrontational proxy war compared to the 2022 to 2024 period. It became a proxy war of which three parties participated in: Russia-Iran (supporting the al-Assad forces and Iranian backed militia groups), the US-Israel (supporting the Kurdish forces) and Turkey (supporting the oppositionist forces).

On 30 November 2024, the Russian forces stationed across the eastern bank of the Euphrates River evacuated to the city of Deir ez-Zor. After the completion of the Russian evacuation, SDF forces launched an attack on the al-Assad-Iranian proxy occupied town of

Khasham, and six other villages along the east bank of the Euphrates River in the Deir ez-Zor province. According to the Syrian Observatory for Human Rights, the SDF's attack was accompanied by American air strikes on Iranian militia positions in Khasham and villages across the east bank of the Euphrates River. The US Air Force also conducted an air strike on IRGC troops in the Deir ez-Zor military airport, killing six. It was widely reported that the SDF's attack on Khasham was repulsed by al-Assad forces, the following day. On 3 December, Iranian backed militias attempted to attack the American MSS Euphrates, but were repulsed by the American defenders. The militias lost one T-64 tank, three trucks with mounted rocket launchers and several mortars, whilst the Americans suffered three casualties.

The Iraqi prime minister claimed that Iraq would not act as a spectator of the reigniting of the Syrian war and diplomatically supported the al-Assad regime. The Iranian-backed Popular Mobilization Forces operated directly under the Iraqi prime minister. It had been widely reported that the Popular Mobilization Forces were among the Iranian-backed forces crossing the Syrian-Iraqi border, in response the HTS offensive. As previously mentioned, American air strikes targeted Iranian-backed forces who crossed the Iraqi-Syrian border in the city of al-Bukamal. Other notable Iranian-backed forces that crossed the Syrian-Iraqi border were the Iraqi Hezbollah factions. Initially, Hezbollah proper in Lebanon announced that it would not send forces to al-Assad's aid, after its mauling by Israeli forces during the 2024 invasion. Iran was adamant to send al-Assad reinforcements to counter the HTS and the Turkish-backed SNA. This was because if al-Assad was toppled from power or if the Syrian oppositionists gained more ground, it would have endangered the Iranian logistical contact with Lebanon and Hezbollah.

Initially, al-Assad forces were able to hold off against the SDF's assaults. However, after the fall of Hama, regime forces and their allies withdrew from Deir ez-Zor on 6 December, in preparation for the Battle of Homs. SDF quickly occupied these abandoned villages, including the city of Deir ez-Zor itself. SDF forces also occupied the city of al-Bukamal and acted as a barrier between Damascus and al-Assad's much-needed Iranian-backed Iraqi militia reinforcements. American officials likely approved of the SDF occupation of al-Bukamal, as it ensured the safety of the American service personnel stationed in east Syria. The SDF presence in al-Bukamal and along the Iraqi border, benefited the US' Syria policy, as it blocked al-Assad's Iraqi reinforcements and severed the Iranian connection to Hezbollah in Lebanon.

On 6 December, HTS forces entered the northern outskirts of Homs. Hezbollah officials in Beirut realised that they had to intervene in the reawakened Syrian war and sent a token number of military advisors to Homs, to help al-Assad's defences. In response, Israel conducted a series of air strikes on several crossings across the Syrian-Lebanon border, to thwart Hezbollah transfer of arms and advisors to Damascus. The Israeli air force also struck several chemical weapon caches in Syria, to prevent al-Assad from using it in desperation against the rapidly advancing oppositionist forces and in fear that it fell into oppositionists' hands. It was widely reported that Hezbollah forces were en route to Homs, and reached the city of Al-Qusayr, until their withdrawal back to the Lebanon border on 6 December, due to constant Israeli air harassment.

Two days after the launch of the HTS offensive in north-west Syria, the oppositionist faction, the Southern Operations Command, began to launch their offensive in the Quneitra, Suwayda and Daraa regions.

On 6 December 2024, the Southern Operations Command had conquered all these regions and pushed northwards, towards Damascus. As the HTS descended on Homs and later Damascus, al-Assad called for Syrian forces in eastern Syria to mobilise to the West to fight off the HTS' advances. On 6 December, al-Assad ordered his troops stationed in the central city of Palmyra to withdraw to Damascus, in preparation of the Battle of Damascus.

Exploiting Palmyra's open-city status, the oppositionist faction, the Revolutionary Commando Army under the SFA, launched its offensive against the city of Palmyra from the co-occupied al-Tanf region. It was reported by *The Telegraph* that Washington gave the green light for the Palmyra offensive in the wake of the HTS' rapid advances and provided logistical aid and preparations to the SFA.[90] The city was fully taken by the 7 December. Damascus was attacked from the south from the Southern Operations Command and from the north by the HTS. The city fell within a day on 8 December 2024. Bashar al-Assad and his family had fled the country prior to the city's capture and was given political asylum in Moscow. The ousting of the al-Assad family and the establishment of a new regime marked what seemed to have been the end of the thirteen-year-long civil war in Syria.

Chapter Eight

IRAN AND THE AXIS OF RESISTANCE

The Iranian Display

Iran has been one of Russia's staunchest allies during the Second Cold War. The Russian military had lost a plethora of vehicles and drones as a result of the initial invasion of Ukraine and the Ukrainian twin offensives. Iran sent Putin a plethora of Shahed drones to replenish the Russian army's depleting drone stockpile in mid-October 2022. Iran also sent drone advisors and technical supporters to Crimea to train Russian drone operators as well as perform drone maintenance. Ten of these Iranian drone experts were killed in a Ukrainian air strike in November 2022. On the night of 28 January 2023, Iranian ammunitions factory in the province of Isfahan was destroyed by Israeli drones. With the news of the factory's destruction, the Ukrainian presidential advisor tweeted with celebration and ambiguously said, 'Ukraine did warn you.' This tweet implies that the Iranian arms leasing to Russia has led to strengthening ties between Ukraine and Israel, who both want to cripple Iran's weapons manufacturing. Iran continues to supply Russia with Shahed drones en masse. Iran faced sanctions from the EU as a result of their support for Russia.

Iran has territorial claims over the Abu Musa, Greater Tunb and Lesser Tunb islands situated in the Strait of Hormuz, which conflicts with the UAE's territorial claim over the islands. Control over these islands was important to Iran and the UAE, as occupying the islands meant certain dominance over the Strait of Hormuz. These territorial disputes were founded in the 1970s, but have resurged following the geopolitical shifts that came after the Russian invasion of Ukraine. The UAE claimed that they were determined to retake the islands from

Iranian occupation in 2022. Iran held their annual drills in the Strait of Hormuz in December 2022, but with much more rigour than the previous drills and utilised more of their military for the drill. Iran continued to hold drills in the Strait of Hormuz during the following months. The islands have been inhabited by the Iranian military since the Iranian invasion of the islands in 1971 and in September 2023, plans were set in place to populate the islands with Iranian civilians, in order to further legitimise Iranian claim to the islands.

Regardless, Iran displayed its dominance in the Strait of Hormuz and the Arabian Sea during 2023, where the Iranian military attacked Western commercial shipping. Iran had been seizing Western ships in the Strait of Hormuz since 2008, but intensified its pirating campaign during the beginning of the Second Cold War.

On 19 April 2022, Greek ships had seized a nineteen-manned Russian commercial ship in the Aegean Sea, which contained Iranian oil, as part of the EU's sanctioning of Russia campaign. Iran seized two Greek commercial ships in the Arabian Sea as a retaliatory response and demanded the handover of the Iranian oil in exchange for the Greek ships. Greece was going to send the oil to the US, but made the deal with Iran after the seizure of the Greek ships. The US seized several Iranian ships and dhows during December 2022 and January 2023. These ships were destined for Houthi controlled Yemen and contained an array of weapons and ammunition. The seized stockpile was later sent to the Ukrainian army to be used against the Russian army.

There was a pause in the Iranian seizure of ships in the Gulf region, until the following year. Iran seized an oil tanker that was destined to the US off the coast of Oman in April 2023. A Panama commercial ship, which was also heading to the US, was seized in early May 2023. The Iranian piracy campaign in the Strait of Hormuz endangered Western shipping and exports as it is estimated that 20 per cent of the world's oil exports go through Hormuz. In response to Iranian seizure of ships, the US sent its naval ships to the Strait of Hormuz in mid-May 2023 and even considered placing armed guards on commercial ships to counter Iranian piracy. In early July 2023, American naval ships had prevented an Iranian capture of a commercial ship on two separate occasions. The American presence in the Strait of Hormuz further escalated tensions in the area and Iran launched a surprise military drill in August 2023 to prepare the Iranian navy for a possible engagement with the Americans. The Iranian seizure of Western ships continued during the Gaza War. Iran never took full advantage of their pirating campaign in the Strait of Hormuz in fear of global condemnation and

American retaliation. The Iranian piracy campaign in the Gulf region acted as a blueprint for the Houthis piracy and harassment campaign in the Red Sea, during the Gaza War.

During the First Cold War, Iran launched its nuclear arms programme with the assistance of its American ally. American aid to the programme came to an end after the 1979 revolution and subsequent Iranian hostilities towards the US and their traditional Middle Eastern allies. The Iranians resumed their programme but the progress of nuclear arms manufacturing was slow. During the turn of the twenty-first century, Iran began making significant progress. This resulted in UN protests and American sanctions, in an attempt to thwart the programme. If Iran was to successfully manufacture nuclear weapons, the nation's regional superpower status would boost spectacularly, diminishing their Saudi competitor and rivalling Israeli positioning in the Middle East. This has become a major concern during the Second Cold War, as Iran has increasingly started to align itself with Russia. This has caused the West to fear that Russia would help Iran in their nuclear weapons programme or downright give Iran their own nuclear weapons, as has been seen with Belarus.

Iran is not a Russian lackey as portrayed by Western media outlets. Iran is attempting to establish regional dominance over its neighbours and is trying to establish itself as an up-and-coming regional superpower. Iranian foreign diplomacy has intervened in conflicts flaring in the Caucasus and Sudan, and cyberattacking the Trump electoral campaign in 2024, all of which conflicted with Russian interests.

The Axis of Resistance refers to the general unofficial military alliance between Iran and certain Middle Eastern militias and paramilitary groups that stand against Israel and American interventionism in the Middle East. The 'members' are numerous, and the reader does not need to know all of them. However, the most notable members include Iran, the political-military Gazan group Hamas, the Yemen opposition group Houthis, the Iraqi militia groups under the umbrella of the Islamic Resistance in Iraq, and the Lebanese paramilitary group Hezbollah and Jordan militias under the umbrella of the Islamic Resistance in Jordan. The listed proxy groups mostly consist of minority Shia Muslims and are heavily supplied and equipped by Shia Iran. The militias acted as Iranian proxy forces and played a huge role in America's second proxy war – the Gaza War and the wider War of Resistance, or as Israeli President Benjamin Netanyahu calls it, the War of Seven Fronts.

Operation al-Aqsa Flood

The Palestinian militant group Hamas, funded by Iran, inflicted an horrific attack, which would cascade a regional war in the Middle East and an international uproar. On 7 October 2023, Hamas launched operation al-Aqsa Flood, which was an offensive into the southern Israel territories neighbouring the Gaza Strip. Hamas broke through the Gaza-Israel fence through the ground, air and sea. Hamas made considerable gains because a lot of Israeli military personnel were on holiday, leaving trainee military personnel stationed at the Gaza borders. The Re'im Festival massacre took place and Israelis were kidnapped and taken hostage by Hamas to be used for bargaining in the future. It is part of Israel's policy to ensure the return of Israel citizens who have been taken hostage through any means necessary. This policy can be seen in 2006, when Israeli soldier Gilad Shalit was taken hostage by Hamas and swapped for 1,000 Hamas prisoners.

Israeli President Benjamin Netanyahu made a statement to the Israeli people that Israel was in a state of war and called for reservists to join the fight. Netanyahu launched Operation Iron Swords, which was the calling of reservists, the reversal of Hamas gains in Israel, the preparation of the Gaza offensive and the deployment of IDF troops to Israel's northern borders to counter possible Hezbollah intervention. The fighting that took place in October resulted in the deaths of 1,200 Israelis and 250 Israelis taken hostage.

The UN condemned Hamas' incursion into Israel, but later condemned the Israeli conduct of the war. Once Operation Iron Swords was complete, the bombing of the Gaza Strip intensified. The official reason why Israel began its mass bombing campaign against the Gaza Strip was to destroy buildings holding Hamas fighters. The density of the urban environment of the Gaza Strips very advantageous for the Hamas fighters and it would be illogical for the Israeli army to enter the strip with the buildings intact. To not bomb the Gaza Strip would lead to a lot of IDF fatalities, which would cause anger within the already angered Israeli public and risked Netanyahu's presidency. Israeli officials had constantly promised to occupy the Gaza Strip to prevent future Palestinian incursions into Israel. Failure to accomplish these promises would lead to Israeli public disgruntlement.

The Israeli government, therefore, made the decision to continue to bomb the Gaza Strip, entailing the state's international isolationism to maintain internal Israeli support. Prior to Operation al-Aqsa Flood, Israel and Saudia Arabia were making efforts to normalise their relations. This was because both countries are competing against Iran in the

Middle East. However, Operation al-Aqsa Flood hindered Israeli attempts to normalise Saudi relations, as the Saudi's liking for Israel began to diminish as the Israeli atrocities on the Palestinians grew more rampant and industrial. This was evident in March 2024, when the US Commission on International Religious Freedom delegation left Saudia Arabia early because the Saudi Arabian delegates demanded the American orthodox rabbi, Anthony Cooper, remove his Kippah to which Cooper refused. This incident demonstrated that anti-Jewish sentiments were heightened significantly, inhibiting the Israel-Saudi Arabian normalisation of relations. Antisemitism within the Saudi government has strained American conduct over their bombing campaign against the Iranian-backed Houthi rebels in Yemen, as Saudi Arabia limited American use of Saudi Arabia as a base for aerial operations.[91] Despite the setbacks of Israel-Saudi relations, Saudi Arabia and other Arabian kingdoms and federal states, such as Jordan and the UAE, have not broken their alignment with Israel and the US against Iran and Iranian proxy groups during the Gaza War.

An Eye for an Eye: The Israeli Revenge

After the completion of Operation Iron Swords, the IDF launched the northern Gaza offensive on 27 October 2023 and raged on until around mid-February 2024. The IDF successfully surrounded the Gaza city and cut the Palestinians from the Gazan western shores. However, the IDF's advances into the Gaza city were met with stiff resistance. The Israeli northern Gaza offensive was met with much resistance and casualties due to the dense urban environment and constructed tunnels favouring the Hamas fighters. The tunnels allowed Hamas fighters to avoid Israeli bombardment and to get from one place to the other with speed and unmolested by the fighting above. It was later discovered during the Rafah offensive that numerous Hamas tunnel networks in the south of the Gaza Strip crossed through the Egyptian border. This meant that Hamas was continuously supplied by Axis of Resistance groups in Egypt, meaning that the IDF could not eliminate the Egyptian groups without encroaching on Egyptian sovereignty.

By late 2023, over 20,000 Gazans had died and over 50,000 were injured by IDF acts of aggression. The surge of injuries and medical needs overwhelmed the Gazan hospitals. The hospitals' supplies of beds, medicine, electricity and other needs had rapidly dwindled, causing the hospitals' conduct to be improvisational in nature and overpopulated. Due to the dwindling hospital supplies there was a high risk of mass stillbirths occurring within the Gaza Strip. Overpopulation within hospitals had surged due to displaced Gazans residing in hospital buildings for refuge and safety, as hospitals are not allowed to be bombed or attacked by the military during a time of war. However, multiple incidences occurred in which IDF soldiers bombed and attacked the Gazan hospitals regardless. The density of the urban environment and the weak durability of high-scale buildings in the Gaza Strip caused people to die in foul swoops from the Israeli bombardments. The overcrowding that was caused by the claustrophobic and now unhygienic urban environment led to the spread of diseases among the surviving population. The spread of diseases intensified with the flight of the northern Gazans to the south of the Gaza Strip. This caused a polio epidemic crisis in the Gaza Strip.

In late 2023, 75 per cent of the Gazan population were displaced and the majority of the dead were Gazan children. The bombardment made it difficult for the Gazan medical emergency and humanitarian teams to travel to and from people who desperately needed medical attention. Famine was a serious risk for the surviving Gazans. Dwindling food supplies left the people of Gaza starving and rationing what little they had. Looting and black marketing became common place due to Gaza's dwindling food supplies. The Palestinians were so desperate for food they climbed over each other like ants to get food from the aid trucks. An incident occurred on 25 February 2024, where this happened and the Israelis fired on the starving crowd, causing over 110 dead and over 700 wounded. The IDF denied this event occurred, but then later acknowledged the massacre and claimed that the IDF believed the crowd was acting hostile. This incident led to European condemnation of Israeli actions and contributed to the decline of American-Israeli relations.

On 21 October 2023, UN aid to Gaza was permitted by Netanyahu due to international pressure on Israel to comply. UN aid trucks arrived in the Gaza Strip via the Gaza-Egyptian border. In early November, the UN attempted to pressure the Israeli government to allow UN aid trucks into Gaza via the Kerom Shalom, which proved to be successful. However, disgruntled Israeli protesters attempted to block the UN aid trucks crossing into the Gaza Strip via the Kerem Shalom border crossing, which were met with various degrees of success. Netanyahu later reopened the Kerem Shalom border crossing for humanitarian aid after much international pressure on April 2024. UN trucks found difficulty getting to areas of interests (especially those in northern Gaza) due to the intense IDF bombings. These trucks were swarmed by mobs of hungry Gazans, causing minor Palestinian infighting, which made fair distribution of foods significantly difficult.

In January 2024, France and Jordan airdropped supplies to the Gazans. The US followed suit in March 2024. However, the airdrops proved to be ineffective, as the number of foodstuffs were around 30,000, which was not enough to feed the surviving population of the Gaza Strip. After the failure of the airdropping campaigns, the UN and the US attempted to provide aid to the Gazans via the sea, accompanied by an increase of aid supply by airdrops.

In August 2024, the UN began supplying Gazans with vaccines to combat the Polio epidemic occurring in the Gaza Strip.

In January 2024, South Africa accused Israel of committing genocide against the Gazan Palestinians. Nicaragua later accused Germany of contributing to Israel's genocidal actions in April 2024. Both perpetrator and complicit states denied these accusations and defended themselves from the genocide accusations in the ICJ. The condemnation efforts to thwart Israel's genocide were not taken seriously in the West. It was in Africa, in late August 2024, Namibia forbade a ship, suspected of embargoing weapons destined for the IDF's war in Gaza, from docking on the Walvis Bay Port.

Netanyahu pressured the northern Gazans to relocate to the south of Gaza. The intent behind the relocation was more so for ideological reasons than security reasons. Netanyahu claimed that the occupation of the Gaza Strip was necessary to ensure that '7th October would never happen again' and that Hamas or any other anti-Israel paramilitary groups were to forever cease to exist. However, these claims served as a pretext for Netanyahu to accomplish his Israeli expansionist goals, and to further Israeli settlement plans in the Gaza Strip. Israeli authorities had been bulldozing Orthodox Christian settlements in Jerusalem during the backdrop of the war in Gaza.

On 7 May 2023, Israeli authorities began settlement construction in Negev in the south of Israel, which was met with Palestinian protests. The Israeli invasion of Syria in December 2024 expanded its settler programme in the Golan Heights. The West Bank was, however, the main site of the Israeli settlement expansionism during the Gaza War. The Israeli expansion into the West Bank during the Gaza war led to the increase of ethnic violence between Israeli and Palestinian citizens in the Palestinian region. The new Israeli settlement expansion in the West Bank began in earnest in June 2023 and continued throughout the Gaza War. The IDF launched several large-scale military operations in the West Bank during the War of Resistance and the Islamic Resistance in Jordan attempted to smuggle lethal aid to Palestinian militias across the border. During the War of Resistance, Jordanian authorities launched surprise crackdowns on the Islamic Resistance in Jordan members in response to their border smuggling activities. Netanyahu openly discussed his desires for a 'new Middle East', which essentially entailed Israel absorbing all the Palestinian territories. Netanyahu claimed that this would be accomplished by displacing Palestinians into Egypt and even Canada.

The International Reaction

The Russian and North Korean governments condemned the Israeli brutality in the Gaza Strip. This act of solidarity led to Palestinians waving Russian and North Korean flags in the West Bank during their pro-Palestine protests. The Chinese government initially took a neutral stance, urging for a de-escalation, but when the bombing of the Gaza Strip began, Beijing was quick to condemn Israel. Many Western governments supported Israel's war against Hamas, with the exception of Spain and the Republic of Ireland, who voiced their criticisms of Israeli actions, deeming them illegal and genocidal. African nations were divided over their support towards Israel and Palestine. Nearly all Middle Eastern countries condemned Israel in the immediate 7 October attacks, with the exception of Saudi Arabia who took a neutral stance and called for a halt in the violence. The majority of South American countries heavily criticised Israel's consistent breach of humanitarian laws, with Bolivia, Chile and Columbia cutting diplomatic relations with Israel altogether. Argentina was the exception as the pro-American President Javier Milei supported Israel.

The US and the majority of European countries condemned Hamas' incursion into Israel on the immediate outset of the war. Because Ukraine was aligned with the US and desired Israeli lethal aid provisions, Zelensky too supported Israel and condemned Hamas' October incursion, stating, 'The whole world knows which terror sponsors could have encouraged and ensured the organisation to attack'. Zelensky was implying that Tehran was the architect of the 7 October attack. Iran denied such accusations and claimed that the world truly underestimated Hamas, as Iran did not aid them in their attack on Israel. Iranian officials claimed that it was rather the wise planning and independent intuition of the Hamas strategists that led to the incursion. Tehran complimented Hamas for their incursion and openly gave solidarity to the Palestinians and supported Hamas' war against Israel. However, nobody bought into Ali Khamenei's denial of Iranian investment behind the Hamas incursion due to Tehran's reputation of sponsoring militia groups abroad.

The US and UK showed solidarity for Israel and sent a couple of their warships close to Israeli shores as a sign of support for Israel. Biden sent missile munitions which were originally destined for Ukraine to Israel (during a time in which the Ukrainians were in desperate need for missile ammunition). The US' Israel policy contrasted with their approach to Ukraine in which Washington was very hesitant to aid Ukraine with certain war equipment and vehicles. The US took a stern pro-Israel stance because Israel is a long-standing ally of the US and because Hamas is an Iranian proxy force. Little did the Americans consider that the missiles sent to Israel contributed to the intensive bombing of Palestinian civilians in the Gaza Strip.

Pro-Palestinian protesters that the author had interviewed in December 2023 described American support for Israel as criminally complicit for allowing Israel to continue the mass killings of Palestinians. However, the US was actively contributing to the Gaza genocide, as they continuously transferred missiles to Israel throughout the conflict, despite rampant reports of Palestinian civilian deaths at the hands of American produced missiles. To be clear, the US did not want a genocide of the Gazan Palestinians. They simply viewed the military aid of Israel as a strategic move to suppress the terrorist paramilitary groups funded by the US' rival in the Middle East: Iran. Washington's geopolitical goals in the Middle East blindsided American politicians to the possibility that Israel would commit mass slaughter on innocent Palestinian civilians. Biden later realised the destruction that Israel wrought on the Gaza Strip and provided the Palestinians with humanitarian aid and later hindered Israel's military conduct in the south of Gaza as shall be discussed later.

The 8 October Attacks

On 8 October 2023, a day after the Hamas incursion into Gaza, Hezbollah launched rockets on northern IDF and Israeli citizens positions and properties. The IDF responded with a general evacuation from northern Israel and conducted retaliatory missile attacks on Hezbollah positions in southern Lebanon. The casualty rates on both sides were minor and the exchange of missile volleys continued at a frequently low rate during October 2023 to August 2024. The Israelis, Lebanese, Middle Easterners and the international community worried that the Israeli-Hezbollah attacks would escalate the Gaza War into a wider regional war, engulfing Lebanon, Syria, Iran, Yemen and even the US into the conflict. As many as 10,000 UN troops were stationed in Lebanon in anticipation of an Israeli invasion of Lebanon. However, the attacks appeared only feeble and did not appear to entail a serious risk of escalation. That was until August 2024. However, there were instances during the period of October 2023 to August 2024, which risked escalating the missile exchanges into an all-out war.

On the 10, 11, 16 and 17 October 2023, the IDF deployed white phosphor on the Lebanese border, which was met with much controversy and global condemnation. The villages of Dharya, Aita-Al Chaab and al-Mari were sites of such atrocities. When the Gaza War reached November 2023, the volley of missiles at the border caused the Lebanese population to worry that they would be plunged into a war that Hezbollah dragged them into, quite like how Hamas dragged the whole of the Gaza Strip into war. On 3 November 2023, Lebanon expected the Hezbollah leader, Hassan Nasrallah, to declare war on Israel in support of Hamas and the Palestinian people. On that day, he refrained from declaring war, saying in his speech, 'You, the Americans, can stop the aggression against Gaza because it is your aggression … Whoever wants to prevent a regional war, and I am talking to the Americans, must quickly halt the aggression on Gaza.' Nasrallah's refrainment from declaring war gave the worried Lebanese population relief. However, it was also controversial from within, as many Hezbollah fighters were fervently ready to attack the Israelis and help the Palestinians. It can be argued that Nasrallah's dissatisfying speech resulted in the Houthis declaring war on Israel a day after Nasrallah's speech.

Al-Jazeera took a fervent anti-Israel stance well before the outbreak of the Gaza War. A week prior to the conflict, *Al-Jazeera* journalists were reporting about Israelis spitting on Christians and various *Al-Jazeera* journalists later became victims themselves of the Gaza blockade and bombardment. However, it was on 13 October 2023, when *Reuters* journalists were shot to death by IDF forces on the Israeli-Lebanese border, that Western media outlets changed their rhetoric from pro-Israel to a more anti-Israel stance. This unfortunate but minor event in the War of Resistance had tremendously changed Western media outlooks on the Gaza War and people started to understand the indiscriminate nature of IDF's conduct of operations.

Sky News took a pro-Israel stance and attempted to paint the picture that the Iranians were really the ones behind Hamas' incursion. It was with the deaths of the *Reuters* journalists that *Sky News* dropped their pro-Israel stance and took a more neutral approach when covering the conflict. American media outlets became more anti-Israel also since American journalists were indiscriminately killed by Israeli forces. Indiscriminate is the best way to describe the IDF's military conduct, as time and time again the IDF has killed civilian Palestinians, neutral observers, such as journalists, UN members, aid workers and even

Israeli civilians as shall be discussed later on. Israeli propaganda claimed that Hamas hid behind civilians and used them as human shields, in order to dehumanise the designated terrorist group. Whilst it has been confirmed that many of these terrorist Iranian-backed groups have constructed underground tunnels and bases below civilian infrastructure, hospitals and UN bases, there is no excuse for the IDF to bomb these cities whilst civilians are residing in them. Israel continued to bomb Palestinian civilians en masse, in order to kill Hamas fighters, without consideration of the civilian fatalities that would entail.

Serious escalations occurred on 2 January 2024, when Israel launched forty missiles in the suburbs of Beirut, killing Hamas' deputy leader Saleh al-Arouri. This was a big shock to the Lebanese people, as their capital was attacked by the IDF for the first time. Hezbollah sent retaliatory missile attacks on IDF positions in Meron air base four days later. In response to Hezbollah's response, the IDF launched missiles on the village of Majdel Selm on 8 January 2024, killing two, including the Hezbollah deputy head of Radwan Force, Wissam al-Tawil, who was believed to be the perpetrator of the Meron air base bombing. Hezbollah then exchanged missiles in response the day after, and the back and forth of missile exchanges ensued. However, the clashes on the border remained minor across the Israel-Lebanese border.

Hezbollah's exchange of missiles was, although daily, not intense and did not present any real risk of instigating an Israeli declaration of war. Rarely did these missiles cause a two-digit number of deaths per day. Hezbollah's initial minor role in the War of Resistance was not because Hezbollah feared escalation or intervention would lead to Israel declaring war on Hezbollah and an invasion of Lebanon. It was likely because Hezbollah was not informed of Hamas' plan to attack Israel in October 2023. The Hamas incursion caught Hezbollah unawares. Hezbollah was unprepared and had insufficient preparation time for a war against Israel. If they were informed of Hamas' plans then Hezbollah would have likely devoted themselves to creating a second front in anticipation to the Hamas incursion of Israel. It is possible that Hamas informed Iran of the upcoming October incursion a couple of weeks prior to the attack taking place, prompting Iran to inform Hezbollah to be prepare a second front. However, it would have been too late for Hezbollah to prepare a second front due to the fact that they had a short preparation time. Hezbollah's missile exchanges across the border were more an act of solidarity than an act of interventionism. Hezbollah's minor role supporting Hamas was unsatisfactory when compared to other groups, such as the Houthis.

The Red Sea Crisis

Prior to the Houthis declaration of war, an American warship operating in the Red Sea, USS *Carney*, intercepted and destroyed a missile heading to Israel from Yemen. This occurred on 19 October 2023 causing much hysteria over a possible Houthi intervention in the Israel-Gaza War, along with reports of US service personnel being drone struck in Iraq and Syria. More drones and missiles were launched from Yemen and were intercepted by the American, Israeli, French and Saudi military prior and after the Houthi declaration of war.

On 19 November 2023, the Houthi seizure of international commercial ships in the Red Sea began. USS *Carney* acted as protectorate of commercial ships entering the Red Sea against Houthi attackers. However, due to the number of ships sailing in the Red Sea, it could not protect them all. Houthi harassment and seizure of commercial ships in the Red Sea took a heavy toll of the global economy, with global shipping being forced to take the longer route around South Africa instead of going through the Red Sea for safety reasons. This was a much more costly endeavour for global trade in terms of time and money. The inconvenience of changing shipping routes away from the Red Sea resulted in an increase in shipping and oil costs and inhibited global business and capital trade. The Israeli cargo ship *Galaxy Leader* was seized by the Houthis on 19 November 2023, which led to the Israeli bombing of Iranian-Houthi weapons depot in Yemen on 30 November 2023 in retaliation.

Even Russian ships containing oil were attacked by the Houthis in January 2024, despite Putin's condemnation of Israel. A similar incident occurred to a Chinese cargo in March 2024. It appears, however, that these two incidences occurred by accident as the Houthis promised that Russian and Chinese shipping would not be targeted in the Red Sea due to their diplomatic support for Gaza. Russia and China held talks with the Houthi rebels to ensure that further incidents did not occur in the future. Moscow's friendly ties with the Houthis enabled their navy to operate stress free and allow them to continue its shipping through the Red Sea.

On 18 December 2023, the US announced Operation Prosperity Guardian, which was an American-led intervention to counter Houthi activities and protect commercial ships in the Red Sea. Participants of the American naval operation included Britain, France, Netherlands, Greece, Canada, Spain, Norway, Bahrain, Italy and Seychelles. Countries joined Operation Prosperity Guardian three days later, such as Denmark, Sri Lanka and Singapore. The EU launched its own naval intervention in the Red Sea – Operation Aspides – in February 2024.

On 20 December 2023, Houthi ballistic missile attacks and aggression intensified as the Houthis began targeting Western naval vessels, which the French navy managed to intercept. This marked the most intense engagement between the Houthi and the Western navies in 2023. This was followed by the attack on the *Maersk* commercial ship. On 30 December 2023, four Houthi ships attempted to seize the *Maersk*. The US navy came to the *Maersk* aid and destroyed three Houthi ships and the fourth fled the scene. The Iranian ship *Alborz* entered the Red Sea a day after the US' victory in the Red Sea, which marked Iranian official entrance into the War of Resistance.

However, USS *Carney* and commercial ships daring to travel through the Red Sea were still attacked by the Houthis. The American-led intervention against Houthi pirating appeared ineffective and the US needed to pressure the Houthis to stop their effective campaign in the Red Sea. On 11 January 2024, the US and Britain bombed Houthi positions in Yemen, which were mostly air bases and military camps. Major General Patrick Ryder claimed that the West's campaign against Houthi acts of aggression was unrelated to Israel's war against Hamas and the Palestinians in an attempt to avoid public outcry. However, the Houthi campaign in the Red Sea as clearly in support of Hamas' war effort as the Houthis claimed that the seizure of commercial ships in the Red Sea would stop once Israeli acts of aggression towards the Gaza Strip had ceased. Ryder made this weak argument to the American public in an attempt to sway public opinion to support American actions in the Red Sea and to distance Operation Prosperity Guardian from the controversial war and bombardment that was occurring in Gaza. Although there were few casualties in the Anglo-American bombings on the first day, this had a huge impact on the region and caused fears that the war in Gaza would escalate into a much bigger conflict. The Anglo-American bombing campaigns in Yemen continued and managed to successfully lower Houthi activities in the Red Sea.

Iran started to undertake similar naval seizures of commercial vessels in the Strait of Hormuz and Arabian Sea, although to a much lesser extent when compared to the Houthi rebels. Iran seized an American oil tanker, *St Nikolis*, off the coast of Oman in January 2024. This was a very tricky situation for the West, as they could not militarily intervene in Iranian naval activities without risking an Iranian-American war. The US and the West, therefore, did not attempt to retake the *St Nikolis* militarily and it was only in late March 2024, that Iran released the crew of the *St Nikolis* from Iranian captivity. This was followed by Iranian missile attacks on Western aligned targets in Iraq and Syria later that January. Tensions rose between Israel, the US and Iran with the bombings in Syria.

Western, Iranian and Houthi battles intensified with the American seizure of an Iranian dhow in the Arabian Sea. This occurred on 11 January 2024 and the dhow was crewed by Yemenite Houthis. The dhow was shipping Iranian arms and missiles to the Houthis and the seizure of the Iranian dhow resulted in two US Navy SEALs' deaths. Western navies continued to intercept Houthi drones, missiles and boats. However, a unique incident occurred on 9 March 2024 in which a Danish naval boat's defence system was not functioning as it was being attacked by four Houthi drones. Fortunately for the Danish crew, they managed to get the ship's weapons working and successfully defended themselves against the drones. The Danish ship's defence malfunctions occurred because the ship did not receive daily inspections, which has been a common theme for European armies' war machines. It is known that Germany faces serious lack of battle-ready tanks at its disposal. Hopefully, this incident acts as a wakeup call for NATO to ensure that their vehicles and ships are 100 per cent operational in preparation for a possible war against Russia, whose war industry is in full swing with the Ukraine War.

State and non-state actors always tried to one-up the other for every act of violence inflicted on each other. Punitive acts of violence further escalate the conflict into a larger war and so it was, therefore, the US and Israel's responsibility to recognise this and to refrain themselves from lashing out at the Iranian proxy groups. The Israeli punitive strikes only resulted in escalation rather than successful deterrence. The retaliatory cycle only played into Iranian interests, as the more atrociously the Israelis conducted themselves, the more disunified Jerusalem was with its American and Saudi allies. The cycle also resulted in an increase in international anti-American rhetoric and heightened Western government-public divide.

The Israeli Implosion

During the early phases of the Gaza War, Hamas kidnapped around 250 Israeli citizens in which some were then subjected to torture, rape and/or execution. On 24 November 2024, a four-day-long ceasefire was brokered between Hamas and Israel in which a significant number of Israeli hostages were exchanged for Palestinian PoWs and allowed for humanitarian aid to enter the Gaza Strip during the temporary halt in Israeli military operations. The ceasefire was perceived as a step towards peace by the international community. They believed that if Israel and Hamas were capable of negotiating agreeable terms, then steps could be taken to further this behaviour. The international community had attempted to create a second major ceasefire thereafter.

However, there were several cases in which Israeli hostages were killed by Israeli bombardment. Cases of friendly fire incidents occurred in October 2023, which resulted in the hostage Efrat Katz being killed. This was initially denied by the IDF until April 2024. The most infamous IDF hostage killing incident occurred in December 2023, when three Israeli hostages, Yotam Haim, Samar Talalka and Alon Shamriz escaped Hamas captivity and approached IDF soldiers with a white flag, only for the IDF to shoot them all dead.

The Israeli 'Bring Them Home Now' protests, which started a week after the Hamas incursion, intensified in Tel Aviv on 31 March 2024. The protests demonstrated their dissatisfaction with Netanyahu's attempts to resolve the Israeli hostage situation. The protests even called for the removal of Netanyahu due to Netanyahu's failure to effectively deal with the hostage situation. In April 2024, around 130 Israelis were under Hamas captivity for 6 months. The life expectancy of these hostages decreased further as the Hamas fighters became increasingly cornered by the IDF advances. The safest way of extracting the hostages was through negotiations, more so than a military offensive or raids to retrieve them. Military offensives or raids were a detrimental way of extracting the Israeli hostages from the Gaza Strip.

It should be made clear that these protests were not anti-war protests. The Israeli protesters condemned Hamas and wished to see the Gaza Strip occupied by the IDF as punishment for the 7 October Incursion. The Israeli population had a deep hatred for Palestinians. The Israeli outrage of Israeli officials' approval of UN evacuation of sixty-eight Palestinian children from the Gaza Strip to the West Bank is evidence for their hatred. Some Israelis protested against the IDF bombardment of the Gaza Strip. These protestors were ostracised and arrested by the Israeli mainstream media and authorities respectively.

In March 2024, American-Israel relations began to decline significantly. Biden began to lose his pro-Israel stance after the Democratic Party was split as to whether the US should continue to supply arms to Israel from a moral standpoint. This caused a great divide in the Democratic Party and led many young left-leaning voters to condemn Biden. This meant that Biden had to take a couple of steps back in supporting Israel in order to win back his voters in time for the American presidential elections in 2024. Biden began to criticise Netanyahu's conduct of the war and warned Jerusalem not to commit to the Rafah offensive, which led pro-Netanyahu Israeli politicians to accuse Biden of 'overthrowing Netanyahu's government'.[92] In February 2024, Biden sanctioned four Israeli settlers in the West Bank who had enacted violence on Palestinians and Israeli pro-Palestine protesters. Imposing sanctions on four Israeli individuals did not shape the outcome of the war nor dissuade Netanyahu from his desires for a Rafah offensive. It can be argued that US sanctions on the Israeli settlers were a political act made by Biden to gain back support from his voters and followers. This proved to be ineffective in achieving its goal as everybody knew that these sanctions would do nothing and were not highly publicised by Western media outlets. The sanctions only served to further ruin Biden-Netanyahu relations and so, arguably, fell against Biden's favour.

The Egyptian Protest

With the siege of Gaza city coming to a near end by late January 2024, Netanyahu prepared for an offensive towards the south of Gaza. Egypt pleaded with the UN to stop Netanyahu's Rafah offensive. Egypt warned that Egypt would not take in Palestinian refugees and, therefore, the Gazans would be cornered between the incoming IDF military and Egyptian border guards, resulting in excessive Palestinian fatalities. Egypt had been denying Palestinian refugees crossing the Rafah border crossing for both economic and political reasons. Egypt's economy during 2023 and 2024 was in complete disarray with debt, currency devaluation and poor industrial and commercial developments. The economic state of Egypt could not bear to accommodate a rapid influx of Palestinian refugees, migrating en masse within a span of two to three months. The state of Egypt would have collapsed as a result.

In April 2024, it was estimated that Egypt experienced an influx of Sudanese refugees seeking sanctuary after fleeing the Sudanese Civil War, which greatly impacted Egypt's economy, resulting in Egypt putting measures in place to stop Sudanese refugees from entering the country, and conducted mass deportations to expel the Sudanese from Egypt. This demonstrated that Egypt was adamant in turning away war refugees in order to secure the stability of the Egyptian economy.

A more political reason as to why Egypt refused to accommodate Palestinian refugees was that in doing so, it encouraged Israel to, one day, invade the West Bank in the hope that Jordan accommodated the refugees and, therefore, allow Israel to properly settle in both the Gaza and West Bank. Therefore, in protest, Egypt refused to allow Palestinian crossings into Egypt despite UN pleads to open the Rafah border crossing. Israel attempted to counter Egypt's protest by airdropping leaflets onto southern Gaza, warning the Gazans of the upcoming Rafah offensive. This was to cause hysteria amongst the Gazan population and to mentally pressure Palestinians to desperately attempt to cross the Gaza-Egypt border. The IDF's propaganda campaign against the Palestinians was an extensive effort to expel Palestinians from the Gaza Strip and was, therefore, an extension of Israeli settler plans in the Gaza Strip. In May and August 2024, Israel requested Egypt to get rid of the Philadelphia Accords of 2005, ridding the Egyptian border guards from the Egyptian-Gaza border. Israel justified their requests, claiming that the Gazans should enter Egypt to escape the war. Egypt saw through the Israeli designs and refused on both occasions.

The International Back and Forth

Drama unravelled in the UN Security Council between 22 and 25 March 2024. With the approach of Ramadan, starvation was a serious risk factor amongst the surviving Gazan population. The US proposed a conditional ceasefire between Israel and Hamas in exchange for all living Israeli hostages to be returned to Israel. This was vetoed by Russia, China and Algeria who claimed that this proposal did not actually ensure a ceasefire agreement and that an immediate unconditional ceasefire should be made instead. They argued that UN and humanitarian aid should be sent to the Gaza Strip immediately. US ambassador Linda Greenfield was angered by Russia's and China's decision to veto, claiming that their veto was a petty act contrived from the concurrent Cold War tensions. Greenfield argued that these petty vetoes came to the detriment of Palestinians and claimed that every passing day meant the prolonging of the suffering of the Palestinians. However, the Russian alternative ceasefire resolution, not the American ceasefire proposal, actually served to lesser the Palestinian suffering. They proposed an alternative resolution, which was decided on 25 March.

The Russian proposal was a power move. If the US vetoed Russia's proposal, they would look petty and it would result in global condemnation. If the US was to approve the Russian proposal, it would be an international humiliation for Washington, as adhering to Moscow's demands would undermine the US' superpower image.

On 25 March 2024, the UN Security Council passed the Russian immediate Gaza ceasefire resolution and Greenfield restrained her spite and raised her hand. The US' sincerity to help the Gazan population was still questionable as after the UN resolution, the US transferred more missiles to Israel days later. These missiles were sent with the intent for the IDF to soften Hamas positions in the south of Gaza, prior to Israel's Rafah offensive.

The US' staunchness with Israel crackled after the IDF indiscriminately bombed and killed seven aid workers belonging to the World Central Kitchen on 1 April 2024. Three were British citizens and one was American, which caused outrage amongst the Democratic politicians. Biden condemned Netanyahu for indiscriminately killing the American aid worker. This resulted in Biden being more adamant for a ceasefire and to providing humanitarian aid to the Gaza Strip. Biden warned Israel thereafter that if Israel was to see a continuous flow of American weapon packages, Israel needed to ensure a significant reduction of Palestinian death rates. Antony Blinken even warned that if Netanyahu and the IDF did not change their way of military conduct, American support would be reconsidered.

True Promise

The Israeli bombing of the Iranian Embassy in Damascus led to Iran threatening to conduct military reprisals against Jerusalem. Israel and the US prepared for the imminent Iranian attack and Israel closed its embassy across twenty-eight countries in fear of an Iranian attack.

On the morning of 13 April 2024, Iran commandos seized an Israeli-linked commercial ship off the Strait of Hormuz via a helicopter. This indicated the start of Iranian retaliatory actions, and so Israel and the US were on standby in anticipation for the coming heavy Iranian attack. On the night of 13 April 2024, Iran launched 170 drones followed by 30 cruise and 120 ballistic missiles from Iran to Israel. Jordanian, French, British and American air forces and the US Navy intercepted Iranian drones and missiles in Iraqi and Jordanian airspace en route to Israel. Saudia Arabia and the UAE provided military intelligence and assistance regarding the destination and time of the Iranian attack. The Islamic Resistance in Iraq and the Houthis launched their air strikes on Israel simultaneously with Iran's Operation True Promise. Iranian drones managed to enter Israeli airspace, but Israel's Iron Dome intercepted 99 per cent of the remaining drones. Nine missiles managed to break through, causing minor damage to two Israeli military bases and a transport plane. There were very few casualties and no fatalities.

Iranian and anti-Israeli analysts and reporters argued that Operation True Promise was a symbolic victory as it shook the Israeli society to its core. It did not. The fact that Operation True Promise failed to break through the Iron Dome defences proved to the Israeli military and public that Iranian made weapons were ineffective against Israel's modern military hardware and the shock of it would be used by

Netanyahu to stir Israeli patriotism. Iran's Operation True Promise was an overwhelming military blunder because not one missile or drone killed a single Israeli.

The wise thing Netanyahu should have done after the Israeli victory over Operation True Promise was to not retaliate. However, on 19 April 2024, Israel launched a missile attack on a nuclear plant in the Ishfana region causing further setbacks to Iran's nuclear programme. Iranian media tried to downplay the Israeli attack because it was a humiliating defeat for Iran. It was humiliating because Iran sent hundreds of drones and missiles to Israel but all were destroyed and ineffective, whilst Israel sent three missiles which the Iranian military were unable to intercept.

Hezbollah launched forty missiles on Israeli positions in the early morning of 13 April, approximately twenty hours prior to an Iran air strike on Israel. Hezbollah's decision to not partake in Operation True Promise was likely to avoid serious escalations with Israel. Hezbollah's Houthi allies launched missiles at Israel simultaneously with Iran in contrast. Israel and Hezbollah continued their retaliatory strikes on southern Lebanon. However, there was a slight escalation in Hezbollah-Israel tensions after Operation True Promise.

After Operation True Promise, Israel conducted land raids, skirmishes and fighter jet bombings in the southern Lebanon region, resulting in the deaths of Hezbollah commanders. This was met with Hezbollah launching missiles on Israeli military bases in northern Israel, on 16 April 2024, killing fourteen soldiers and injuring many. Hezbollah successfully missile struck an Israeli base in the north of Acre, making this the deepest Hezbollah attack in Israeli territory during the War of Resistance. Tensions escalated after Israel launched the Rafah offensive and news headlines pondered the idea of Israel invading Lebanon again.

In June 2024, Israel used white phosphorous against Hezbollah forces in south Lebanon. Hezbollah discovered that Cyprus secretly held air bases for the Israeli air force. Significant escalation occurred on 3 July 2024, where successful Israeli air strikes killed Hezbollah Commander Muhammed Nimma Nasser. Hezbollah responded with a 200-missile attack on Israel, of which most were intercepted by Iron Dome operators.

After Operation True Promise, the Islamic Resistance in Iraq launched a missile attack on an American military base in Syria from the Iraqi city of Zummar. The Iranian proxy group then claimed responsibility and announced the resumption of the groups' issile attacks on American military bases in Iraq and Syria. The mysterious explosion at the Islamic Resistance in Iraq's base in Baghdad may have played a role in the proxy group's return in the War of Resistance. However, it is likely that Iranian intervention gave the group confidence to intervene in the conflict again.

In June 2024, the Islamic Resistance in Iraq also announced that it would hold joint operations with the Houthis against Israel.[93] The Houthis also declared that they aimed to extend their attacks on commercial ships to the wider Indian Ocean after Operation True Promise. The Houthis began concentrating more attacks in the Arabian Sea and in the months of May and July 2024, the Houthis claimed to have struck commercial ships in the Mediterranean Sea. As a symbolic gesture to the Axis of Resistance's unified effort against Israel following the Iranian attack, the Bahraini Axis of Resistance group al-Ashtar Brigade claimed responsibility for the 27 April 2024 Eilat drone attack. Although Operation True Promise did not result in an Israeli-Iranian War as expected by analysts a and journalists, it did unite all the Iranian proxy groups to fight Israel with intensity and unity. This made Iranian proxy forces outside the Gaza Strip a much more dangerous threat to the state of Israel than they were prior to the Iranian bombardment.

The Rafah Offensive Begins

On 7 April 2024, Israel had regrouped its forces from northern Gaza to the Gaza Strip's southeastern borders. Israeli forces learned from the hardships of the northern Gaza offensive and took their time to prepare to counter Hamas drones, tunnels and military tactics. The Rafah offensive needed a much-dedicated military logistical preparation. During the wait for the anticipated Rafah offensive, South Africa and eventually the rest of the UN and even the US warned Israel not to launch the Rafah offensive. The US was very adamant against the Rafah offensive and delayed and eventually halted shipment of munitions to Israel in late April and early May 2024 respectively.

In April 2024, the Cairo peace talks were mediated by Egyptian and Qatar mediators, calling for a permanent ceasefire to be made between Hamas and Israel. Hamas agreed to the terms, which was met with Palestinian cheers in southern Gaza on 6 May 2024. During the ceasefire, Hamas exchanged Israeli hostages to Israeli authorities and Israel exchanged Palestinian POWs (disproportionately in Palestinians favour) thereafter. The ceasefire also demanded the withdrawal of Israeli troops stationed at the Israeli-Gaza border and the reconstruction and removal of the Israeli blockade of the Gaza Strip. However, the

Israelis did not agree to the terms, believing them to be 'far reached' and favouring Hamas.

Israel then launched the Rafah offensive on 6 May 2024, closing the Rafah and Kerem Shalom border crossings and cutting international humanitarian aid to the Gaza Strip. The UN condemned Israel for the Rafah offensive, and even held an assembly for Palestinian membership of the UN in protest to which Israeli representative Gilad Erdan shredded the UN charter as a petty form of counterprotest. American spokesperson Matthew Millers stood up for Israel's actions against Rafah by claiming that the Hamas leader's approval of the Cairo peace agreements was not an official agreement but a formal response. Miller elaborates that the Palestinians and the world misinterpreted Hamas' agreements in the defence of Israel's controversial decision to launch the Rafah offensive. Of course, Netanyahu's disregard for the exchange of Israeli hostages were met with condemnation by the families of the hostages and the anti-Netanyahu protesters. The Cairo peace talks were still ongoing despite Israel's Rafah offensive. It can be argued that the Rafah offensive was launched to pressure Egypt, Qatar and Hamas to revise the peace agreement in Israel's favour.

The international scene showed further solidarity towards Palestine during the IDF's offensive into Rafah. On 11 May 2024, the UN began to consider the membership of Palestine. On 21 May 2024, the ICC threatened to declare an arrest warrant on Netanyahu which Rishi Sunak opposed, and Joe Biden was outraged by and claimed that the IDF's actions in the Gaza were not a genocide. On 22 May 2024, the Republic of Ireland, Spain and Norway officially recognised Palestine as a country. On 2 June 2024, Zelensky urged for an end to the Israel-Gaza conflict and for both states to recognise each other's rightful sovereignty and international law.

Further drama occurred during the Rafah offensive in which the combined forces of Israeli navy, air force, defence forces, Shin Bet and Yamam conducted a rescue operation in Nuseirat in May 2024, rescuing three Israeli hostages. The rescue mission caused the deaths of over 274 Palestinians deaths with over 700 injured according to the Gaza health ministry. In July 2024, Palestinians located in and to the east of the Rafah were ordered to evacuate to Khan Younis by the Israelis, causing further displacement and hardships to the Palestinian people. Many pro-Israeli observers commend the Israelis for warning the Palestinians to evacuate from places that were going to succumb to Israeli bombardment and become a battlefield. However, they do not realise that these evacuations were more intended for the benefit of

Israel rather than for the common Palestinian. The evacuations made it easier to pacify territories of the Gaza Strip as a lot of Palestinians fled from Israeli aggression. This made it easier for Israeli expansionism into Palestine, which the Israeli public supported as a reward for winning the Gaza War.

Assassination Run

On 27 July 2024, Hezbollah carried out an air strike on a football pitch in the Golan Heights as a response to Israel's never-ending retaliatory attacks. The air strike killed twelve teenagers and Israel responded by air striking a Hezbollah arms depot and then a Hezbollah commander, Fuad Shukr, in Beirut. The Hezbollah strike in the Golan Heights and the Houthi attack on Tel Aviv led many to fear that Israel would declare war on these proxy groups as a response. Retaliatory attacks continued as normal, but Hezbollah vowed to deal a significant blow to Israel soon in response to Shukr's death.

On 31 July 2024, Israel assassinated one of Hamas' leading figures, Ismail Haniyeh, in Tehran using an explosive. This assassination was condemned by Iran and various nations around the globe. The Israeli assassination was more controversial than other air strike assassinations of Hamas and Hezbollah leaders, as Haniyeh was an important negotiator on behalf of Hamas during the Israeli-Hamas Cairo peace agreements. The mediators of the Cairo peace agreements, Qatar and Egypt, condemned the assassination, claiming that his death setback the already strenuous peace talks. Qatari diplomat Sheikh Mohammed bin Abdulrahman bin Jassim Al Thani claimed, 'political assassinations and continued targeting of civilians in Gaza while talks continue leads us to ask, how can mediation succeed when one party assassinates the negotiator on the other side?'[94] The Israeli government approved of the assassination to thwart Hamas' progress at the Cairo peace table. Iran and Hamas later vowed to avenge Haniyeh and to punish Israel, resulting in a second Iranian interventionism scare.

The 25 August 2024 marked the most intense combat exchange in the Hezbollah-Israel border war, with 100 Israeli fighter jets bombing Hezbollah positions across southern Lebanon within a span of 30 minutes. Israel claims that it was a pre-emptive strike against a Hezbollah attack on Israel. Regardless of Israel's claims, it was undeniable that Hezbollah's preparations for retaliation against Israel had to thereafter be reorganised. This was because if Hezbollah were to gather an army force or any form of military grouping in southern Lebanon with the intent to launch a cross-border attack or offensive, they had to it covertly without Israel finding out the positions and destroying them via air strikes and fighter jets. The Israeli thirty-minute bombing campaign further delayed a possible joint Hezbollah-Iranian retaliatory operation.

The Invasion of Lebanon

On the night of 8 September 2024, the Israeli military conducted air strikes and a commando raid into an underground Iranian missile production facility in Maysaf, north-west Syria. The attack resulted in several Syrian deaths and hindered Iranian-Hezbollah medium-range missile production rate in Syria.

On 15 September 2024, Netanyahu vowed the return of northern Israelis to their homes as part of the ongoing Cairo peace deal terms.

On 17 September, around 2,700 Hezbollah members across Lebanon and Syria suffered injuries from the pagers-explosion attack. Another wave of casualties occurred the following day, with Hezbollah walkie talkies exploding. The perpetrator of the pager sabotage was likely Israel. However, Israel did not publicly confirm their involvement. The pager attacks caused hysteria and decline in morale in Lebanon, it also inhibited Hezbollah communications.

On 23 September 2024, Israel launched several hundred missiles against Lebanon, targeting southern Lebanon and Beirut, killing over 200 people and injuring over 1,000. The IDF dropped leaflets across Lebanon, telling the Lebanese to flee north, in a similar way to how they warned the Gazans prior to the northern Gaza and Rafah offensives. Masses of people started migrating to northern Lebanon and to Syria in fear of a looming Israeli invasion. The Israeli bombings continued the following days, targeting other key cities, such as Acre and Tyre. The bombings of Beirut continued also, with particular emphasis in the southern suburb districts in which Hezbollah commanders were stationed.

On 26 September, Israeli bombings hit the Matraba crossing bridge, to prevent smuggling of arms to Hezbollah from Syria. Hezbollah intensified their bombardments of northern Israel in response to the mass destruction caused by the IDF. War appeared inevitable and the intensity of the Israel-Hezbollah tensions during August to September 2024 contrasted sharply with the early months of the border missile exchanges. The US and France demanded a twenty-one-day ceasefire. However, Netanyahu declined the ceasefire proposal and sent many elite brigades to the Israel-Lebanon border in anticipation for the invasion. British and American troops were sent to Cyprus in preparation to evacuate their nationals from Lebanon. The UN condemned Israel's breach of Lebanese sovereignty, however were ineffective in pressuring Israel to reverse course.

On 27 September 2024, Israel struck the southern suburbs of Beirut with a bunker-buster bomb, injuring approximately 200 people and killing around 30, including several Hezbollah and Iranian Guards members. The Israeli strike killed Nasrallah, which was a great blow to Hezbollah morale.

On the 29th, Nasrallah's supposed-to-be successor was assassinated by Israel, further disrupting the Hezbollah chain of command, fuelling disorganisation during a time where an Israeli invasion was pending.

On 1 October 2024, Israel invaded Lebanon. Netanyahu claimed that the invasion was only a limited and regional operation, aiming at creating a buffer zone in the south of Lebanon. This was to get rid of Hezbollah presence in the south, in order to ensure the safe return of northern Israeli citizens. The Lebanese army was ordered to withdraw behind the Litani River, away from the Israel-Lebanese border.

On the night of 1 October, Iran launched two waves of missile attacks on Israel in retaliation for 27 September bunker-buster bombing and in defiance of the Israeli invasion of Lebanon. Most Iranian missiles were intercepted by Israeli, Jordanian, American and British air forces.

On the second day of Israel's invasion of Lebanon, eight Israeli soldiers were killed in action, which was a great blow to Israeli morale. On the third day, the Lebanese army fired on IDF positions after being hit in southern Beirut. Hezbollah had managed to repel several Israeli advances into southern Lebanon. However, Israel continued striking Lebanon, killing Hezbollah members and their chain of command.

Beginning on 9 October 2024, Israel attacked numerous UN outposts in southern Lebanon, injuring over forty. Israel claimed that Hezbollah tunnels were under the outposts and demanded the UN withdraw, but the UN troops refused. In mid-November, Israel conducted several air strikes on Hezbollah affiliated outposts and infrastructure across Syria.

With the Israeli invasion of Lebanon, French President Emmanuel Macron greatly condemned Israel's aggressive actions and called for all Western nations to halt arms shipments to Israel. Biden had been critical of Netanyahu's decision to invade Lebanon, claiming that it was thwarting the Cairo peace agreements and any chance of peace in the Middle East. Vice President Kamala Harris promised her voters during the presidential debate in 2024, that the two-state solution would be a pursued outcome of the Gaza conflict, much to the dismay of Netanyahu. This resulted in many Americans speculating that Netanyahu was interfering in the US elections in 2024 against Biden in favour for a more supportive candidate.[95] Throughout the Gaza conflict, Trump had been steadfast in supporting Israel's war against Iranian proxies and had not once questioned Israel's conduct of the war. Even during his electoral campaign, Trump had been commemorating Israel's war effort despite his pro-isolationist remarks.

During his time as president, Donald Trump had been a staunch ally of Israel and antagonist of Iran. It had been revealed in September 2024 that Iran had intentions to assassinate Trump, displaying a sort of proxy-war campaign between Israel and Iran over the US election results in 2024.

Dangerous Developments

During the early days of the Gaza War, Russia invited Hamas officials to Moscow to negotiate over the release of Russian nationals that were captured during the 7 October attacks. Israeli officials scorned Moscow's dialogue with Hamas. Moscow was successful in the negotiations and the Russian hostages were returned.

In April 2025, in a televised event, Putin sat alongside one of the freed hostages and gave Hamas his thanks towards their decision to release the Russian hostages and champion Russian-Palestinian ties. Moscow condemned Israeli conduct in the Gaza Strip: firstly, for Russian domestic anti-West propaganda consumption and secondly, to regain Russian positioning amongst the international community by tapping into the Arab, African and Latin American protest against Israel's breach of humanitarian law.

During the early days of the Hezbollah-Israel clashes, the Pentagon received intelligence reports indicating that Wagner Group troops stationed in Syria were planning to supply Hezbollah with Russian made SA-22 anti-aircraft systems. The Pentagon feared that Moscow was planning on providing Hezbollah with more lethal aid to establish a new proxy war in Lebanon.

During the early weeks of the Israeli invasion of Lebanon, Netanyahu claimed that the IDF found Russian 'state-of-the-art' weapons in Hezbollah possessions.[96] These were presumably anti-tank weapons and Netanyahu contemplated shipping them off to Ukraine as an act of defiance of Moscow's meddling in the War of Resistance. According to the ISW, Iran had tried to persuade Putin to supply the Houthis with anti-ship cruise missiles to attack Western ships in the Red Sea.[97] Moscow had considered it, acknowledging the benefits of curbing Western trade Red Sea routes and began to send missiles and military packages in July 2024. Putin was inclined to send the Houthi military packages after he had warned the West that he would send lethal aid to the US' enemies across the globe if Washington were to give the Ukrainian armed forces permission to use Western long-range missiles against Russian infrastructure in June 2024. However, the Russian military packages were paused last minute after the US and Saudis persuaded Moscow against transferring weapons to the Houthis.[98]

In October 2024, it was alleged by *Wall Street Journal* that Victor Bout ('the Merchant of Death') was providing the Houthis with AK-47s on behalf of Russia. The report claimed that Houthi officials were sent to Moscow for Russian supplied arms in August 2024 to counter Western drones.[99] Moscow also provided the Houthis with satellite intelligence about the whereabouts of Western commercial ships in the Red Sea for them to attack. The Russians likely provided intelligence as to where Western commercial shipping was in order for the Houthis to hinder Western trade and to strengthen Russian presence in the Red Sea.

In April 2025, Washington accused China of providing the Houthis with satellite intelligence about Western commercial shipping in the Red Sea.[100] If Washington's accusations are true, then Beijing, like Moscow, are shaping the Red Sea front of the War of Resistance into a proxy war to further curb Western trade.

On 6 October 2024, during the Rafah campaign, the Israeli 828th Bislamach Brigade engaged with several Hamas fighters, killing three. One of the dead Hamas fighters was Yahya Sinwar, the head of Hamas and architecture of the 7 October attack. The killing of Sinwar was unexpected and a deadly blow to Hamas as many of its high-ranking leaders were killed during the conflict, greatly impacting the Cairo peace agreements in the Israelis' favour. Sinwar's death also led to increased calls amongst the Israeli public and Western governments for the end of the war and the return of the hostages. The Israeli public believed that justice was had been served and now wanted the hostages to be returned and to end the war. The families of the remaining Israeli hostages feared that with the killing of a number of Hamas leaders, the fates of the hostages were now at the hands of their captors. Israeli demands for the hostages return had became more difficult with the death of Hamas leaders who had been taking part in the Cairo peace arrangements.

With Iranian-Israeli tensions rising, following Operation True Promise II, the US deployed 100 troops with THAAD anti-missile weapons to Israel in mid-October 2024, to strengthen Israeli air defences. An Israeli retaliation was imminent and Washington feared that tensions could possibly escalate into a full war between the two countries. The US air-defence personnel stationed in Israel later participated in the country's defence against the Houthi and the Iranian missile attacks the following year.

On 26 October 2024, Israel responded to Iran's Operation True Promise 2. Codenamed Operation Days of Resistance, Israel struck Iran with three waves of aerial bombardments. The aerial attacks struck ballistic missile production facilities (one of which was presumed to be a hidden nuclear facility) and anti-air weapon positions in Tehran.

An Uncertain End

The Israeli invasion of Lebanon made gains as the weeks progressed, but not to the extent that was desired. Hampered with logistical issues, accompanied by increasing international condemnation and Hamas' gruelling insurgency campaign in Jabalia, Zeitoun and Rafah, Israel approached Macron and Biden to settle a ceasefire with Hezbollah. The ceasefire agreement entailed the complete withdrawal of both Hezbollah and Israeli forces from southern Lebanon. UN and Lebanese troops occupied the southern Lebanon and established a buffer zone between Israel and Hezbollah. The ceasefire agreements were agreed by all parties and on the early morning of 27 November 2024, the ceasefire was initiated. Biden claimed that this ceasefire was designed to be permanent and wished to implement a permanent ceasefire in Gaza before he left presidential office. However, both Israeli and Hezbollah were distrustful of each other and were sceptical of whether other would uphold the ceasefire demands.

The ceasefire was met with international relief and Israeli disappointment. Netanyahu promised to eliminate Hezbollah. However, this was not accomplished due to the IDF's unsatisfactory progress in the invasion. Netanyahu attempted to recover from the failed Israeli invasion by making the Israeli public aware that the ceasefire agreement ensured the return and safety of northern Israeli citizens. Despite the ceasefire, IDF and Hezbollah forces committed several ceasefire violations by attacking one another across the IDF-Hezbollah line of contact. Israel also continued to harass Hezbollah trade routes across the Syrian-Lebanon border and conducted several air strikes on Hezbollah members in Damascus and other areas of Syria. Israeli targeting of Hezbollah members outside Lebanon did not violate the ceasefire agreements. The Lebanese army's inadequate role of controlling south Lebanon from Hezbollah led to discussions of whether the IDF presence in southern Lebanon should be extended for thirty days in January 2025.

With Hezbollah officially exiting the War of Resistance and the fall of al-Assad, Israel began negotiating for a peace settlement with Hamas in Doha. The Cairo peace agreements had stalled and with Hamas' most uncompromising negotiator, Yahyah Sinwar, being dead and Hamas being more isolated than ever, Israel was in a much more advantageous position at the peace table. The American-Qatari-Egyptian Doha mediated talks began on 17 December and it was reported that both parties were adamant on securing the peace. Not much was known of the peace table demands. However, it was widely reported that the remaining and replacement Hamas leaders were willing to compromise to Israeli demands. Initially, it was rumoured demands were the release of Israeli hostages and IDF presence in the Gaza-Egypt border to prevent Hamas weapons smuggling in the future.

On 5 January 2025, Hamas proposed, online, to release thirty-four of the remaining ninety-six Israeli hostages as the first phase of ceasefire negotiations. The names of the thirty-four hostages were listed, prompting much emotional responses amongst the Israeli people online. Hamas released a video of one of the hostages pleading for Netanyahu to agree to a ceasefire in order to save the hostages from their plight. This intensified Israeli protests for a ceasefire in exchange for the return of the hostages. Hamas' public hostage exchange offering was a tactical manoeuvre to pressure Netanyahu into compromising his expansionist goals in order to avoid isolation from not only his Western allies, who urged Israel to agree to the Doha ceasefire terms, but from his own citizens. The Hamas insurgency and regathering in northern Gaza likely played a role in Netanyahu's reconsideration of the feasibility of occupying the Gaza Strip. Israel simply did not have enough men to successfully occupy the Gaza Strip. Netanyahu's political goal of the eradication of Hamas was void, as the traumas of the Israeli bombardment of the Gaza Strip had resulted in more Palestinians being radicalised and recruited into the Hamas movement.

On 15 January 2025, it was announced by Qatar and the US that the Doha peace agreements were agreed by both parties. They announced that the ceasefire had three phases:

Phase 1
Initiated on 9 January 2025. Immediate ceasefire from both warring parties. Hamas to return thirty-three Israeli hostages – consisting of the American, elderly, children and critical injured Israeli hostages. Palestinian prisoners returned to Gaza. The beginning of the Israeli military withdrawal from the Gaza Strip. Negotiations continue with

the US, Qatar and Egyptian mediators to ensure that Doha peace agreements are seen through and to effectively tackle oversights or unforeseen events that jeopardised the peace process.

Phase 2
Hamas to exchange of all remaining hostages. The completion of the IDF withdrawal from the Gaza Strip.

Phase 3
Hamas to return the bodies of the dead Israeli hostages and the reconstruction of Gaza.

Israel's War of Resistance against Hamas and Hezbollah appeared to have come to an end in 2024 and 2025. With the blockade and bombing of the Gaza Strip ceasing, the Houthis stopped their campaign in the Red Sea. However, everyone across the globe knew that the ceasing of the wars in Gaza and Lebanon served as a mere pause in the wider Israel-Arab conflict. This mindset had been exploited by forces and actors who did not want the war to end. When Trump returned to the White House, he trashed Biden's peace plan and goaded Netanyahu to recontinue the Gaza War with his Riveria of the Middle East proposal.

In March 2025, Israel and the US re-engaged their wars against Gaza and the Houthis. This was part of Trump's wider front to pressure Iran into accepting a deal to stop their international funding of the Axis of Resistance groups and to end the Iranian nuclear weapons programme.

Chapter Nine

DRAMAS IN THE FAR EAST

The majority of historians declared that the fall of the Soviet Union in 1991 was the end of the First Cold War. They fail to mention that the Chinese threat remained unresolved and slowly grew from an influential superpower in the global south into a major global superpower across the world. The People's Republic of China was formed in the immediate communist victory over the Chinese nationalists during the Chinese Civil War. The remaining nationalist forces evacuated to Taiwan to evade the wrath of the communists. There the nationalists declared Taiwan as an independent nation from the People's Republic of China.

China has vowed to invade Taiwan and played a global superpower rival between the West and the USSR during the First Cold War. The last great communist nation has exploited the West's capitalism and have embedded their economic influence in Western nations' economy. It is because of China's economic embedment in countries' economy that it is very difficult for nations to untangle themselves from Chinese influence. During his first term at the presidential office, Donald Trump engaged in an economic trade war against Chinese economic influence during his presidency, but he appeared to have lost. Despite the failure of the trade war, President Joe Biden engaged in a new phase of the Sino-American competition during the Second Cold War. Biden's Asia policy was to establish an anti-China coalition of nations in the far eastern Asian region to curb China's growing expansion in the region. This anti-China coalition policy procedure was later realised as a miscalculation as it made isolated China perceive its neighbours as hostile and aligned with the United States. This pressured Beijing to pivot away from its initial neutral stance during the Second Cold War, into joining the Russian bloc.

All Eyes on Taiwan

Sino-Russian relations have increased during the early decades of the twenty-first century. It was, therefore, a surprise to Putin when Beijing did not support Russia during the international condemnation of Russia from February to March 2022. There are various reasons why China was so hesitant in supporting Russia's action at that time. One reason was that China rarely supports nations who invade other countries as they view these military conducts as colonial behaviour. The Marxist doctrine views colonialism as the final phase of turbo-capitalism. A more likely reason behind Beijing's hesitancy was because they did not want to immediately support Russia due to the worldwide condemnation of Russia in 2022. They wanted to remain neutral and see how events played out until they were in Beijing's favour. If China had supported Russia in February 2022, they risked facing sanctions and Western isolation, which hindered China's growth. It can be argued, however, that the Russian invasion of Ukraine played in Beijing's favour. China has observed the international consequences of Russia's invasion of Ukraine, which has helped them predict what consequences would similarly happen to Beijing if their army finally committed itself to the invasion of Taiwan. China, therefore, will take their time to prepare to withstand these consequences when China invades Taiwan.

Biden was very adamant to defend Taiwan from a possible Chinese invasion, dropping the strategic ambiguity of his predecessors regarding American military support to Taiwan. This was likely because China was rapidly becoming a global superpower aiming to compete with the American economy and superpower status. Taiwan is, therefore, a symbol of American defiance against Chinese growth and Biden was bent on thwarting Beijing's constitutional goal to unite the Chinese lands under one flag. This served to increase both Taiwan's confidence and anxiety. Taiwan was very confident that the US' firm stance in backing Taiwan assured them that they had a fighting chance against China. But it also made many Taiwanese on edge because Biden's firm stance in support for Taiwan suggested that events around the globe were heightening Sino-American tensions, meaning that the invasion date of Taiwan became more imminent.

Nancy Pelosi's visit to Taiwan in August 2022 marked an intensification of Sino-American tensions, and China's entry as a significant player in the Second Cold War. Pelosi made a diplomatic visit to Taiwan on 2 August 2022. President Xi Jinping was outraged by the Pelosi visit as she did not ask permission from Beijing to enter Taiwan. Beijing does not recognise Taiwan as a country. It views

Taiwan as a region of China that harbours separatist rebels. Beijing perceived Pelosi's visit as an American encouragement of Taiwanese separatism. After Pelosi left Taiwan, China initiated air and naval military drills around Taiwan using live fire rounds on 4 August 2022. The world was watching the events unfold in Taiwan with anxiety as they feared that Chinese military exercise would naturally lead to the invasion of Taiwan and risk of a third world war, akin to the global anxiety of February 2022. Chinese military drills occurred around the Taiwan Strait, Taiwan's Kinmen Islands and Japan's Yaeyama Islands.

Taiwan began their own military drills utilising exercise live rounds on 8 August 2022, as a counter-deterrent to Chinese aggression. The turbulent scene in Taiwan was so ferocious that the US Navy delayed its military drills near Taiwan in fear that it would be in the crossfires of the Chinese aggression. On 10 August 2022, the Chinese military exercises around Taiwan came to an operational end. The Chinese military drills acted as a response to the Pelosi visit and acted as a message to the US to not intervene in China's 'internal' affairs.

However, the Pelosi visit made Biden more fervent in supporting Taiwan against China. In November 2022, Biden proposed a $10 billion aid package to Taiwan. In August 2023, the US approved the immediate $314 million aid package to Taiwan and the annual $2 billion military aid package to Taiwan that would end in 2027. Taiwan has become more militaristic in the wake of the Pelosi visit and the Kinmen beaches were littered with anti-vehicle obstacles. Beijing continued its military exercises around Taiwan, which has led to some minor incidents between China, Taiwan and the West.

Similar to the Pelosi visit, US House of Representatives' Speaker Kevin McCarthy made a diplomatic visit in Taiwan in April 2023. McCarthy voiced America's support for Taiwan against Chinese aggression, which led to Beijing sanctioning McCarthy. Following McCarthy's visit, Chinese air and naval forces conducted military drills around Taiwan similar the Pelosi visit. On 10 April 2023, the US Navy circled around one of China's Artificial Islands, which led to the de-escalation of Chinese aggressive military drills around Taiwan. In May 2023, UK politician and former Prime Minister Liz Truss made a diplomatic visit to Taiwan displaying Britain's support for Taiwan against Chinese aggression. The Chinese did not bother to instigate a major military drill at the Taiwan Strait.

In June 2023, the Chinese naval ship *Luyang III* harassed the US naval destroyer USS *Chung-Hoon* and the Canadian naval ship HMCS *Montreal* by manoeuvring around them in the Taiwan Strait. *Luyang III*'s unsafe manoeuvres were aggressive in nature as it risked USS

Chung-Hoon colliding with *Luyang III*. On October 2023, Chinese fighter jets made similar manoeuvres around a US fighter jet in the South China air. On April 2024, China and the US held a diplomatic meeting about the Taiwan Strait for the first time since the Pelosi visit. During this meeting, another Chinese and American non-lethal clash occurred in the Taiwan Strait.

On February 2024, six Chinese fishermen were fishing extremely close to the Kinmen Islands when the Taiwanese navy chased them out of Taiwanese waters, resulting in two of the Chinese fisherman drowning. A joint effort between Taiwanese and Chinese lifeboats was sent to save the capsized ship. The event was highly condemned by Beijing and led to heightened tensions between China and the Kinmen province the following month. Fears of Chinese annexation attempts over Kinmen during March 2024 were heightened to an extent where Washington deployed Green Berets to Kinmen and Penghu Islands on 8 March 2024. The Green Berets' mission was to help train Taiwanese soldiers and defences. However, it also served as a deterrent against possible Chinese annexation attempts over Kinmen. Chinese naval and air drills occurred around the Kinmen Islands within the subsequent weeks and months, despite the presence of the Green Berets.

The US tried to thwart Chinese economic expansionism and military aggression against Taiwan and the Philippines by establishing a series of American bases across Pacific islands and Asian countries in the Far East. There are 120 American bases in Japan (with over 53,000 troops stationed) and 73 American bases (with over 26,000 troops stationed) in South Korea. American troops stationed in South Korea act as a deterrent to North Korea from invading South Korea. The US has also a significant military presence in Okinawa and a series of American bases on the strip of Japanese islands east of Taiwan. These bases act as both a barrier against Chinese encirclement manoeuvres around Taiwan and as a corridor of drop off points for American shipment of aid to Taiwan. American lily-pad bases in Guam and Hawaii act as an in-between logistical hub where American goods and supplies are dropped off before going to bases in Taiwan, South Korea, Japan and surrounding lily-pad bases. An American base was established in Singapore to block Chinese shipping transports, in case of a scenario in which China invades Taiwan.

China's Neighbours

The US and Taiwan are not alone in their fight against Chinese aggression in Asia. In 2021, the US agreed to provide nuclear-capable submarines to Australia as a countermeasure against Chinese expansion. Australia has been very concerned with the spread of Chinese economic, diplomatic and military influence in neighbouring islands, such as the Maldives, Fiji and the Solomon Islands. China made a security deal with the Solomon Islands in 2022 involving joint Sino-Solomon policing of the country and the establishment of a Chinese naval base in the country. In 2023, Fiji renewed its security agreement with China. Growing Chinese influence spread across the Indo-Pacific waters means the straining of Australian trade. This has caused Australia to attempt to strengthen its ties with Papa New Guinea in an attempt to stave off Chinese influence. This came after Papa New Guinea allowed the US to establish military bases in the country. Australian aircraft had experienced Chinese interception on multiple occasions in May, June, July and November 2022. Australia aims to double its navy to prepare themselves for a possible war against China.

Japan aimed to do the same by increasing its military spending to 2 per cent. The increase in Japanese military spending demonstrates the severity of the tensions in the Far East as the US is willing to overlook its decades-long policy to minimalise the Japanese army after the Second World War. The current militarisation of Australia and Japan is the first since the Second World War.

Japan intercepted around 133 suspicious Chinese and Russian navy vessels between April 2022 and March 2023. Russian navy has been manoeuvring and intercepted around the north, west and south of Japan. A Russian helicopter violated Japanese airspace in March 2022. Chinese naval ships were intercepted in the south of Japan, Taiwan and Philippines. In February 2024, Japan intercepted two Chinese H-6 Bombers above the Miyako Strait. Japan also faced renewed tensions with Russia over the Kuril Islands, which has been a lengthy land dispute between the two countries since the Second World War.

The Nine Dash Line

Countries belonging to ASEAN, such as Indonesia, attempt to play off both Chinese and American foreign policy, knowing that if they were to adhere solely to one, this would result isolation and antagonism from the other. However, Chinese desires to legitimise its rights over the Nine Dash Line has pressured the ASEAN county of the Philippines to align with the US. The Nine Dash Line refers to the disputed waters of the South China Sea between China, Taiwan, Malaysia, Brunei, Vietnam and the Philippines. It is located between Indochina, the Philippines and Malaysia, encompassing the Parcel Islands, Pratas Island, Spratly Islands, Macclesfield Bank and Scarborough Shoal. Artificial Islands have been created by China, Taiwan and Vietnam, as a geopolitical instrument to help legitimise their claims to the Nine Dash Line, which has been disputed over since 1946.

The Nine Dash Line tensions became a highly contested arena between China and the Philippines during the early years of the Second Cold War. Chinese desires over the Nine Dash Line violated the Philippines' Western waters and sovereignty over the Scarborough Shoal. The Chinese-Philippines tensions began with the presidency of Bongbong Marcos who pledged to not allow Chinese expansionist desires to violate Philippine sovereignty in June 2022.

On 6 February 2023, the Chinese navy utilised a military grade laser to blind a Philippine navy crew in an attempt to disrupt Philippine resupply of Philippine personnel in the disputed islands. Shortly after this incident, the Philippines announced the establishment of an American military base in the Philippines in February 2023.

In April 2023, the number of American bases in the Philippines increased to four, further establishing the American encirclement around China and establishing a military aid corridor to Taiwan. In the same month, Chinese boats attacked and blocked Philippine ships using water cannon in the disputed waters. A similar Chinese-Philippine clash incident occurred again in August 2023.

On 10 November 2023, dozens of Chinese ships chased Philippine ships, tasked with a resupply mission, away from the Second Thomas Shoal island.

On 10 December 2023, the Philippine-Chinese tensions exacerbated drastically after both sides accused each other of ramming their ships into each other in the disputed waters. Thereafter, the rate of Chinese-Philippine non-lethal clashes in the South China Sea increased drastically and continued until May 2024. The waters of Scarborough Shoal and the Spratly Islands were both highly contested arenas between the two countries. The intensity of the Philippine-Chinese tensions had escalated so much that Antony Blinken warned China that their support for the Philippines was 'Ironclad'. Due to Chinese expansionism in the South China Sea, Vietnam increased their military cooperation with the Philippines to counter their mutual aggressor.

The Balikatan military exercise was conducted by Philippine, American, French and Australian navies in the South China Sea in April 2024. Fourteen countries acted as observers to the exercise, including Japan, South Korea, India, New Zealand, and various EU and ASEAN countries. Over 16,000 Filipino and American forces participated along with 250 French and Australian forces. The Philippine Coastal Guard participated also, as they were the ones who usually clashed with Chinese Coast Guard in the disputed South China Sea. China condemned the Philippines for bringing international countries into the Nine Dash Line dispute and warned that the exercise would escalate tensions. China announced their own military drills in the South China Sea, which involved stalking, observing and disrupting the joint Philippine-West navy ships during the Balikatan exercise beginning on 25 April 2024.[101]

The Chinese military drills from April to May 2024 also saw Chinese aircraft and naval ships operating in Taiwanese airspace and waters, which struck international fears of an imminent Chinese invasion of Taiwan. The Chinese military drills around Taiwan came after the Taiwanese president's inauguration speech which condemned Chinese aggressive policies towards Taiwan. This coincided with the American naval ship, USS *Halsey*, operating in the Taiwan Strait, which the Chinese naval fleet pressured from the waters.

In June 2024, Chinese boats confronted a Filipino ship with spears and machetes, resulting in Filipino casualties and the Chinese capture of Filipino M4 rifles. The regional disputes escalated into another international flashpoint of the Second Cold War.

India's Position Against Chinese Expansion

India has been a competing superpower against China in Asia since the beginning of the First Cold War. In the Second Cold War, Indian foreign diplomacy doctrine has been to side with Russia to counter Western influence and to side with the US in order to counter China's global-superpower goals. India has, therefore, exploited China's aggressive behaviour in Asia, to solidify its borders and insert their influence over ASEAN countries against Chinese influence. As a result of Indian foreign policy, Indo-Philippine relations increased in the wake of the Nine Dash Line tensions.

India displayed support for the Philippines during the Nine Dash Line tensions by sailing a naval ship to the Manila docks as a display of support for the Philippines after the Filipino-Chinese ship collision in December 2023. In February 2024, India sent BrahMos supersonic missiles to the Philippines, increasing Indo-Philippines military ties. As part of India's foreign policy, India increased its influence in ASEAN countries to counter Chinese trade expansionism. In May 2024, the Indian navy took part in naval academic and community activities with the navy of Singapore.

In the beginning of the Second Cold War, India had abstained from condemning Russia's invasion of Ukraine. Indian-Russian relations had increased thereafter, and India purchased a significant amount of

Russian oil and S-400 missile systems. These Indian purchases were strategic in nature, as India wanted to continue its trade with Russia as usual to ensure Indian stability. Indian President Narendra Modi purchased Russian oil to help their ally to lessen the West's sanctions on Russia, which led to the US considering sanctioning India in response. However, the US would eventually withdraw these notions.

By mid-May 2023, Russo-Indian relations were strained due to Putin's increasing economic ties and dependence with India's main superpower competitor, China. Not only this, but Russia was delaying the shipment of the Indian purchased S-400, because Russia needed them for the Ukraine front. Seeing that Russian dependence on China was increasing as a result of Western sanctions, India switched its alignment with Russia towards the US and began to establish talks with Kyiv concerning Russo-Ukrainian peace talks.

China's robbery of India's ally and the prospect of a Chinese invasion of Taiwan had made India significantly more aligned to the US under the Biden administration. Indo-American relations had improved in 2023 onwards as seen with the increase of diplomatic talks between the two countries concerning military cooperation, intelligence sharing and a partnership in the Second Space Race. This is not to say India had turned on Russia, as India maintained friendly relations with Russia, rather it was in India's strategic interests to align with the US against the Chinese threat. The US has utilised India as a counterbalance against the growing superpower competitor, China. India's alignment with the US in the Far East theatre led to a rise in Sino-Indian border tensions, the Chinese seduction of the Maldives from India, and an intensification of Sino-Pakistani military trade and cooperation.

The Second Space Race

The Second Cold War started a Second Space Race between the superpowers, especially the US, Russia, China and India. The Second Space Race began in earnest on 19 August 2023, with the unsuccessful launch of the unmanned Russian Lunar-25 spacecraft to the Moon, which resulted in its destruction. This was followed by the Indians successfully landing their unmanned spacecraft on the south pole of the Moon on 23 August 2023, marking the first time a spacecraft has landed on the dark side of the Moon. The success of India's landing pressured the US and China to contribute to the Second Space Race, with the goal of landing the first astronauts on the dark side of the Moon.

The US aligned itself with India and Japan to compete against Russia and the Sino-Pakistan team. Two weeks after the Indian landing, Japan launched its unmanned spacecraft to the Moon, with the intent for scientific and technological research, in preparation for landing future spacecraft and astronauts. The US planned to send its astronauts to the south side of the Moon by September 2026. The US unsuccessfully launched a commercial spacecraft in January 2024 and made a successful lunar landing on 23 February 2024.

On 3 May 2024, China with the help of Pakistan, launched the unmanned Change-6 robotic lander to the southside of the Moon.

A Second Space Race has commenced because space is becoming a unique area for potential military dominance. Such a claim appears absurd. However, it has been a huge project for many nations since the late 2010s.

In 2019, for example, Donald Trump created a new branch of the military, US Space Force, displaying the US' serious commitment to the militarisation of the space front. Starlink has been utilised by Ukrainian and Russian forces during the Ukraine War. The Second Cold War has seen the first ever space combat in which during the War of Resistance, where Israel intercepted a Houthi ballistic missile above Earth's atmosphere on 31 October 2023. Spy satellites have been increasingly launched into space with North Korea warning in December 2023 that any American interference on their launching would be a declaration of war.

During a UN Security Council resolution in April 2024, Russia vetoed a draft resolution that called for all states to prevent a nuclear arms race in outer space. The draft resolution was sponsored by the US and Japan. China abstained from the vote, presumably because they had ambitions to station weapons in space too. Although it may appear absurd, the Second Space Race serves as a huge step towards innovating modern military warfare.

The Second Space Race is occurring in the hope to of discovering and collecting samples of the Moon's natural resources that could fuel nations' economies and technologies. NASA was very concerned about the successful Chinese lunar landings as it meant that China could make territorial claims on the Moon, which inhibited NASA's scientific discoveries and exploration. People have speculated that the Second Space Race would result in a 'scramble for the Moon' of sorts and would play out in a similar way to how Antarctica was divided.

In 2021, Russia and China announced plans to establish a joint lunar research base on the surface of the Moon. This indicates that the superpowers wish to establish space stations on the Moon for scientific research, akin to how scientific bases were established in Antarctica.

Cold War Allies

Returning back to Earth, Chinese espionage was a huge concern for the US and Europe.

In January 2023, a Chinese spy balloon was seen in American and Canadian airspace. There was much hesitancy from the American military to shoot it down, fearing that the debris from the destroyed balloon would harm civilians.

However, by 4 February 2023, American fighter jets shot it down. Xi Jinping claimed that the spy balloon was for environmental observations and research. However, this proved to be a weak alibi. China launched more spy balloons in Canada, Michigan, Alaska and in Latin American countries a couple of days later, which were subsequently shot down. In June 2023, Chinese spy balloons were detected in Taiwanese and Japanese airspace. Chinese spy balloons again monitored Taiwan in February 2024.

It has been well documented that TikTok has been encroaching on people's privacy. Because of the dangers of TikTok, British politicians and officials are forbidden from having the app and American lawmakers were planning on passing a bill to ban it. Akin to the Beijing security agreement Fiji, the Solomon Islands and Hungary signed a joint police patrol agreement with China in March 2024. This serves to encroach Chinese influence and espionage in Europe and the Pacific.

During March to May 2024, China and Russia increased their hacking and cyber attack capabilities on Western nations. The West responded by imposing multiple sanctions. Chinese cyber attacks particularly targeted Western nations' electoral infrastructure in 2024 and produced media propaganda about each nation's electoral candidates in order to sway public opinion (and hitherto public votes) to Beijing's favour.

On 24 April 2024, Antony Blinken arrived in China to speak to Xi Jinping to warn China against supplying lethal aid to Russia. It had been reported that China and Russia had been establishing joint modernised war manufacturing industrial factories, which produce drones, missiles and microelectronic gadgets. China has provided nitrocellulose to Russia to help them with ammunition production. China has also sent spare military parts and war components, such as scopes, tank parts and rocket fuel. These Chinese factories and provisions to the Russian army were to help the Russian army's war efforts in Ukraine.

In response to growing Sino-Russian military ties, the US sanctioned hundreds of Chinese businesses that were contributing to helping Russia's war effort in Ukraine. Blinken notes that the Chinese backing of Russia marks a significant worsening of Sino-American bilateral relations. April 2024 also saw the increase of Chinese harbours being used as in-between port for North Korean transfer of arms and ammunition to Russia. In late 2024, it was discovered that Russia established a drone manufacturing company in China, further suggesting China's pivot away from its neutral stance towards the Russian camp.

China now faces multiple antagonists and lacks strong neighbouring allies. This made China more aligned to the Russian bloc, and to support North Korea and Russia in their efforts against the US, in order to maintain status quo in Asia. If Putin lost the war in Ukraine, it risked a regime crisis in Russia, which could play in the US' favour. China wanted to play the 'third neutralist bloc' during the early years of the Second Cold War, but increasing aggressive foreign policies from the US and India pressured China to align with the Russian bloc in order to counterbalance the superpower competition. Putin's desperation for foreign aid was taken advantage of by Beijing, who supplied the Russian army with military equipment and manufacturing. Beijing's exploitation of Russia's international ostracisation and uncertainty in the Ukraine War, were the first steps of Beijing establishing its influence over Moscow. Due to the West's economic sanctions, the Russian economy had become increasingly reliant on China, risking the country becoming economically in debt with China. If Russia were to fall under economic debt to Beijing, China would be very influential over Russia and subsequently Russia's neighbours. Regardless of whoever wins the war in Ukraine, it is likely that China will arise as the victor of the Second Cold War as they would make the Russian economy heavily dependent and in debt to the Chinese economy, which will boost the Chinese superpower status enough to effectively rival the US.

Chapter Ten

THE UNITED STATES IN THE AGE OF CONSPIRACY THEORIES AND POLITICAL EXTREMISM

The 'Woke-Left' and 'Alt-Right' Trench Lines

Like most empires when they fall, the US is currently experiencing fierce competition from external forces and internal divisions. The populist divide is a new phase of the never-ending culture war in the Western world.

The populist divide is a culture war between the left and the right that has been going on since around 2016. The Progressivist-Left is a general term that shall be used to refer to modern leftists who campaign against social and political injustices, and support equal rights for women, ethnic minorities and the LGBTQ community, as well as campaigning against climate change.

Initially, the Progressivist-Left was a voice for those suffering from the inequalities inherent in their society. However, some argue that the Progressivist-Left's voice became increasingly more hostile and demanding after Donald Trump's presidency in 2016. Some believe that during Trump's first term in the presidential office, some of the Progressivist-Left was a force that advocated for cancel culture.

Cancel culture was a movement created by some of the Progressivist-Left to ostracise and eliminate those who did not agree with their political views or made remarks or actions that could be perceived as culturally offensive.

'Politically incorrect' has been a phrase used by the Progressivist-Left to label their political enemies. However, some allege that the hostile individuals within the Progressivist-Left use the label to villainise the right to fearmonger others to subscribe to the progressivism movement. Many Western nations' governments have sided with the progressivist movement to increase their control and appeasement over the public. The Biden administration adopted the movement as part of their domestic policy. Some believe that businesses and Hollywood pander to the Progressivist-Left for monetary gain.

The West's support and indulgent in the movement has made a number of people amongst the populist feel abandoned by the government in favour of the minority. The progressivist movement caused a whiplashing change in the culture of Western societies. The rapid alteration of social norms and fearmongering tactics made by certain leftist groups, individuals and governments, have made many amongst the Western populist reject the switch to progressivism. These are the Traditionalist-Right who oppose the rapid spread of the progressivist movement and are generally nationalistic in nature because they believe that the government should utilise its resources and time over the socio-ethnic majority rather than towards the socio-ethnic minority.

The reasons behind how and why people choose to join either the Progressivist-Left or Traditionalist-Right are numerous and varied. The populist divide has seen a series of political violence in Western societies, such as volatile verbal remarks between individuals in both the public and internet spaces, harassment, riots and even coup attempts, resulting in mass arrests, suppression and deaths.

The Progressivist-Left and the Traditionalist-Right accuse each other of starting the populist divide. The Traditionalist-Right claim that the Progressivist-Left's recent hostility towards those deemed politically incorrect caused the reactionary formation of the modern Traditionalist-Right, to counter the hostilities caused by the rapid and ever-changing Progressivist-Left movement. Whereas the Progressivist-Left claim that they were formed in response to decades-long oppression and discrimination from conservatives and from those inheriting traditionalist values and characteristics.

The populist divide is present in Europe and Western nations, but the US has been the most focal and self-destructive country during this period of political infighting.

During the Second Cold War, notable events of which can be associated with the populist divide are the attempted German coup in

2022, the assassination attempt of right-wing Slovakian Prime Minister Robert Fico, the Nahel Marzouk protests in 2023, the French elections in 2024 and the anti-immigrant Southport stabbings protests in England also in 2024. However, this chapter shall explore the populist divide in the US during the Second Cold War as Russia has exploited the internal dividing of the US to benefit Russia's foreign policy.

The Russians have exploited the populist divide and the West's identity politics by increasing the Western public's attention to their domestic issues and controversies. This aimed to increase Western political and civil infighting, while distracting their attention away from the war in Ukraine.

American politics and society in the twenty-first century is a mess of volatile beliefs that are so embedded in people's minds that it is now nearly impossible to sway them away from their ingrained political beliefs and ideologies. So many sub-politics belong under right and left wings, such as the well-known ones Antifa, LGBTQ, BLM and QAnon believers and other more niche groups most known and active online, such as Incels, 'Alpha male movements', neo-Kazinksyiists and online Marxists. Within these groups are extremist individuals who are fervently devoted to their political group and do not listen to other political groups' ideology or proposals. Then there are some within these groups that are more reasonable and do not force their beliefs on others. And then there are people who support the movement but are not wholly invested into it. Then there are people who follow these groups from afar, out of spite and/or to laugh at, but in doing so unconsciously listening and adopting their beliefs. There are so many of these political groups who bicker about so many social and political issues that it is impossible for the author to write about all of them. Therefore, the author will do his best to write about the most important ones and how Russia exploited the US' internal political and social polarisation.

The American Implosion

After Trump's succession, the world began to consider the consequences of his presidency. Europeans started to consume American media outlets that condemned and praised Trump. This resulted in the West taking a side: leftism extremism or rightism extremism. Brexit further polarised UK and even mainland European politics. A great divide occurred in American politics with the American presidential elections in 2016. The left and the right began digging into their self-believed 'righteous' politics and dug themselves against each other. Trump was compared to Hitler, and Clinton was called a war criminal for leaking classified US documents. During the elections in 2016, disinformation campaigns circulated around social media, to which many Americans consumed and subscribed, such as the Pizzagate conspiracy.

Both Clinton and Trump indulged these disinformation stories. Trump talked about government scandals and ill deeds whilst Clinton claimed that Putin was rigging the American electoral polls in favour of Trump. These conspiracy theories increased dramatically during the Second Cold War, where news outlets would double down on these stories. Leftist television news outlets claimed that Prigozhin and several other Russians rigged the elections in 2016, resulting in Trump's presidency. Right-wing Western internet outlets double downed on the Pizzagate conspiracy during the Second Cold War by claiming that the American deep state was operating an underground child-sex-trafficking operation.

In 2017, an anonymous 4chan user known as Q, claimed that they worked in the American government and was exposing the deep state of the US. Q claimed that the American government was a puppet of the wider deep state. The American government alongside the deep state were agents of the devil and ran a mass underground child trafficking ring. Q named Democratic figures, such as Hillary Clinton and Barack Obama, as agents of the devilish deep state. Q claimed that Donald Trump and his Republican peers were combatting the devil-worshipper politicians. Q also claimed that certain events were going to occur to American celebrities and politicians, but the events never happened. Q's 4chan post gained a huge following in the US and was the spark of the rise of anti-government conspiracy theories in the US. The 4chan post led to the QAnon movement, which was a series of incidents and events in which individuals and mobs would attack the American political establishment, leading to the deaths of individuals.

The Republican Party has exploited the rise in conspiracy theories in order to gain votes. This can be seen with Republican politicians making speeches in at QAnon events whilst claiming that they did not know what QAnon was. It can also be seen during the Trump-Harris presidential debate in which Trump spread lies about Haitian migrants' eating domesticated animals in Springfield and killing babies after they were born. Both claims do not have evidence to back this up and have been proven to be false. Russia too exploited the QAnon movement.

In 2017, in an interview with Western journalists, Putin claimed that men in dark suits and ties tell the American presidents what to do and say in an attempt to stir Cabal conspiracy theories in the West.[102]

The populist divide intensified during the Covid-19 pandemic in which people across the world faced lockdown, and subsequently financial struggles too numerous to list. Boredom and increased social media consumption during lockdown has led the American online users to learn about past scandals, domestic and foreign tinkering and conspiracy theories involving the American government via the internet. This introduced many people to the deep state conspiracies and to adhere the Traditionalist-Right thinking. The murder of George Floyd caused by police brutality resulted in the Progressivist-Left protesting for racial equality in the streets of the US. The protests turned violent and counter-riot police were sent to put down the violence. The protests were initially peaceful and stood against police brutality and racism.

Internet consumerism increased during the Covid-19 pandemic, which paralleled with the rise of 'right wing toxic masculine' influencers, such as Andrew Tate and the rise in circulation of American authority scandals, such as the Ruby Ridge incident and the CIA involvement in the assassination of President John F. Kennedy. Financial troubles and increasing social media consumption further coiled the American people into the turbulence of the populist divide.

Social media has exacerbated the political divide of the West. Algorithmic apps and features, such as TikTok, Instagram reels and YouTube Shorts, incite extremist opinions. If a person likes, shares, comments or interacts with a certain right- or left-leaning short, their algorithm will increasingly display more of that content to the user. When the user receives more right- or left-leaning content, they become more entrenched in that political leaning belief. For example, if a user interacts with a right-leaning post of TikTok and subsequently receives more right-leaning posts from the algorithm, their reality of politics becomes warped.

Their sense of reality is warped by these algorithmic posts produced by Russian bots, extremists and misinformation. They consume various political messages at an unprecedented rate with every swipe. Due to this underlying extremist messages are unconsciously processed. The user will not spend the time to research and verify the messages of these posts due to confirmation bias, lack of personal time to research something so trivial or lack of interest to do so. Confirmation bias has been extremely prevalent during the populist divide, as evidence to disprove a person's argument or narrative are dismissed as false news created by the opposition.

The Opposition to Trump

In 2020, Joe Biden took candidacy for American presidency under the Democratic Party against Donald Trump. Joe Biden won the American elections in 2020 with 51.3 per cent public votes. Donald Trump was enraged by the loss and claimed that the votes in 2020 were rigged in Biden's favour. He called for his Republican voters to protest in Washington DC in late December 2020, leading to the 6 January attacks. This was a violent storming of the Capitol in which Republican voters clashed with police personnel and displayed dangerous intentions towards the politicians and officials inside the Capitol building. The clashes led to several deaths and fatalities on both sides and Trump eventually called off the Capitol riots, which his followers obeyed. Joe Biden later compared the events of 6 January to 9/11 and to the Pearl Harbor attack in 1941 to sway public opinion against Trump.

The results of such comparisons were weak in effect as at this point, the American people had already picked a side and refused reconsideration. Biden and the Democrats thereafter called the American people who participated in the 6 January attacks as 'Insurrectionists'. This was a fearmongering tactic, and several participants did face prosecution, which furthered the Traditionalist-Right's hatred towards the left, as they were now in power, and were actively taking down the Capitol riots participants and oppositionists in an authoritarian manner.

Trump presented a real danger to American democracy and to the West's hybrid war during the Second Cold War, and so the Democratic government attempted to shut him down and erase his credibility.

In 2023, Trump faced a series of thirty-four indictment cases, which included multiple cases of keeping unauthorised classified documents, several cases for inciting the violent 6 January Capitol riot, falsification of business records (involving hush money payments to a porn star), and for attempting to rig the Georgia electoral votes in 2020, which was pretty damning. Several dramas occurred during the Trump indictments.

On 20 April 2024, an American citizen, Maxwell Azzarello, burned himself outside the Manhattan court where Trump was being tried for one of his cases. Azzarello was handing out conspiracy theory leaflets, which claimed that both Biden and Trump were part of the deep state, and that the American people were being played. Prior to his self-infliction, Azzarello held a cardboard placard, which had the following engraving, 'Trump is with Biden and they're about to Fascist Coup Us.' Azzarello survived the initial self-burning, however, later died in hospital.

Another drama surrounding the Trump indictments was the circulation of Trump's mugshot photograph, which became viral on social media. The mugshot was circulated on television news outlets to mock Trump and scare his followers. However, on social media, it appears that the hoped-for effect had the opposite result amongst the Traditionalist-Right, as they used the photograph as a symbolic image against the 'authoritarian' government's discriminatory agenda towards Trump and his followers. The Traditionalist-Right backed up their claims of a two-tier system by pointing out that Biden was found accused of mishandling classified documents too, but never faced extreme scrutiny by the media and the law.

Trump encouraged such beliefs as he compared the indictments to Nazi persecution of the Jews and Black prejudices in order to gain public sympathy. Despite the Trump indictment cases, which proved to be damning, American public opinion did not change. The Progressivist-Left cheered for Trump's downfall whilst the Traditionalist-Right were enraged by Trump's loss. In April 2024, Trump was convicted on all thirty-four charges. It can be argued that the indictments pressured Trump to stand for presidency again in order to pardon himself from the charges.

'Sleepy Biden'

Despite the controversies of Donald Trump, Joe Biden was a near equal as a controversial president in the eyes of Americans. During the electoral campaign in 2020, Trump claimed that Biden was mentally incapable of running for presidency and mockingly referred to Biden as 'Sleepy Joe' at a rally. The phrase 'Sleepy Joe' became popular and a running joke online and amongst the Traditionalist-Right. Countless jokes and memes made people aware of Biden's mental capabilities to run as presidency. Images and videos of Biden falling over, failures to understand questions, inaudible speeches and reading notes guiding him what to say and do became viral. Biden's cognitive abilities became a serious concern online by 2024, with Biden mistakenly introducing President Zelensky as President Putin, and Kamala Harris as Vice President Donald Trump in his speeches.

Biden's first major blunder was with the withdrawal from Afghanistan. The incompetence of the American withdrawal had been hugely criticised, and Republicans claimed that the withdrawal gave the Russians confidence to invade Ukraine, without facing serious repercussions from the US. Biden's aid to Ukraine and Israel has been met with criticism online, which Russian propaganda exploited to cause further infighting in the US.

The US had undergone various economic crises under the Biden administration, causing much disgruntlement towards Biden for his inability to effectively solve them. The Traditionalist-Right perceived Biden as tearing down the American rights, such as free speech and the right to bear arms. However, the most controversial failure of Biden was the migration crisis in the southern border. Since the Biden administration, illegal immigration rates from Mexico had peaked at an all-time high. The Traditionalist-Right labelled the surge in illegal migrations from the south as an 'invasion', in order to stress Biden's blunder in securing the American border. The Traditionalist-Right feared the surge in illegal immigration and the government housing for them, as they feared the rise of illegal immigration corelates with the rise in crime rates and the endangerment of the American people's safety. This was a huge concern in Europe also. The illegal border crossings from the Mexican border had been a highly contentious issue in the US, and many Republicans claim that the investments into Ukraine were diverting funding away from the security and control of the American-Mexican border. Russia spread both awareness and disinformation concerning the illegal border crossings online in order to sway the American people to vote for the Republicans. This was part of the Russian propaganda campaign to undermine and eventually disconnect American support towards Ukraine.

The state of Texas has been enduring legal back and forth with Washington over the Texan National Guard's activities, such as establishing razor wire on the Texan-Mexican borders, and arresting and deporting illegal migrants without the authorisation of the federal government. However, on January 2024, the Texan-Washington antagonism peaked, with the Eagle Pass Park standoff. On 11 January 2024, the Texan National Guard seized Shelby Park, as its topographical position provided strategic value in combatting the illegal border crossings. The Texan National Guard had prevented Border Patrol from entering Shelby Park and cruising the nearby rivers. In doing so, Border Patrol were unable to process asylum seekers into the country. The Democratic government condemned the Texan National Guard, but the Republican Party supported them and claimed that they would support further activities once they were in power. News outlets' headlines labelled the standoff as 'the beginning of an American Civil War'. However, politicians from both sides of the debacle claimed this was no more than a legal dispute. Despite this, the ramifications of Texas bypassing the American constitution cannot be understated.

In March 2024, the Texas National Guard were confronted by illegal immigrants at the El Paso border, who breached the border fences and caused a riot, injuring several Americans in the process. The incident confirmed the Republican's beliefs that the Biden administration's effort towards securing the border was ineffective and neglected in nature. Russian bots online thereafter targeted their propaganda campaign at the State of Texas, in order to continue to undermine American support to Ukraine. The neglect of domestic concerns on Biden's part played a contributing factor as to why Americans did not want to send money to Ukraine and to the rise of American isolationism.

The Mexican border migration crisis, accompanied by criticisms of American spending abroad, led to the America First movement across the US. The America First movement was the demand for the White House to significantly reduce, or even abandon outright, its commitments abroad and to stop accommodating migrants and asylum seekers. The America First movement's logic was that if Washington were to reduce their commitments in these two areas, more American spending would be diverted towards American lives and prosperity, ensuring that American culture and values are not altered by migrant and external influences. Russian propogandists have egged on this sentiment in the American media, influencing the American public to advocate for the abandonment of Ukraine, altering American values away from universal liberty and freedom. When Trump finally entered office, he let it be known that America's foreign diplomacy adopted an American First approach, causing a rift in American-EU relations.

Trump also began mass deportations of illegal immigrants and cartel members, as well as dismantling pro-LGBTQ organisations in order to restore the US' Christian values and culture. Interestingly, although Americans are not truly the native people of North America and are a collective of ethnic groups, the America First movement has led to a rise in Xeno-nationalism in which the collective ethnic American groups spout nationalist rhetoric and venomous rejection of outsiders. American Xeno-nationalism goes far beyond the regular American patriotism as they strive to preserve the American from outside cultural deprivation. A rise in counter-cancel culture has emerged from these Xeno-nationalist groups, which condemn Progressivist-Left, immigrants and external influences or presence of nations. Despite this, they repeat anti-war propaganda rhetorics which they found from pro-Russian influencers and media.

Putin's Exploit During the Populist Divide

The Iraq War is the most controversial war in American history. More so than the Vietnam War because in the Vietnam War, people did not fully understand why they were being drafted to fight in Indochina, whereas in the Iraq War, the American people were tricked and lied to by the American government to fight a war. The invasion of Iraq occurred despite UN disapproval and it was later revealed that Saddam Hussein did not possess weapons of mass destruction as had been alleged. The American government knowingly lied to the post-9/11 American public for the sake of gaining wealth from Iraq's oil. This shifted American public's attitudes towards the War on Terror from pro-war to anti-war in the Middle East and the seeds of American isolationism in the twenty-first century were sown. Thereafter, American military intervention into any conflict has been heavily scrutinised by the American people, and the Ukraine War was no exception.

Many American citizens, especially right-leaning ones, questioned why the US was willing to send Ukraine a mass of funding, but failed to help American individuals' with their financial difficulties. They also questioned if it was moral or worthwhile to fund a faraway nation against the Russian army. Their concerns derive from American reactions of American intervention in the Middle East and how that ruined the region. Such fears contributed to the rise of American isolationism, and the belief that the US should not get involved in other countries' politics as they have proven to be ineffective in displaying understanding and constructive implementations. Donald Trump and the Republican Party capitalised this emerging sentiment to help them gain the advantage over the Democrats during the 2024 Presidential elections. American isolationism served to Russia's favour as it weakens the US' global-superpower abilities as American leaders fear that any form of interventionism would be met with public backlash. American scrutiny of aiding the Ukraine War was exploited by Russian propogandists who claim that American taxes do not contribute to the American people, but to the Cabal elitists' wallets and foreign interventionism.

In 2024, it was discovered that Moscow gave financial backing to American social media celebrities to spread Russian propaganda and endorse Trump.

On 8 February 2024, Putin partook in an interview with Tucker Carlson. In the interview Carlson failed to maintain the focus of the interview, leading to Putin making a long-winded dialogue about how Ukraine belonged to Russia and how the West started the war. The interview was widely controversial, but nothing of substance was made of it due to the interview's poor direction. Putin's interview with Carlson was an attempt to sway Traditionalist-Right sympathy and make them anti-Biden due to his victimisation stance on the Ukraine matter.

As part of Russia's propaganda campaign in the American populist divide, Putin criminalised LGBTQ affiliated movements in Russia, which were designated as terrorist extremist ideological organisations in November 2023.

This was also a counter to Ukraine's legalisation of homosexual marriage in 2022 (which can be viewed as an effort to appeal to the American people and to display Kyiv's alignment with the Western ideals over Russian traditionalist ideals). Putin even offered political asylum to Westerners who believed themselves as oppressed citizens within a Western neo-liberal extremist state in August 2024. This was a propaganda stunt to make the Traditionalist-Right Americans believe themselves as an oppressed minority under the Democratic government and the Biden administration. This was an attempt to influence Americans to vote for the Republicans during the elections in 2024, and to further destabilise the imploding populist crisis in the US. It was also used to recruit Americans to spread Russian values in the US. In many cases, the cause of most Westerners volunteering into the Russian army, was in response to the shift in Western lifestyle and how their society was abandoning conservative, nationalist and family values.

Russia's propaganda campaign has successfully brainwashed a handful of Westerners to commit treason and fight for Russia in Ukraine, due to the appeal of the more conservative lifestyle of Russia. Moscow's Western foreign fighters spout the same anti-West and anti-Cabal rhetorics that Russian propogandists produced on the internet, when asked why they had joined the Russian army.[103] It has been revealed that most Westerners who have sought political asylum in Russia did so to avoid criminal charges in the US or because they held genuine Traditionalist-Right ideological reasons.

The Republican Party exploited American concerns by endorsing Putin's views and lies on Ukraine in order to gain votes. Republican candidate Vivek Ramaswamy ran his entire candidacy campaign regurgitating American conspiracy theories and using conspiracy theory social media platforms in an attempt to gain votes. His candidacy campaign was short lived and failed to gain significant support. It was rhetorically claimed that whilst Putin was being condemned for invading Ukraine nobody condemned the US for what it did it in Iraq in 2003. These remarks derived from Russian Minister of Foreign Affairs Sergey Lavrov's comparisons of the Iraq and Ukraine invasions. Lavrov's comparisons led to many Americans attitudes changing from pro-Ukraine to suspicion towards the way the West's foreign diplomacy operated.

The Republican Party stood firm on their anti-Ukraine stance by blocking the Democrats' $61 billion aid package to Ukrainian, Israeli and Asian allied nations in December 2023. This was a power move by the Republicans to thwart the Democrats and claimed that this package should be diverted to securing the Mexican-American border from illegal migrants 'invading' the country. This was to also alter Republican voter doubts of Republican stance towards stopping the diversion of American taxes away to Ukraine. It also demonstrates that Russia's information campaign successes in exacerbating American domestic public's discontent towards certain domestic issues and foreign interventionism, indirectly influenced government policy implementations to Russia's favour.

Trump had leaned into American concerns of the country funding Ukraine by reiterating propaganda tales of Zelensky money laundering the American economic packages to Ukraine and claimed that he would end the Ukraine War within twenty-four hours. Trump did not elaborate how he would accomplish such a task, but during the Harris-Trump presidential debate, Trump claimed that he would simply talk Zelensky and Putin into signing a peace deal. It is well known that by 2023, Putin refused to adhere to any peace talk negotiations with the West, until Trump was elected to presidency, as he would give a beneficial peace proposal to Russia.

In June 2024, Putin offered a peace deal with Ukraine, saying that the war would end if Ukraine respected Russian annexation of the four eastern oblasts, and to reverse Ukraine's application to NATO. These demands were refused by Kyiv and were condemned by the EU. It could be argued that this was a propaganda stunt made by Putin to villainise the Ukrainian government for rejecting peace for their country. Putin knew that these demands were too harsh to be taken seriously by Kyiv and hoped that the peace deal's rejection would sway the Traditionalist-Right in the US and Europe to condemn Kyiv.

During Trump's electoral candidacy campaign in 2024, he claimed that during his first presidency, he warned his NATO allies that they would not receive American military support if they did not contribute more to their funding obligations. Trump also claimed that during his presidency, he began to re-evaluate American membership in NATO. Trump's story ramified the Traditionalist-Right's beliefs that American spending for other countries was an inappropriate use of American taxes. These remarks, as well as Trump's positive relationships with Putin and Hungarian Viktor Orban, and Trump electing anti Ukraine James David (better known as J.D.) Vance as his vice president, made NATO beware of the dangerous change in NATO directions of the hybrid war. It also ignited NATO fears of American withdrawal of US funding towards Ukraine's war effort and American appeasement to Putin's expansionist desires. Germany, Ukraine's second biggest lend-leasing supporter, aimed to halve their lend-leasing aid to Ukraine in 2025, as Chancellor Olaf Scholz believed that if the US was to cut its funding to Ukraine, then it was a lost cause. Other NATO nations conspired a 'Trump-proof' plan so NATO could continue to aid Ukraine whether Trump was re-elected or not. NATO's observations of the Republican's blocking of the military package to Ukraine prompted NATO officials to begin the 'Trump-Proof' in earnest.

Joe Biden rightly stated, 'History will judge harshly those who turn their back on freedom's cause'.[104] Biden is correct in his assumption, as the US has been creating a long track record of abandoning its allies to their fates. This can be seen during the Second Indochina War, which saw the Americans abandoning the South Vietnamese, Laotians and Cambodians to the various brutal communist regimes in 1975. It can be seen during the War on Terror where it abandoned its Iraqi, Kurdish and Afghan allies to their fates with various Islamic extremists in 2011, 2019 and 2021 respectively. And now we see a potential risk of the US abandoning its Ukrainian, and hitherto European-NATO allies during the Ukraine conflict due to alt-Right Traditionalists and isolationist-American voters and politicians. How can European NATO allies trust their American counterparts to help them in a war when they consistently abandon their allies?

This is comparable to Armenia's relations to the CSTO. Why should Armenia fight Russia's wars when its CSTO counterparts refuse to fight in theirs? The US, like Russia, will see a decline in military allies, which will be a huge blow to American foreign policy and economy, as European nations will look elsewhere to find a strong nation to protect them against foreign threats, and so shall be under their economic and military influence as a result. The European NATO allies were steadfast with the US during 9/11 and the invasion of Afghanistan, for which Americans were grateful. However, Americans are quick to abandon their allies when Europe is antagonised. For a country that boasts of being the most moral and courageous country in the world and seeks the spread of its democratic and liberal ideals, it is too afraid to see such accomplishments through. American maintenance of its superpower status is essential for its prosperity and isolationism will only further its decline.

It should be noted that Moscow's exploitation of the populist divide serves several purposes aimed at achieving Russia's Ukraine and Second Cold War goals. The dividing of Americans serves to destabilise American unity and subsequently global hegemony, weakening Washington's global- superpower status and inhibiting European nations' sovereign security. Russian propaganda has demonised the Democrats and championed Trump's macho Traditionalist-Right character and values. This was to hinder the Biden-Harris electoral bid for presidency, paving way for Trump be re-elected. Trump's critical views of European nations' defence spending and trade could serve to embed American isolationism and even antagonism towards the EU, hindering European nations' military strength. Trump's apologetic rhetoric towards Putin could be exploited by Moscow to have a favourable mediator in the eventual Russo-Ukrainian peace negotiations. The promotion of Traditionalist-Right values online serves not only to divide Western societies but to also dismantle NATO, paving the way for Russian expansionist conflicts in Poland and the Baltic states in the distant future. The consequences of dynamics of the populist may cause a divide between NATO countries.

American isolationists argue that NATO should not fear a Russian invasion of NATO countries due to 'mutually assured destruction'. However, it is obvious that despite Poland and the Baltic states' NATO membership, Moscow still wants to cede them into Russia regardless. Russian propaganda and intervention in the populist divide are a means to dismantle the NATO alliance. Once the NATO alliance is dismantled via pro-isolationist propaganda, Russia's neighbours are thereafter vulnerable to Russian invasion. The growing 'Why die for Danzig?'-esque rhetoric is jeopardising European sovereignty, yet people are too preoccupied with the consumption of other Traditionalist-Right and Russian disinformation to realise it.

Civil War Tensions

Although Europe and Ukraine worried over the possibility of a second Trump term, Zelensky tried to persuade Trump to be on the same page regarding the Ukraine conflict. Kyiv grew wary of the possibility of a second Trump presidency due to Trump's history of Russian sympathies and growing isolationist rhetoric. If Trump were to win the 2024 elections, then Kyiv had to make efforts in ensuring that the American aid to Ukraine was not disrupted by the Presidential transition. In January 2024, Zelensky offered Trump to visit Kyiv to personally witness the devastation that the Russians had brought unto Ukraine in order to sway Trump to support the US lend-leasing programme to Ukraine. Although he declined Zelensky's offer, Donald Trump publicly stated that Ukraine was important to American interests on Truth social in April 2024. In the same post, Trump criticized the European NATO allies for allegedly spending disproportionately less than the US towards Ukraine's defence. Despite Trump's criticism towards the Europeans, Trump's recognition of Ukraine as geopolitically important to US interests was a positive shift in Trump's views of Ukraine. Shortly after the first assassination attempt on Trump's life, Zelensky held a "positive" phone-call with Trump. Despite this positive blip in Zelensky's relationship with Trump, it was shortly disintegrated near the pending months of the 2024 elections, as Trump publicly reversed his stance towards Ukraine to ensure that he secured votes from the American people, who were steadily becoming disillusioned from the War in Ukraine.

As the Presidential elections grew closer, the American civil tensions and divide was in full hysteria. American foreign policy was a highly discussed topic amongst the American population during the 2024 elections. American domestic and foreign investments became increasingly intertwined in political discussions and debates. During their electoral campaign, the Republican Party criticised the Democrats' over-spending towards nations abroad, as they did not translate to American welfare - rather it produced the opposite, as it diverted government finances away from domestic investments. This proved to be a very profound argument by the Republicans, as many middle class American citizens were suffering from economic hardships and began to believe that the Biden administration was prioritising Government spending abroad over the American people's welfare. Amid the civil tensions during the impending US presidential elections, Zelensky made a state visit to the USA in September 2024. Zelensky visited the presidential candidates Biden, Harris and Trump, to propose a 5-point "Victory Plan." The proposed peace plan entailed several security clauses between Ukraine and the West, that ensured that Russia would be deterred from invading Ukraine again after the war's conclusion. When Zelensky laid out his 5-point peace plan to Trump, Zelensky informed Trump of Russia's terror campaigns against civilian infrastructure and of Ukraine's recent gains in the Kursk Offensive, to instill Trump's sympathies and confidence towards the Ukrainians. Zelensky's US visit aimed to ensure continuity in American support towards Ukraine after the 2024 presidential elections were concluded. During his visit, Zelensky also visited a munitions factory in Pennsylvania that produced artillery ammunition to the Ukrainian armed forces, as a public stunt to convince the US to permit the Ukrainian use of Western long-range missiles against Russian infrastructure. Many Republicans, such as JD Vance and Eric Schmitt, to name a few, criticsed Zelensky's Pennsylvania stunt as a form of electoral interfering in the battleground state in support of the Democrat Party. Zelensky in the past had feuded with Vance over his "radical views" that the US should withdraw US assistance from Ukraine and reengage in dialogue with Moscow for the sake of American interests. The Zelensky-Vance feud exacerbated during Trump's second presidency, when Vance entered Vice Presidency, which facilitated the alteration of US-Ukraine relations.

On 13 July 2024, 20-year-old Thomas Matthew Crooks attempted to assassinate Donald Trump, during a Trump rally in Bethel Park, Pennsylvania. Trump narrowly avoided death, and several Trump supporters were injured, one being fatally shot. Crooks was killed by the American Secret Service sniper team. The attempted assassination was a shock to the American people and was condemned by Biden and the Democrats. Trump defiantly fist pumped the air and shouted 'fight!' to assure his audience that he was okay and courageous in face of the danger. Images of his defiance was used by Trump's team to boost Trump appeal during the electoral campaign. Incompetency from the Secret Service team allowed Crooks to position himself on the roof of The Home Depot store, in preparation to snipe Trump. An investigation as to why the Secret Service team were unable to prevent Crooks from positioning himself on roof led to the resignation of the director of the Secret Service team. Due to the populist divide dynamics, many Traditionalist-Right Americans speculated online that Biden ordered Crooks to assassinate his candidate rival.

Shortly after the Trump assassination attempt, Biden was forced to withdraw his presidential candidacy, after making countless blunders during the Biden-Trump presidential debate in 2024. During the debate, Biden displayed his inability to properly answer and understand questions and counterarguments directed towards him. Biden's blunders instigated fears from both Democrats peers and voters concerning Biden's cognitive ability to run the country or a second term, putting a dent in American confidence in voting for the Democrats. Biden resisted his peers' pleas to step down as candidate and frequently claimed to reporters that he had no intention of dropping out of the candidacy race. On 21 July 2024, Biden eventually gave in and dropped out of the presidential race. Kamala Harris stood in for the presidential candidacy.

On 15 September 2024, five days after the Harris-Trump presidential debate, a pro-Ukrainian activist, Ryan Routh, attempted to assassinate Donald Trump at the Trump International Golf Club in West Palm Beach. Routh had waited in a bush at the golf course for several hours in anticipation for Trump to arrive, intending to kill the former president with an SKS rifle. Routh failed at his attempt and fled the scene but was apprehended several hours after the incident. The Traditionalist-Right yet again believed the Democrats were behind the attack. However, Biden and Harris publicly condemned Routh's actions. The motives behind Routh's attack likely stemmed from his support of Ukraine and his belief that by assassinating Trump, the Republicans' chances of coming into power would diminish after losing their charismatic leader, ensuring that American lend-leasing to Ukraine continued.

Chapter Eleven

ENTER TRUMP

The Seventy-Six-Day Window

Following Trump's electoral victory in November 2024, the West began to prepare for the coming changing dynamics of the Ukraine situation. NATO leaders discussed alternative NATO proposals to ensure that the Ukraine continued to receive Western supplies, regardless of the shifting Trumpian dynamics of the Ukraine War.

Keir Starmer and Emmauel Macron discussed how to best put Ukraine in a strong position against Russia, before Trump entered presidency on Armistice Day. On 23 November 2024, the head of NATO, Mark Rutte, visited Trump in Florida to discuss foreign security and to understand Trump's approach to the Ukraine conflict.

On 15 November 2024, German Chancellor Olaf Scholz broke his two-year long silence with Putin and held a telephone call with him, demanding the Russian war in Ukraine come to an end. This telephone call was highly controversial among Germany's European allies as it displayed NATO weakness and open uncertainty with the changing geopolitical situation of the Ukraine War.

In response to the Scholz telephone call, Yuila Navalny, Alexei Navalny's wife and self-declared candidate for Russian presidency in the event that Putin loses his leadership role, protested in Berlin against Western reapproach with Putin. Zelensky described the Scholz telephone call as 'opening pandora's box' as it could result in a domino effect of NATO leaders telephoning Putin, reversing the effects of Western imposed isolation on Russia or relaxing NATO's Second Cold War policy against Russia. It also risked encouraging Western leaders to pursue a peace approach (likely involving a compromise to Russian demands) rather than continuing the lend-leasing approach.

During November 2024, the Russian army intensified its offensive efforts in the Donbas and made rapid gains in the Pokrovsk direction and in the Kurakhove-Velyka Novosilka direction. Putin intended to occupy all of the Donetsk and Luhansk oblasts before Trump entered presidency. This was so that when peace talks commenced, with Trump as mediator, Russia's terms for the annexation of the Donbas region would be more obtainable. Despite Russian army's intensification along the Donbas front, elite Ukrainian brigades were sent from the to the Kursk front. Elite troops were sent to hold onto the gains made in Kursk, especially after the halt in advances following Russia's first major Kursk counteroffensive in September 2024 and after the rapid Russian retaking of territories during the second Russian major Kursk counteroffensive in November 2024.

On 5 January 2025, it was reported that Ukrainian forces were attempting a significant push in the northern Sudzha settlements in Kursk. This push made little Ukrainian gains. Coincidentally, Russia launched its third major Kursk counteroffensive on the same day. The Ukrainian army launched a more successful 5-kilometre push in the south-east of Sudzha on 7 February 2025.

Zelensky wanted to hold onto the Kursk region as long as possible in order to use it as a bargaining chip in exchange for Russian occupied regions in the south or east of Ukraine. As the Trump inauguration (and prospects of the Ukrainian peace table) neared day by day, Putin realised that Ukrainian presence in Kursk undermined Russia's position in the peace talks. The Ukrainian army had to be pushed out of Russia to ensure that Zelensky could not use Kursk as an effective bargaining chip. This pressured the Russian counteroffensives in Kursk to become more intense and rapid in nature compared to the Russian army's slow and steady paced operations in the Donbas region. The gradual and cathartic advances in the Donbas ensure that Russian casualty rates remain lower than they would be had they advanced at a more rapid rate and ensure that the Russian army secures their rear and not face pockets of Ukrainian resistance. The swathing and rapid Kursk counteroffensives resulted in high Russian casualties, and it can be assumed that North Korean troops were specifically deployed to the Kursk region to soak up Russian casualties, negating Russian public outcry of Russian men being thrown to their deaths. The seventy-six-day window between Trump's electoral win and inauguration saw an intensification of the Ukrainian front lines, in the attempt for these countries to have an advantageous position at the peace table.

With Trump's electoral win, the Democrats began to intensify their aid provisions to Ukraine, in order to ensure that Ukraine would be in a strong position against the Russians in the event that Trump would withdraw support from Kyiv.

On 8 November 2024, Biden lifted the ban on American private companies being deployed in Ukraine. These American PMC contractors were not allowed to engage in direct combat against Russian forces or be stationed in the Russo-Ukrainian front lines. Contractors were permitted to be deployed far behind the front, repairing and maintaining Kyiv's Western supplied weapons and war machines. Prior to the PMC deployment to Ukraine policy, Ukraine had to transfer damaged Western supplied war vehicles to its Western neighbours in order for them to be repaired by NATO armies and factories who are familiar with the advanced vehicles and then be sent back to the Ukrainian front lines. The presence of Western contractors in Ukraine, therefore, saved time and money, with maintenance and repairing of Western military vehicles.

Biden gave in to his Western allies' pleads and approved Ukrainian use of American long-range missiles on Russian territory on 17 November 2024. Starmer and Macron approved Ukrainian use of Storm Shadow missiles on Russian territory shortly after. Biden's decision to approve Ukrainian use of long-range missiles in Russia was likely in response to North Korea's entry into the Ukraine War. It can be argued that Biden's rationale was that Ukraine used long-range missiles and caused as much damage to the Russia army's logistics as possible before Trump's inauguration. Trump had been vocal in not sending long-range missiles to Ukraine. Biden's gamble relied on Putin and Trump's friendly relations. Russia would not use serious escalatory actions against NATO in response to Biden's approval, as Russia only had to wait until Trump was inaugurated and persuade him to reverse Ukrainian use of Western long-range missiles on Russian territory.

Biden subsequently sent anti-personnel mines to Ukraine on the 20 November 2024, to inhibit future Russian advances after he left presidential office. Ukraine began using American ATCAMS against the Bryansk region on 20 November 2024. Six missiles were launched, but only one managed to successfully strike its target (military base), as the other five were shot down by the Russians. On 21 November 2024, Ukraine began using Strom Shadow missiles on Russian territory.

On 18 and 19 November 2024, the Germany-Finland and Lithuania-Sweden connected undersea cables were sabotaged. The Chinese cargo ship *Yi Peng 3* was initially suspected for the sabotage by the European authorities, as it was travelling from Russia through the Baltic Sea during the time of the double undersea cable sabotages. The cable sabotage was a great scare for European nations, as it was feasible that Russia was behind the attack, in response to Biden's approval of Ukrainian use of American long-range missiles against Russian territory.

Biden's gamble was a significant escalation of the Russo-NATO Second Cold War. Putin responded in several escalatory ways. On 19 November 2024, Putin revised Russia's nuclear doctrine by claiming that Russian nuclear weapons can be used if its sovereignty is attacked by a non-nuclear capable country that is supported by a nuclear capable country. Putin's revision of the Russian nuclear doctrine was another form of nuclear blackmail to persuade the West to reverse its approval of Ukrainian use of Western long-range missiles. If Putin's revision of the Russian nuclear doctrine were genuine, the world would have seen nuclear Armageddon on 20 November 2024.

Russia also threatened to attack the American Embassy in Kyiv using missiles, resulting in a temporary closing of the embassy on 20 November 2024. The Russian threat seemed to be a lie as the embassy was not attacked. Such direct threats towards NATO made many fear that NATO's Article 5 was bound to be enacted, as an attack on a NATO embassy can be considered a declaration of war.

On 21 November 2024, Ukraine claimed that Russia had used intercontinental missiles against Ukraine in the Dnipro. Ukraine's panic was met with scepticism by Western officials, as if it had been an intercontinental missile, Western nations would have detected the Russian attack and subsequently responded. If Russia had launched an intercontinental strike on Ukraine, it is likely that a subsequent exchange of nuclear strikes between NATO and Russia would have ensued. Shocking videos of the missile attack on the Dnipro circulated online. Putin later declared that the missile attack was the new Oreshnik hypersonic missile that Russia was testing. Putin continued that the Oreshnik missile attack was in response to the West's approval of Ukrainian use of long-range missiles.

No Prisoners: The New Trade War

In late December 2024, the newly elected American President Donald Trump publicly announced his desire to acquire Greenland, Canada and the Panama Canal to become more aligned with American hegemony. Trump later reaffirmed and justified that his desires were to combat encroaching Chinese and Russian influences and military presence during the Mar-a-Lago press conference on 7 January 2025. His justification claims are not unfounded, as Chinese and Russian presence in the Arctic had increased in 2024, endangering recognised Western sovereign rights in the region. During the press conference,

Trump remained ambiguous as to whether military force would be used to acquire them. Trump did, however, claim to use economic force to pressure the leaders of these lands to relinquish their rule of Greenland and the Panama Canal to Washington. Trump outright claimed that he would use tariffs against Denmark to pressure Copenhagen to give up Greenland. Military force was, therefore, a last resort if the economic pressures were to fail. Greenland and the Panama Canal contained economic value in which the US would revel if they were annexed or administered by Washington. Trump claimed that the Panama Canal needed to be required as external forces, such as Chinese investors were exploiting the economic surplus of the canal. Trump described Chinese presence in the Panama Canal as a form of occupation.

Trump had interests in Greenland during his first presidency. In 2022, Greenland was the site of NATO unity, as Denmark and Canada finally resolved their territorial dispute over the Hans Island peacefully. This served as a symbolic message to Putin, to show that territorial disputes should be finalised via peaceful diplomatic talks rather than military force. In 2025, Greenland became a source of internal NATO tensions. Greenland was a highly contentious claim, as Greenland is an autonomous region of the NATO country of Denmark. Denmark's prime minister repeatedly stated that Greenland was not for sale. Trump's strategically ambiguous threats towards Denmark's sovereignty made many reporters and observers fearful that a conflict between the US and Denmark would ensue as a result of the dispute. Regardless of whether Trump annexes Greenland via military or economic force against Denmark, Putin benefits from the NATO disarray. Trump's ambiguous threats led to an increase in Danish spending in the military and caused the EU to consider whether to send troops to Greenland as a form of deterrence to an American invasion.

Trump claimed that Canada would be annexed via economic force rather than via military conflict, but suggested that the American force was needed to stop gang supremacy in Mexico. American military intervention against the Mexican cartels had been a repeated proposal by Trump during Biden's presidency, as the cartels had improved and increased their human smuggling operations in the Mexican-American border, contributing to the US' migrant crisis. Regardless, Trump's desires over these provinces in the North American continent was an attempt to encroach on other nations' sovereignty and influences in order to establish a firmer American hegemony across the continent.

On 1 February 2025, Trump attempted to apply pressure on achieving his expansionist goals by demanding a 25 per cent tariff on Canadian and Mexican exports, inhibiting the neighbours' economy.

The following day, Canada and Mexico responded in kind by imposing 25 per cent tariffs on American businesses.

On 3 February, Mexico agreed to adhere to Trump's list of demands (such as the deployment the Mexican army on the Mexican side of the Mexican-American border to prevent migrant and drug smuggling into the US). Mexico's bending of the knee resulted in a temporary reversal of American imposed tariffs on the country. This left Canada without a diplomatic ally in Trump's tariff war. Judging by Trump's use of tariff threats on Mexico and Columbia, it is likely that Trump uses tariffs was a means of pressuring nations into abiding by his commands. For Canada's case, Trump's 25 per cent tariffs was a means to economically pressure Canada into accepting American annexation.

Following the 25 per cent tariffs on the US' northern and southern neighbours, Trump reiterated his past threats to apply a 25 per cent tariff on EU exports, resulting in rising tensions between the EU and Washington. Following Trump's threat on the EU, Trump reasoned that the UK could be spared from tariffs, due to his liking of the British prime minister. Starmer downplayed Trump's tariff threats to the UK and EU in a bid to maintain good relations and to avoid tariffs. Trump's tariff threats to the EU did, however, endanger British exports as the EU was a key British economic trading partner. Trump's tariff threats resulted in the EU stocks seeing a dramatic decline.

On 4 March 2025, despite Canada and Mexico's yielding, Washington initiated 25 per cent tariffs on Canada, Mexico and China. Justin Trudeau responded with retaliatory tariffs and publicly claimed that Trump's trade war with its neighbours served only to the benefit of the West's enemies. With the US-Canadian trade war commencing, former governor of the Bank of Canada and Bank of England, and now Prime Minister Mark Carney, Justin Trudeau's successor, vowed to beat the US in the trade war.

The Transatlantic Split

Trump's expansionist threats towards Canada and Greenland, accompanied by Trump's tariff threats and demands for NATO European nations to increase their GDP spending to 5 per cent into the Atlantic alliance, were the first official seeds of what appears to be an EU-American split. Initially, Trump appeared to take a pro-Ukraine stance and a tough attitude towards Russia. As he signed his memorandums, Trump claimed that if Russia failed to stop the war, the US would launch an international-wide sanctions campaign against Russia.

On 25 January 2025, Donald Trump and Elon Musk ordered a ninety-day freeze in USAID spending and then dissolved USAID on 30 January 2025 on grounds of mismanagement of American expenditure. This was condemned worldwide by NGOs as it froze international humanitarian expenditure, which put millions of lives at risk across the global south and in conflict zones. This completely cut Ukraine from lethal and humanitarian aid. Ukrainian officials negotiated with Washington to secure American resumption of American aid to Ukraine. Trump proposed that aid would continue in exchange for Ukraine's natural uranium and other rare minerals that would be used for nuclear, AI and infrastructure production. This served to Washington's interests as it would boost their economy and ensure that Russia would not obtain and extract them and later exchange them to Iran or China. This was met with optimism by Ukrainians as a huge portion of the rare minerals were under Russian occupation – American lethal aid would be required if Ukraine were to extract them.

In February 2025, Trump announced that all metal and steel imports entering the US would be tariffed by 25 per cent in March 2025. This further fuelled the European-American split. However, it would be on 12 February 2025 that the split began to reach a critical point.

On the same date, Trump held a ninety-minute telephone call with Vladimir Putin in an attempt to establish grounds for Ukrainian peace terms and to establish bilateral talks between American and Russian officials. The following day, a prisoner exchange occurred between the US and Russia, as a gesture of good will between the two countries.

Zelensky criticised the telephone call and demanded that Ukraine take part in the peace talks. Kyiv was deeply disturbed by Trump's telephone call as it was seen as informal peace talk negotiations. What further disturbed Kyiv and the EU was Trump's demand for Russia to be accepted back into the G7 and for there to be Ukrainian elections despite the country's war-time status. Such demands for Zelensky to hold elections can be commonly found in Russian propaganda, making Ukraine and its Western neighbours afraid that Trump's impressionability was being exploited by Putin to hinder the White House's perspective of Ukraine. Furthermore, American Secretary of Defense Pete Hegseth made it clear that Ukrainian ambitions for the return of pre-2014 borders and entry into NATO were unrealistic. This was met with pushback by NATO members and Keir Starmer counterargued Hegseth's pessimistic outlook on post-war Ukraine by claiming that Ukraine was on an irreversible path to NATO. Kyiv was very critical of Hegseth as they demanded American security guarantees in order to prevent a future Russian invasion of Ukraine. Hegseth's dismissal of Ukraine's path to NATO membership was a serious blunder on the US' part, as it undermined Kyiv's use of NATO membership as a bargaining chip at the peace table. To the shock of their European allies, the Republican administration dismissed Ukrainian NATO membership as non-negotiable, limiting Zelensky's hand at the peace table.

It is debatable whether Hegseth's dismissal of Ukrainian NATO membership bargaining chip was deliberate or not. If it was a deliberate act, then the Republican administration acknowledged Ukrainian entry into NATO was a strong bargaining chip against the Russian negotiators, but played down its significance as 'impossible' as part of Trump's appeasement approach to Russia during the peace negotiations in 2025. If it was not deliberate, then Hegseth's dismissal of Ukrainian NATO membership as a 'reality check' to the Europeans was a major political blunder as he did not understand the value of Ukrainian NATO membership as part of the peace negotiations. Whether deliberate or not, Hegseth's 'reality check' of Ukrainian NATO membership further exacerbated the emerging EU-American split.

Much to the chagrin of Ukraine and the EU, Russia and the US held official Ukrainian peace talks in Riyadh, Saudi Arabia, without Ukraine or European members being invited. Following Trump's telephone call, Russian officials claimed that they would reject any form of Ukrainian security guarantees or return of territory, worrying Kyiv and the EU. Objections needed to be established in the initial peace talks in order to prevent notions of Russia being handed absolute victory on a silver platter. American pushback against Russian demands under the Trump administration was an inconsiderable question.

At the same time as the American and Russian foreign ministers were preparing to go to Riyadh to hold Ukrainian peace talks, the sixty-first Munich summit was held in which Western leaders attended to discuss the security of Europe. Zelensky was furious with Trump's betrayal and briefly rejected his mineral extraction proposal. In Munich, Zelensky fearmongered his European peers by claiming that a European army was needed to counter the Russians as they were capable of launching an invasion into Europe by 2026. Zelensky utilised the EU's uncomfortableness of American isolationism as a means to make European NATO members apply pressure on the US for a security guarantee for Ukraine.

During the conference, the American Vice President J.D. Vance claimed that Europe's greatest threat was not Russia but the migrant crisis. Vance also criticised European nations for their violations of democratic processes, citing Germany's attempt to block the AfD from electoral process and Romania's decision to make Călin Georgescu's first round win null. He criticised how European nations attempted to attack the Traditionalist-Right's free speech. Vance's criticisms of European nations were initially met with silence and then open disagreement. Vance's concerns over freedom of speech are a valid discussion to be had in the Western world, but the timing and place of Vance's speech was miscalculated and inappropriate. Europeans interpreted Vance's criticism of Europe's freedom of speech limitations as the Republican administration's indication of pivoting the US away from Europe.

The timing of Vance's speech came after Trump's criticism of his European allies, anti-Ukraine rhetorics and apologetic approach to Russia, hence the European's criticisms of Vance's speech. The Munich summit was an inappropriate place for Vance to deliver his freedom of speech argument as the summit was about security. The out-of-pocket jab at speech laws at a security summit made Europeans interpret Vance's speech as an indication of Washington's desires to discontinue American security cooperation with Europe due to disagreements over Europe's domestic-ideological differences. Vance's dismissal of Russia as a security threat to Europe as an exaggeration and his insistence on migrants being the real security threat indicated to the Europeans that American security interests and ideological stances were fragmenting away from European.

Following Vance's speech, European leaders took Zelensky's word seriously and an emergency summit was held in Paris between European leader's concerning Ukraine and the US. After the summit Starmer announced that he was committed to send British troops into post-war Ukraine to ensure Ukraine's security. Starmer's commitment demonstrates the UK's pivot away from the US and towards the EU, despite strong historical ties with the US and Brexit.

The Riyadh talks were held on 18 February 2025 in which the American and Russian foreign ministers negotiated over the framework of the Ukrainian peace terms. Many EU members and Ukraine criticised the Riyadh talks as it sidelined Ukraine's input and terms. Following Marco Rubio's positive reception in the post-Riyadh talks, many speculated that Washington would dismiss Ukraine's bargaining chips and pressure Kyiv into signing an unfair peace treaty. Zelensky demanded for the EU and Turkey to be in subsequent peace talks alongside Ukraine, as the EU understood Ukraine's need for security guarantees and Erdoğan publicly demanded the return of Ukrainian territory. Zelensky further stated that he would not agree on any peace deal that was conceived without Ukrainian input.

Following the Riyadh talks, drama between the American and Ukrainian presidents ensued. On 19 February 2025, Trump publicly regurgitated Russian propaganda, claiming that Ukraine was at fault for the Russian invasion in 2022 of Ukraine. Zelensky responded in a kind manner, that it was a pity that Trump had fallen into a Russian disinformation bubble. Trump took to X (Twitter) and regurgitated further disinformation and insulted Zelensky's character. Trump ranted of how Zelensky was a dictator as he refused Ukrainian elections to take place. Trump indirectly accused Zelensky of money laundering and accused Zelensky of 'playing Biden like a fiddle'. He mocked Zelensky's career background as a comedian and accused Zelensky of prolonging the war to maintain power at the expense of 'MILLIONS' of Ukrainian lives. Trump also regurgitated Russian bot arguments that American expenditure into Ukraine was a waste as it did not concern American security.

US envoy Keith Kellogg and Zelensky held discussions following Trump's open disapproval of Zelensky in order to re-establish friendly dialogue. Despite Kellogg's initial hesitancy towards further American aid to Ukraine, Kellogg's stay in Ukraine made him realise the horrors that the Ukrainian people endured every day.

In March 2025, Russian complaints towards Kellogg's growing pro-Ukraine stance made Trump feel pressured to limit Kellogg's role as US envoy and he became increasingly excluded from high level mediation discussions.[105] Kellogg would be one of the few vocal supporters of Zelensky within the Republican government. Despite the positive discussion held between Kellogg and Zelensky, and Kellogg's appraisal of Zelensky as a leader, Trump continued to reiterate his beliefs of Zelensky and other Republican politicians, such as Musk, repeated Trump's false accusations of Zelensky's character. Zelensky responded to these false accusations by claiming that he was willing to step down as president in exchange for security guarantees for Ukraine. As Macron and Starmer were preparing to travel to Washington, Trump complained to *Fox News* reporters that the two European leaders never attempted to negotiate the peace settlements during the Biden administration. Trump's complaints of the lack of peace negotiating attempts by Macron and Starmer likely stemmed from Russian victimisation propaganda, which portray the West as an aggressive bloc.

On the third anniversary of Russia's invasion of Ukraine, the US alongside Russia, Belarus, North Korea and fourteen other countries, voted against the UN resolution of condemning Russia for the invasion of Ukraine. Sixty-five abstained from the resolution and ninety-three remained in favour. Some speculated that the US' decision to support Russia against global condemnation was a means to avoid bad faith towards the Russians during the Ukrainian peace talks.

Macron and Starmer visited Washington in February 2025, to persuade Trump to provide American backing for the Coalition of the Willing project. Trump gave evasive answers when questioned to comment on whether the US would respond or support UK if the British peacekeepers were attacked by the Russian army in the post-war Ukraine. Starmer reminded Trump that the UK had always stood by America's side during several conflicts throughout the years. Starmer had repeatedly emphasised the benefits of America and Britain backing each other during his visit to Washington. Trump openly claimed that he was not opposed to the idea of a peacekeeping force in post-war Ukraine. However, he argued that such a peacekeeping force should be exclusively comprised of European troops. Trump did not want American troops to be stationed in Ukraine and as of now only speculation can be used to explain why. One such speculation can be made that the US decision to not partake in the peacekeeping force was an isolationist policy. However, what can be said is that Washington's decision to not be involved in such a peacekeeping force indicates the US' shift in alignment and a display of the EU-America split.

In the Oval Office a reporter asked Trump if he still believed that Zelensky was a dictator and responded with 'Um … did I say that? I can't believe I said that.'[106] Trump backed down on his past 'dictator' accusations towards Zelensky in light of the Ukrainian agreement of rare minerals deal on 25 February 2025. Kellogg managed to restore the dialogue between Trump and Zelensky following the Trump-Zelensky row and the rare minerals deal was back on the table. However, Moscow tried to undermine Ukraine's attempts to re-establish American support by offering Washington their own rare minerals in Russia and in occupied Ukraine via joint Russo-American extraction projects. This was proposed by Sergey Lavrov during the Riyadh talks alongside other economic cooperation, such as the relaxation of American sanctions, and cooperation in access to the Arctic (a growing concern of the Russians during Trump's public announcement of expansionist desires over Greenland).

Regardless, Zelensky agreed to the minerals deal after several redrafts and visited Washington to sign the deal on 28 February 2025.

However, during the Oval Office press conference, Vance criticised Zelensky's desires for continued American lethal aid to Ukraine and claimed that diplomacy was the correct solution to the war. Zelensky corrected Vance's criticism, citing how diplomacy and agreed ceasefires during the Obama, Trump and Biden administrations failed to prevent Russian aggression on numerous occasions. Diplomacy, for which Vance advocated, proved to be a tried, tested and ineffective conduct. Zelensky told Vance that he should visit Ukraine so that he could understand the severity of Russia's aggression against Ukraine, to which Vance answered that he understood the severity via his consumption of news outlets and the media. Zelensky further explained that American assistance is needed to prevent the spread of Russian influence across the West and the US.

Zelensky's warnings of the spread of Russian influence across to the US irritated Trump, who then raised his voice claiming that Zelensky had no cards on the table and that Zelensky was 'gambling with world war three'. Humiliated by Zelensky's answer and exploiting Trump's irritation, Vance accused Zelensky of being disrespectful towards Trump and the Republican Party. Vance continued to accuse Zelensky of supporting the opposition Democratic Party during Zelensky's visit to the US in September 2024 and that he 'never said thank you once'. Trump began to adopt Vance's views that Zelensky was being disrespectful. Following the argument, Trump cancelled the minerals deal and Zelensky left the White House early.

On 2 March 2025, Starmer held a European summit in London to discuss prospects of sending peacekeeping-European troops to post-war Ukraine. Zelensky was invited but Slovakian and Hungarian representatives were excluded. Following the summit, Starmer publicly announced that he was setting up the Coalition of the Willing, which referred to European nations who were willing to participate in an international-peacekeeping force in post-war Ukraine. Starmer also announced that the UK was setting up munition factories to produce munitions for the Ukrainian army in Belfast to ensure that Ukraine would be capable of withstanding Russian aggression in the current and foreseeable wars with Russia. Starmer also pressed for American backing to pull of the Coalition of the Willing project, indicating that the Europeans were willing to reverse the EU-American split. Putin had repeatedly rejected the idea of sending a European peacekeeping force in Ukraine since its conception and during the Russo-American peace talks, Russia persisted that Moscow would not accept it as part of the peace terms. Moscow's staunchness on the matter was likely a means to pressure

Trump into rejecting the European-peacekeeping force by portraying the European peacekeepers in Ukraine idea as a jeopardy to the peace talks. Zelensky was thankful to the European leaders who had showed up to the summit and their attempts to subsequently insert Ukrainian security guarantees in the peace talks. Zelensky thanked Trump for the US' support for Ukraine in order to amend the debacle of 28 February that was instigated by Vance.

Zelensky publicly declared that he was ready to make amends and to sign the minerals deal, much to Trump's appeal. Despite this rapprochement, Vance mocked Europe's Coalition of the Willing, and Trump suspended American cyberattack efforts against Russian infrastructure on 4 March 2025.

On 6 March 2025, European leaders met in Brussels where they held talks concerning the need to become less dependent on American military provisions and boosting the EU's defence budget in order to operate independently. Prior to the summit, Macron publicly announced that he proposed the idea of sharing information with France's European allies on how to construct nuclear weapons as a means to deter Russian expansionism in the future. Macron bluntly stated that the US' allegiance to Europe was questionable, and steps must be made in the event that the US would abandon Europe. European nations, such as Germany, Denmark, the Baltic states and Poland, displayed their interest in Macron's proposed European nuclear-umbrella programme. With the nuclear American pillar of NATO in question, increased European acquirement of nuclear weapons was essential as an effective deterrent against Russian aggression.

On 15 March 2025, Starmer held a virtual meeting with nation leaders who were unofficially part of the Coalition of the Willing. The meeting included all EU members (except Hungary and Slovakia) and was also attended by the leaders of Australia, New Zealand, Canada, Ukraine and Mark Rutte. The meeting did not include President Trump. During this meeting, the leaders established groundwork for the Coalition of the Willing's stance in terms of supporting post-war Ukraine from future Russian aggression by investing in the enhancement of the Ukrainian army and prospects of sending in peacekeeping troops to the country. The leaders also discussed the Coalition of the Willing's proposed peace terms.

Trump's unpredictable mood swings towards Europe served as a detriment to Europe's security and talks of the establishment of an EU army resurfaced as a result to ambiguities over the US' continued support towards European defence. Trump voiced his desires to withdraw American presence from European countries, such as

Germany, and even the idea of withdrawal of American forces from NATO throughout the years (including during his second term).

On 8 April 2025, it was revealed that the American military was preparing to withdraw from the crucial military base and logistical hub in the Polish city of Rzeszów. The Europeans realised that it was very possible that their main defence spending and military ally would no longer have Europe's backing in the near future. Trump's anti-European foreign policies served as a louder wakeup call for Europe to remilitarise against Russian aggression, compared to the Russian invasion of Ukraine in 2022. In the early days of the EU-American split, numerous European countries made extensive measures to be combat ready against the Russian aggression as American withdrawal from the NATO alliance appeared incoming. Starmer diverted investment from British foreign policy into the British defence security. Many countries sought economic measures to fulfil its obligation to commit 5 per cent of their GDP into NATO. Poland underwent processes of implementing universal military training to all Polish men. Ideas of mandatory service and establishments of foreign legions were circulated as ideas towards resolving the Europeans' manpower shortages issue. Many European nations, in light of the EU-American split, ceased their purchases from American arms manufacturers in favour of a single European defence market.

Trump's emotional and impulsive switches and exploitative naïvety and impressionability served as a danger to the European and Ukrainian security partnerships with the US. The American U-turn in allegiances and Trump's global revolution has significantly shifted the global status quo, arguably even more so than the Russian invasion of Ukraine in 2022. Russian isolationism is nearing its end, and the EU will likely approach China as an economic partner to rely on instead of Trump's US. Trump has made a plethora of enemies across nearly all continents of the globe, which would further solidify the US' self-imposed isolationism, much to the benefit of China. Although the populist divide did cause geopolitical infighting within Europe during the onset of the Second Cold War, the cytokinesis of the West began with Trump's second entry into the White House.

The West is now divided into two blocs: the Traditionalist-Right bloc and the occidental powers. The occidental powers are a collective of nations whose goal is fighting the hybrid war against Russia's invasion of Ukraine. The occidental powers bloc consists of the UK, France, the Baltic states, Poland and other nations within the West. All Western nations who volunteered to participate in the Coalition of the Willing can be considered part of the occidental power. The

Traditionalist-Right bloc consists of nations which hold a strong nationalist-isolationist ideology. The bloc also reserves an anti-West/anti-NATO, isolationist/non-interventionist and anti-woke/anti-Progressivist-Left set of beliefs. These nations also contain Russian sympathies and retort Russian propaganda. This bloc consists of the US, Hungary, Slovakia and other political oppositionist parties, such as the AfD and Romanian Georgescu supporters. The populist divide and the subsequent cytokinesis of the West was partially engineered by Russian propaganda to cause Western infighting, harming their sovereignty security and enabling Russia to achieve its goals in Ukraine. With the US' pivot away from the EU, Europe's security is greatly in question and Moscow's Second Cold War goals become more feasible.

The American vote to elect Trump to presidential office has had a serious ripple effect across the globe. Although Trump wishes to see himself as a peacemaker, he has put peace in Ukraine and Palestine in jeopardy with his outlandish rhetorics. Trump's re-entry into the White House has boosted the Traditionalist-Right prestige, tolerability and confidence across the West. With Trump's adoption of American isolationism within the White House, the US has become an unpredictable power to both friendly and antagonistic nations. Trump's increasing alignment with Russia is likely a means to use Russia as an ally against China's goal of succeeding the US on the world stage as the ultimate global superpower. The EU-American split has further threatened Europe's stability and security. If the EU-American split were to derail at breaking point, the occidental powers will likely approach China as a means to maintain economic and military security in response to American isolationism and Russian aggression respectively.

Some may argue that Trump desires to re-establish Washington's relationship with Moscow to gain a new ally against Chinese superpower expansionism. Trump voiced his desires to 'un-unite' Russia from China, prior to his second term presidency.[107] Trump believed that an American-Russian coalition of sorts would strengthen its leveraging capabilities against Chinese economic global expansionism and Iran's nuclear weapons programme. This comes at the expense of the US' European allies' security.

Sibling Rivalries

As Trump framed the portrait of President Andrew Jackson in the Oval Office, Trump eyed for American expansion. Trump wanted to accomplish the annexation of Canada by imposing a series of tariffs on Canada to break their economy. The sovereignty of Canada was in jeopardy, causing a rise in anti-Americanism and a rise in Canadian patriotism amongst the Canadian public.

The Liberal Party of Canada, previously looked on with controversy due to Justin Trudeau's domestic and economic policies, now garnered much love for their deterministic vow to protect Canadian sovereignty. Mark Carney took advantage of the scene and called for a snap election. The cocky Conservative leader, Pierre Poilievre, knew that he was at a disadvantage due to his well-known philia towards Donald Trump, which served to undermine his support from Canadian voters during the snap Canadian elections in 2025. Carney won the elections in April 2025 and championed that Canada would not falter to American pressure. It should be noted that during the Canadian electoral campaign, Carney informed the Canadian people that Canada's economic and military relationship with the US was now over due to Trump's aggression against the country. The longstanding-American-Canadian relations reached a historic low point.

In March 2025, Carney visited Starmer and Macron in Paris to seek their nations' support for Canada's sovereignty and to pivot Canada away from the US and towards Europe.

Trump's expansionist desires for the US were of great disturbance to the EU, as it served to further the West's decohesion and complicated Europe's efforts to realign the US with Europe. Trump's continued coercion of Canada to become the fifty-first state of the US made the EU fear that Trump was also committed to annexing Greenland. Trump continued to publicly promise his American voters that he was pursuing the annexation of Greenland.

In late March 2025, Vance visited Greenland and failed to persuade Greenlanders to show up to his speech about why the US should acquire Greenland. This was a complete humiliation to the Republican administration and Denmark greatly condemned Vance's pleading to Greenlanders to show up for his speech. Various conducted surveys and studies found that an overwhelming majority of Greenlanders did not want Greenland to become part of the US. Vance retreated to the American military base in Greenland to assemble an audience of military personnel to listen to his speech. Vance criticised Denmark's weak naval security over Greenland against the increasing naval presence of China and Russia. Vance urged that American control over Greenland was required to ensure American security and deemed the Danish naval presence to be too ineffective and unreliable.

Security concerns was Washington's official justification for wanting to acquire Greenland. However, if security was a true concern, Washington could have asked Denmark permission to allow for an increase of American naval presence in Greenland and Denmark would have been more than willing to adhere to the request. Many have speculated that Trump wanted to acquire Greenland in order to have access to untapped natural resources that would emerge in the future following the reduction of ice in Greenland as a result of global warming. It can be argued that Trump feared Russia and China extracting the natural resources illegally from Greenland before the Americans and the Danish could acquire them. Regardless, Russia took Trump's annexation threats seriously and feared of greater American presence in the Arctic Sea. Moscow ordered an increasing military presence of Russia's northern territory in response. The Danish prime minister vowed to uphold Danish sovereignty and invested in naval spending to combat the growing American and Russian threats in the Arctic Sea.

In April 2025, Danish Chief of the Army Major General Peter H. Boysen made it known that Copenhagen was considering sending some brigades of the Danish army to West Ukraine to receive drone training from the Ukrainian army.[108] The Danish contemplation was likely made in response to Trump's threats and Russia's increasing presence in the Baltic Sea and Arctic Sea. The Danish reaction to American aggression led to the EU trying to de-escalate the inter-West tensions.

In May 2025, Danish authorities uncovered a secret American intelligence ring tasked with monitoring and spurring independence movements in Greenland. Denmark expressed its concerns over the US' aggressive policy. During the Trump administration, American propaganda and spy networks tried to interfere in the EU's political discourse to steer European electoral results in Washington's favour. Trump has promoted Traditionalist-Right parties from the Republic of Ireland to Romania in order to establish Traditionalist-Right governments in Europe, who are more aligned to Trump's ideology and political thinking.

Shortly after his electoral victory, on 5 November 2024, Trump and Putin held a telephone call in which Trump urged Putin to stop the conflict in Ukraine. Zelensky congratulated Trump on his electoral victory and Trump in return claimed that the US would continue to back Ukraine. Elon Musk was invited on the call and promised Zelensky that he would continue supplying Ukraine with Starlink satellites.

Trump appointed many prominent figures who supported him during the electoral campaign in 2024 to top governmental positions. As Biden was exiting the presidential office, he described Trump's inner circle as a formation of an American oligarchy. One such was Musk, who was appointed as head of government efficiency. Musk's intentions behind having a governmental position in the US has been met with scepticism by Westerners and Ukrainians. This was because Musk made various anti-Ukrainian remarks and actions publicly. Since Musk purchased Twitter in October 2022 and renamed it X, Russian bot activities have skyrocketed and had made various contacts with Russian officials.

In October 2022, Musk proposed a peace plan on X (Twitter) in which Ukraine recognises Crimea and the Donbas as Russian sovereignty and that Ukrainian ambitions for NATO membership should be abandoned. Musk had spread false information on X (Twitter) during the UK riots, which resulted in the riots becoming more violent and popular. Musk's appointment as head of government efficiency was, therefore, a frightful reality to Ukrainians and European nations, as Musk could use his position to divert funds away from Ukraine towards domestic issues.

The instalment of Musk as head of government efficiency worried many European leaders, as he opposed many of their domestic policies. British Prime Minister Keir Starmer's policies and politics were vehemently opposed by Elon Musk online. Musk briefly gave donations to Nigel Farage's Reform UK Party to skewer Starmer's political positioning in Parliament. Musk also displayed his support to the German right-wing political party AfD, further fuelling and instigating the populist divide in Europe. Musk's support of the AfD led to Musk being accused of electoral interference by European leaders. Musk's interferences, accompanied by rising migrant violence against native Germans, and political-economic disgruntlement, led to the AfD winning a second majority position in the German coalition government on 23 February 2025.

Musk's anti-Ukrainian sentiments and promotion of opposition right-wing parties in Europe has caused European leaders to be more unsure of the US' obligations of European security. Musk's unmoderated 'interferences' in German, British and European politics are not simply an act of an individual, rather a politician of the American Republican Party. Many speculate that Musk's promotion of right-wing parties in Europe is a Republican effort to align Europe with the Traditionalist-Right ideology of the Trump White House. In doing so, it would contribute to European alignment with the US, strengthening American influence in a much-divided Europe. Musk's intervention in European electoral processes can be considered building blocks towards the EU-American split.

It is known that Trump has supported European Traditionalist-Right leaders and parties in the past, such as Orban and displayed his willingness to give full backing to the controversial Traditionalist-Right leaning UFC fighter Conor McGregor's fight for Irish presidency in March 2025, much to the chagrin of Irish politicians.

Although McGregor's American-backed 'make Ireland great again' campaign faltered in the Republic of Ireland, it managed to interfere with Irish political discourse about immigration and the EU, leading some Irish right-wing parties to adopt McGregor's political takes in order to gain support. Trump failed to bring McGregor to presidency but did succeed in persuading some Irishmen to adopt the US' Traditionalist-Right thinking. Europe cracked down on far-right political parties in an attempt to prevent the emergence of a Traditionalist-Right bloc within Europe.

In February 2025, Vance visited the AfD as an act of solidarity during the German elections. In February 2025, the Trump administration pressured Romania to lift the house arrest charges on the very popular Traditionalist-Right online influencer Andrew Tate. Immediately following the reversal of his house arrest, Tate fled to the US. Trump likely pressured Romania in order for Tate to regain popularity in the US and spread his Traditionalist-Right thinking in a more effective manner outside of his house in Romania in order to convert more Americans and Westerners into the Traditionalist-Right ideology, which is more aligned to Trump's political and personal thinking.

In February 2025, the Romanian far right-wing leader right-wing leader Călin Georgescu was arrested by Romanian authorities due to his suspected connections with the Romanian mercenary, Horatiu Potra, who was amassing an illegal weapons stache in Romania. The Romanian authorities suspected that Georgescu was planning to violently overthrow the Romanian government with the aid of Potra and his gang of mercenaries. Romanian authorities had discovered the weapons cache and arrested several Romanians in March 2025. It is well known that Potra has friendly relations with Russia and publicly opposes Romanian support to Ukraine. It has been discovered that 800 TikTok accounts, linked to Russia, were promoting Georgescu's electoral campaign in 2024. Georgescu's arrest was condemned by Washington who viewed the arrest as political repression of the Romanian right-wing movement, breaching Romanian democracy. Georgescu's arrest also came as a shock to his supporters who demonstrated in the streets of Bucharest in the their thousands for his release and in protest against Romanian infringement on democracy. Georgescu was subsequently barred from participating in the Romanian electoral processes on 7 March 2025.

In April 2025, the French Traditionalist-Right right-wing Marine Le Pen was charged guilty for with embezzlement of EU finances and was banned from running for office for five years – disqualifying her from the French presidential elections in 2027. Le Pen publicly continued to plead innocent to the charges. Trump's team lambasted the charges and accused the French court of being hosted by the radical left who conspired to oust Le Pen from political power. Trump compared Le Pen's trial to his own, claiming it was a political witch hunt aimed at curbing Traditionalist-Right freedom of speech. Viktor Orban tweeted, '*Je Suis Marine*' in solidarity with Le Pen. This cascaded numerous Traditionalist-Right leaders to show solidarity with Le Pen, calling the trial an act of political suppression. The '*Je Suis Marine*' movement aimed to portray the Traditionalist-Right as a victim of political repression to garner global sympathy, whilst diverting public attention from their controversies and crimes. Even Putin condemned the Le Pen verdict.

The Traditionalist-Right bloc reacted similarly with German authorities designating the AfD a far-right wing political party known for their connections with Moscow, as an extremist organisation. Vance condemned the designation, as 20 per cent of Germans had voted for the AfD (mostly from eastern Germany). Rubio and Vance called this verdict an act of tyranny and an act which divided Germany into two political camps, quite like during the First Cold War. The AfD and Le Pen's party were becoming increasingly popular in Europe and possessed a real challenge to the current European governments. The Traditionalist-Right have been a major concern for the EU due to their general alignment with Russia. However, it can be argued that due to the Trump administration publicly backing these parties to win their respective elections, European leaders felt obliged to take them down before they had garnered serious momentum from Washington's backing. It was in the interests of the occidental powers for the Traditionalist-Right to be kept at bay. This was because if a Traditionalist-Right bloc was to emerge in Europe, it would undermine the formation of the EU and NATO. The Traditionalist-Right groups pressure current leaders to oppose their country's financial obligation abroad. This could result in said countries to voluntarily exit from various international organisations. If Traditionalist-Right political groups manage to enter power across Europe, this would increase chances of European countries exiting international organisations, such as the European Union. This, in turn, would contribute to the redundancy and eventual collapse of the EU and NATO.

During this period of tension, Trump released a plethora of tariffs on the EU and other Western allies. Trump enacted substantial tariffs on countries as a means to pressure them into accepting Washington demands for a substantial reduction of their tariffing of American imports. In March 2025, the aluminium tariffs came into effect and the EU responded by threatening to enact counter tariffs on American goods. In response, Trump threatened to put 200 per cent tariffs on European wine and beer and also implemented 25 per cent tariffs on car manufacturing goods, which were aimed towards Canada and the EU. Germany expressed their concerns and the EU began to plan for counter tariff measures. The head of the EU, Ursula von der Leyen, realising the US as both an unreliable economic and military partner, began to look towards China and India to strengthen its economic ties with the Asian superpowers. Von der Leyen looked past the political and ideological differences between India and China, to ensure the EU would cope with the American tariffs. Many European leaders have, in response to the EU-American split, realised that China is not a direct threat to European security and so was more willing to engage with Beijing as a means of compensating for the foreseeable loss of American trade.

Washington's tariffs against the UK were noticeably lower than the EU and Trump voiced his desires to enact a trade deal with the UK early on during the trade war. Starmer was rather quiet during the initial onset and uproar of the US-EU trade war and later voiced that the UK would not be engaging in a trade war with the US. It is likely that Trump's favouritism towards the UK was a means of swaying them into the American camp of the US-EU split.

Despite Trump's success in convincing Starmer to accept a UK-US trade deal in May 2025, Trump failed to sway the UK to the US camp. In the backdrop of the US-EU trade war, Trump had interfered in European political discourse, enacted controversial domestic policies that clashed with Starmer's ideological thinking and, most importantly, criticised Zelensky and cosied up to Putin during the peace negotiations in 2025. For these reasons, London did not view the US as a reliable ally and so entrenched itself with the EU.

Vance and Witkoff's aggressive public dismissal of Starmer's Coalition of the Willing project, let alone Musk's efforts to remove Starmer from power, served to further embed the UK's alignment with the EU during the US-EU split. Following the signing of the US-UK trade deal, Starmer declared that the UK would invest more in its trade relations with the EU. Starmer strengthened the UK's ties with the EU over the migrant crisis and the Coalition of the Willing's stance over Ukrainian peace terms. In a sense, Starmer enacted a policy of soft return to the EU. This soft-return policy saw the UK increase its trade and security cooperations with Europe without the UK officially returning back into the EU.

On 2 April 2025, Trump signed an executive order to enact reciprocal tariffs on all international exports coming to the US. This was hard felt especially in Asia, where the tariff demand was exceptionally high. Although the UK and the EU received comparably lower tariffs, it was still a major blow to the European countries. A couple of days later, Trump announced a ninety-day postponement of the reciprocal tariffs, allowing for countries across the globe to contact Washington to offer their trade deals in an effort to reduce or avoid American tariffs. The EU was no exception and paused their retaliatory tariffs on American imports to allow for EU-US trade negotiations to commence without back-and-forth tariffs disrupting the trade negotiation processes. As the negotiations were undergoing, EU diplomats continued to finalise their EU tariff countermeasures and attempted to rally a counter-Trump tariff bloc with their allies in the Indo-Pacific.[109]

Peace Within Twenty-Four Hours

Trump publicly claimed that he would like to be remembered as a peacemaker.[110] A modest title of remembrance, but many worried that Trump's desire for peace in Ukraine would not be a just peace or one that would ignore the potential ramifications of the war in Ukraine, for the sake of ending the US' obligations to Ukraine and reopening Washington's relations with Moscow.

As mentioned in the previous section, Putin has exploited Trump's peace-making desires to push for favourable peace terms, such as conceding all 'annexed' Ukrainian territories in the east and south, and for there to be no Ukrainian security guarantees of any kind. Putin's unflinching demands were seen as a hurdle to Trump's 'peacekeeping' image, and it was feared that instead of confronting Putin's unjust terms, Trump pressured Kyiv into accepting them.

With growing anti-Americanism and anti-Trumpism rhetoric circulating in the West, many observers feared that Trump would simply allow Putin to achieve his goals in both the Ukraine and the Second Cold Wars. Online users accused Trump of being a 'Russian asset' for his apologetic attitude towards Russia. Some believed that Trump's Russian sympathies and geopolitical ignorance was being exploited by Putin to dupe Trump into unknowingly leverage Russian peace terms. The Republican Party's ignorance of Ukrainian affairs can be seen in Steve Witkoff's interview with Tucker Carlson. The American envoy explained that the Ukrainian people in the Donbas, Crimea and other Russian-occupied places have displayed their desires to be integrated into Russia and cited 'referendums' that had taken place in Russian occupied Ukraine in September 2022 as evidence of this.[111]

Witkoff's improper understanding of Russian 'democracy' and how Moscow pressured the occupied-Ukrainian voters into voting in favour of annexation, displays the Republican Party's blind eye towards Moscow's repressive and corrupt democratic systems and processes. The Trump administration knowingly or unknowingly chose to overlook how these 'referendums' in occupied Ukrainian territories do not actually reflect the Ukrainians' desire to be annexed and how they are a very direct and unapologetic product of Russian interference. In February 2025, Witkoff claimed that he struck up a personnel friendship with Putin.[112] Like Trump, Putin exploited Witkoff's naïvety, ignorance and friendliness to warp the envoy's understanding of the conflict to a pro-Russian standpoint.

On 5 March 2025, Trump suspended both military aid and intelligence sharing to Ukraine. This was a draconian and arbitrary means to pressure Kyiv to accept the US brokered 30 day ceasefire between Ukraine and Russia. The Trump administration's policymaking was met with criticisms by the EU and reduced Ukrainian soldiers' morale and life expectancy. The American intelligence cut was immediately felt in Ukraine, as Ukraine no longer received American warnings of incoming Russian air strikes, causing unnecessary excess deaths of civilians and late air warning sirens. Exploiting the American intelligence cut off, Russia launched its fourth major Kursk counteroffensive on 7 March 2025, attacking the Ukrainians' rear. The surprise attack utilised the Avdiivka tactic of subterranean manoeuvring, endangered the Ukrainian army's logistics and put the Ukrainian soldiers stationed in the city of Sudzha at risk of encirclement. Russian forces made significant and simultaneous gains in the northern Kursk front line, engulfing the Ukrainian forces into a tight salient. It can be argued that Trump's closing off of Ukrainian aid was a means to pressure Zelensky into signing the minerals deal whether Kyiv wanted to or not. However, Trump later realised the unnecessary deaths that the American intelligence cut off caused and later openly threatened Russia with further tariffs and sanctions if the Russian army continued to inflict excess Ukrainian casualties. On 12 and 13 March 2025, Russia retook the city of Sudzha, undermining Kyiv's 'Kursk bargaining chip'.

In light of the American cut off, Musk boasted on X (Twitter) that if Starlink were to be cut off from the Ukrainians, the Ukrainian front would collapse. Polish Minister of Foreign Affairs Radosław Sikorski interpreted the tweet as a threat to Kyiv and countered Musk's tweet by saying that Poland was paying millions for Starlink to be operating in Ukraine and that a cut off would be unlawful. Rubio and Musk countered Sikorski's argument by berating him and claiming that he was spreading false information. Ukrainian morale was low after it had appeared that the Americans were boastfully abandoning Ukraine to Russian aggression online. However, on 12 March 2025, after a meeting in Saudi Arabia, Zelensky agreed to Trump's thirty-day ceasefire deal. The agreement led to the reversal of the American cut off and put global pressure in Putin to do the same.

On 13 March, Putin claimed that he was willing to agree to a ceasefire but also claimed that issues needed to be addressed, such as what to do with the Ukrainian forces encircled in Sudzha (which later turned out to be a lie that Trump believed in). Putin's hesitancy in the ceasefire served to stall any ceasefire processes and pressures whilst the Russian army's fourth Kursk counteroffensive was in full swing. The façade behind the hesitancy also served to alleviate international pressure into agreeing to the ceasefire proposal.

By 17 March 2025, the Ukrainian army began to make a partial withdrawal to southern Kursk, and it was reported that the Russian army began to make incursions into the Sumy oblast. Despite Russia's incursions into the Sumy oblast, Trump did not impose sanctions on Russia for its continuous 'pounding' of the Ukrainian army.

By 26 April 2025, the Russian forces had liberated the last slither of land that the Ukrainians held in Kursk.

Beginning on 19 March 2025, the Ukrainian army launched a limited incursion into the Belgorod region, as a means to divert Russian troops away from the collapsing Kursk front and to compensate for the losses in the Kursk region. After a telephone call with Trump on 19 March, Putin agreed to a limited thirty-day ceasefire on energy infrastructure targeting. The following day, Trump and Zelensky held a telephone call discussing prospects of American ownership of certain Ukrainian power plants, including the Zaporozhe Nuclear Power Plant. Although Zelensky was publicly against American ownership of the Zaporozhe Nuclear Power Plant, the loss of the Kursk Nuclear Power Plant made Zelensky reason that the Zaporozhe Nuclear Power Plant could only be wrestled out of Russian hands if the Americans were to own it or have some sort of cooperative hold on it. The riches that the nuclear power plant possessed would give a strong incentive for the individuals within the Republican Party to wrestle the Zaporozhe Nuclear Power Plant out of Russia's hands during the peace talks. Trump made it clear that it was in Washington's interests for Ukraine to be capable of paying back its debt to the American lend-leasing programme.

American control over Ukrainian nuclear power plants would ensure that the Ukrainians would pay their debts to Washington, despite the economic plight of post-war Ukraine. The American-Ukrainian minerals deal also serves this purpose.

In March 2025, Trump sought an energy infrastructure and Black Sea ceasefire agreements between Ukraine and Russia. During energy infrastructure ceasefire talks, Russian and Ukrainian air attacks on Ukrainian and Russian infrastructure intensified.

On 19 March 2025, the energy infrastructure ceasefire was agreed. However, Russia continued striking Ukrainian energy infrastructure on a lower intensity, thereafter, violating the energy infrastructure ceasefire. The failures of the energy infrastructure ceasefire led to both parties refusing to renew the ceasefire in April 2025. After the failed energy infrastructure ceasefire, which was mistakenly deemed a success by the Republicans, ceasefire negotiations in the Black Sea theatre commenced in late March 2025.

Talks were tedious and prolonged, but Zelensky accepted the Black Sea ceasefire deal proposed by Trump. Putin however, refrained from signing the deal. Putin claimed that Moscow would accept the ceasefire proposal if both the US and Ukraine accepted the following terms: the alleviate of American sanctions on Russia, for there to be a new presidential election in Ukraine and for the removal of the 'illegitimate' Zelensky from presidential power. Trump was infuriated by Putin's constant demands and refusal to sign the ceasefire agreement. After a furious telephone call with Putin on 30 March 2025, Trump threatened to increase tariffs on Russian oil exports if Moscow did not sign the Black Sea ceasefire deal. Within the same breath and red from his humiliation with the ceasefires, Trump also gave an ambiguous warning to Zelensky of what would come if the minerals deal was not signed.

In April 2025, the Republican Party was split on how to secure peace in Ukraine. An idea championed by Witkoff was to allow Russia to annex the four provinces under its occupation. However, Kellogg was vehemently against Witkoff's idea. The Witkoff and the Kellogg camps within the Republican Party argued over what the post-war Ukraine should look like, and a schism of sorts ensued between the negotiators. Anonymous Republican politicians admitted to *Reuters* that there was confusion amongst themselves as to what Washington's take on Ukrainian peace terms was, inhibiting their duty to pursue Washington's input on the Ukrainian peace efforts.[113] The schism between the Republican negotiators suggests that Trump never had a clear, concise and committed plan as to how to accomplish his 'twenty-four hour' peace plan.

Russia's genocidal pacification campaign in occupied Ukraine would be greatly enhanced if Washington were to adhere to Witkoff's ideas of allowing Russian annexation of occupied Ukraine and to recognise Crimea as Russian territory. Some Republican negotiators, like Witkoff, perceive the rigged Crimean and Donbas referendums as legitimate-voter input and so believe it to be righteous to integrate these regions into Russia and officially recognise it as such. For Washington to allow a continued Russian occupation in the eastern and southern oblasts of post-war Ukraine, even if temporarily, would serve to benefit Moscow's Russification of Ukrainian territories. The deportations of Ukrainian children and the massacres of Ukrainian civilians are a means of Russifying the Ukrainian populations and to deter Ukrainian violent rejections against Russian rule respectively.

By Russifying and terrorising the ethnically and linguistically mixed Russo-Ukrainian populations of eastern and southern Ukraine, Russia could expand Russian territory without facing a prolonged insurgency conflict after the Ukraine War. Once Moscow completes its Russification programme in the occupied lands of Ukraine, the Ukrainian population there would reject being reintegrated into Ukrainian sovereignty regardless of whether the Russian occupation was supposed to be temporary or permanent. The Russian genocide of the Ukrainian people is a means to permanently integrate eastern and southern Ukraine into Russian sovereignty.

During this period of Trump's attempts in resolving the Ukrainian conflict, numerous reports indicated that Russia was intensifying its Russification campaign in Crimea by encouraging its citizens from Russia proper to migrate to Crimea, boosting the ethnography of the peninsula to predominantly Russian. It can be argued that Moscow's Russification campaign is a foreign policy tool, exploiting the Republican schism and ignorance, to legitimise their claim over territories of Ukraine at the peace table. The genocide of Ukraine plays an important role in the Ukrainian peace talks.

In March 2025, the Trump administration stopped funding university departments' research into the Ukrainian genocide and withdrew the US from the EU's International Centre for the Prosecution of the Crime of Aggression Against Ukraine programme.[114] By intentionally overlooking and allowing the Russian annexation and pacification campaign of occupied Ukraine, Washington has become complicit of in the Ukrainian genocide.

In mid-April 2025, Marco Rubio and Donald Trump were frustrated by their inability to achieve peace in Ukraine and threatened to withdraw from the mediator role if both parties did not display commitment or desires to follow American peace terms and demands. Zelensky agreed to sign the American minerals deal and Putin announced a (farce) thirty-hour Easter ceasefire. Both served as political gestures that they wanted to continue the Ukrainian peace negotiations under American mediation.

Thereafter, Trump kept reiterating to reports that serious peace talks between Russia and Ukraine were imminent in the coming weeks. They did not materialise. Trump and Rubio's frustration with the peace negotiations displays the Republicans' realisation that the Ukrainian peace could not be achieved within a short timeframe as anticipated. The Ukraine conflict is complex, and a lengthy back and forth is required to ensure a definitive end to the conflict. If both parties are not satisfied with the treaty, a second Ukraine war is certain.

Trump's peace proposal expectations were too simplistic to meet reality. The prolonging nature of the peace negotiation is frustrating to the Republicans as it serves to undermine their face. During the 2024 Republican electoral campaign, Republican officials promised to end the war within a short timeframe but, in their eyes, the Russian and Ukrainian counterparts were hindering the Republicans' ability to carry out that promise. The Republicans' infighting over how to produce a fair deal display that, from the outset, they never conjured a clear plan on how Washington could negotiate both parties to agree on the US' suggested peace terms.

It is clear that during the years 2022 to 2024, the Republican Party spent too much time promising that they were going to end the war within twenty-four hours and less time actually sitting down and planning how to achieve peace in Ukraine. Trump attempted to save face with the American supporters and international leaders by blaming Zelensky and Putin for the failures of the Ukrainian peace negotiations in 2025.

BIBLIOGRAPHY

Primary Sources

ABC News, 'Russia Destroys 13,000 Tonnes of Ukrainian Grain Destined For Egypt and Romania', *ABC News*, 23 August 2023, https://www.abc.net.au/news/2023-08-23/russia-attacks-ukraine-port-and-school/102768324, consulted 5 May 2024

Ahmadi, A.A., 'Trump Administration Withdraws From Russian War Crime Investigations', *BBC News*, 19 March 2025, https://www.bbc.co.uk/news/articles/c0rzygdn8w2o, consulted 19 April 2025

Al-Jazeera, 'Freed Russian Arms Dealer Viktor Bout Back in Business: Report', *Al-Jazeera*, 7 October 2024, https://www.aljazeera.com/news/2024/10/7/freed-russian-arms-dealer-viktor-bout-back-in-business-report, consulted 11 October 2024

Al-Jazeera, 'Niger Becomes Hotbed of Disinformation After July 26 Coup', *Al-Jazeera*, 18 August 2023, https://www.aljazeera.com/news/2023/8/18/niger-becomes-hotbed-of-disinformation-after-july-26-coup, consulted 25 March 2024

Al-Monitor, 'Pentagon Floats Plan for Its Syrian Kurd Allies to Partner With Assad Against ISIS', *Al-Monitor*, 26 January 2024, https://www.al-monitor.com/originals/2024/01/pentagon-floats-plan-its-syrian-kurd-allies-partner-assad-against-isis, consulted 15 April 2024

Askew, Joshua, 'Disloyal Views: Lithuania Strips Russians of Residency Permits', *Euronews*, 18 July 2023, https://www.euronews.com/2023/07/18/disloyal-views-lithuania-strips-russians-residency-permits, consulted 6 March 2024

Banco, Erin, Slattery, Gram and Pamuk, Humeyra, 'Trump Envoys Embrace of Russian Demands Worries Republicans, US Allies', *Reuters*, 11 April 2025, https://www.reuters.com/world/trump-envoys-embrace-russian-demands-worries-republicans-us-allies-2025-04-11/, consulted 19 April 2025

Barnes, Joe and Rothwell, James, 'British Soldiers Helping Fire Ukrainian Missiles, Olaf Scholz Reveals', *The Telegraph*, 28 February 2024, https://www.telegraph.co.uk/world-news/2024/02/28/british-soldiers-help-ukraine-fire-missiles-olaf-scholz/, consulted 14 May 2025

Barnes, Julian E., 'Russia Pushes Long-Term Influence Operations Aimed at the US and Europe', *The New York Times*, August 25 2023, https://www.nytimes.com/2023/08/25/us/politics/russia-intelligence-propaganda.html, consulted 12 August 2024

Barseghyan, Arshaluys, 'Armenian Parliamentary Speaker Says Russia Is Waging "A Hybrid War" Against Armenia', *OC News*, 6 May 2025, https://oc-media.org/armenian-parliamentary-speaker-says-russia-is-waging-a-hybrid-war-against-armenia/, consulted 9 May 2025

Barseghyan, Arshaluys, 'Armenia Sending Three Citizens Accused of Organising Coup Attempt to Court', *OC News*, 27 February 2025, https://oc-media.org/armenia-sending-three-citizens-accused-of-organising-coup-attempt-to-court/, consulted 9 May 2025

BBC News, 'Nord Stream 2: Trump Approves Sanctions on Russia Gas Pipeline', *BBC News*, 21 December 2019, https://www.bbc.co.uk/news/world-europe-50875935, consulted 10 July 2024

Beale, Jonathan, 'Rogue Russian Pilot Tried to Shoot Down RAF Aircraft in 2022', *BBC News*, 19 September 2023, https://www.bbc.co.uk/news/uk-66798508, consulted 5 August 2024

Berman, Lazar, 'Egypt, Qatar: Strikes in Beirut and Tehran Harm Hostage Talks; Blinken: Ceasefire Vital', *Times of Israel*, 31 July 2024, https://www.timesofisrael.com/egypt-qatar-strikes-in-beirut-and-tehran-harm-hostage-talks-blinken-ceasefire-vital/, consulted 31 July 2024

Bertrand, Natasha and Lilli, Katie Bo, 'Russia Pulled Back Weapons Shipment to Houthis Amid US and Saudi Pressure', *CNN News*, 2 August 2024, https://edition.cnn.com/2024/08/02/politics/russia-weapons-houthis-saudi-arabia/index.html, consulted 19 March 2025

Biden, Joe, 'Remarks by President Biden and President Zelenskyy of Ukraine in Joint Press Conference', https://www.whitehouse.gov/briefing-room/speeches-remarks/2023/12/13/remarks-by-president-biden-and-president-zelenskyy-of-ukraine-in-joint-press-conference-2/, consulted 27 September 2024

Binley, Alex and Beale, Jonathan, '43,000 Troops Killed in War With Russia, Zelensky Says', *BBC News*, 8 December 2024, https://www.bbc.co.uk/news/articles/c5yv75nydy3o, consulted 18 December 2024

Birch, J., 'Border Disputes and Disputed Borders: Border Disputes and Disputed Borders in the Soviet Federal System', *Nationalities Papers*, 15:8 (1987), pp.43–70

Borger, Julian, 'Divers Used Chartered Yacht to Sabotage Nord Stream Pipelines – Report', *The Guardian*, 10 March 2023, https://www.theguardian.com/world/2023/mar/10/divers-used-chartered-yacht-to-sabotage-nord-stream-pipelines-report, consulted 10 July 2024

Bromfield, Adrain, 'US Prepared Syrian Rebel Group to Help Topple Bashar al-Assad', *The Telegraph*, 18 December 2024, https://web.archive.org/web/20241218220120/https://www.telegraph.co.uk/world-news/2024/12/18/us-prepared-syrian-rebel-group-to-help-topple-bashar-assad/, consulted 21 December 2024

Butenko, Victoria, Elbagir, Nima, Mezzofiore, Gianluca, Qiblawi, Tamara, Goodwin, Allegra, Carey, Andrew, Munsi, Pallabi, Zene, Mahamat Tahir, Arvanitidis, Barbara and Platt, Alex, 'Exclusive: Ukraine's Special Services "Likely" Behind Strikes on Wagner-Backed Forces in Sudan, a Ukrainian Military Source Says', *CNN News*, 20 September 2023, https://edition.cnn.com/2023/09/19/africa/ukraine-military-sudan-wagner-cmd-intl/index.html, consulted 7 March 2024

Camut, Nicolas, 'Russia Strikes Kyiv Amid Visit by African Leaders On Peace Mission', *Politico*, 16 June 2023, https://www.politico.eu/article/russia-strike-kyiv-africa-leader-visit-ukraine-war/, consulted 30 April 2024

Carlson, Tucker, 'Steve Witkoff's Critical Role in Negotiating Global Peace, and the Warmongers Trying to Stop Him', https://www.youtube.com/watch?v=acvu2LBumGo, consulted 22 March 2025

Carlson, Tucker, 'Tucker Carlson Live Tour Grand Finale With President Donald Trump LIVE in Glendale, AZ', https://www.youtube.com/watch?v=9J0cdq_0SPE, consulted 17 April 2025

Chul-hwan, Jung, 'Exclusive: Captured North Korean Soldiers Speak Out on Deployment to Russia', *Chosun*, 19 February 2025, https://www.chosun.com/english/north-korea-en/2025/02/19/2TUJ44HQBVGJNJFEA6XD2A4IPU/, consulted 10 March 2025

Clash Report, 'Video footage confirms presence of Ukrainian special forces in Sudan. Ukrainian special forces conduct operations in Sudan against the Russian Wagner PMC and their local allies from the Rapid Support Forces (RSF), who tried to stage a *coup d'état* in April.', X (Twitter), 6 October 2023, https://x.com/clashreport/status/1710241167751671844?ref_src=twsrc%5Etfw%7Ctwcamp%5Etweetembed%7Ctwterm%5E1710241167751671844%7Ctwgr%5E536d6cb1ecf01b0d96aedcc0df4a0ac9fb960d12%7Ctwcon%5Es1_&ref_url=https%3A%2F%2Fwww.bellingcat.com%2Fnews%2F2023%2F10%2F07%2Fexamining-videos-of-suspected-ukrainian-riflemen-in-sudan%2F, consulted 7 March 2024

Court, Elsa, 'Moscow Issues Protest Note to Yerevan After Armenian Delegation Visits Bucha', *Kyiv Independent*, 9 June 2024, https://kyivindependent.com/moscow-issues-protest-note-to-yerevan-after-armenian-delegation-visits-bucha/#:~:text=Russia's%20Foreign%20Ministry%20issued%20a,TASS%20reported%20on%20June%209, consulted 6 August 2024

Danish Defence, 'Comment on Danish Media Story About "Danish \soldiers to Ukraine"', Danish Defence, 16 April 2025, https://www.forsvaret.dk/en/news/2025/comment-on-danish-media-story/, consulted 2 May 2025

de Waal, Thomas, *Black Garden: Armenia and Azerbaijan Through Peace and War* (New York University Press, New York, US, 2013) de Waal, Thomas, 'The Nagorny-Karabagh Conflict in Its Fourth Decade' in de Waal, Thomas and Twickel, Nikolaus von, and Emerson, Michael (ed.), *Beyond Frozen Conflict: Scenarios for the Separatist Disputes of Eastern Europe* (Rowman and Littlefield International, London, 2020), pp.206–227

Elbagir, Nima, Gianluca Mezzofiore, Qiblawi, Tamara and Arvanitidis, Barbara, 'Exclusive: Evidence Emerges of Russia's Wagner Arming Militia Leader Battling Sudan's Army', *CNN News*, 21 April 2023, https://edition.cnn.com/2023/04/20/africa/wagner-sudan-russia-libya-intl/index.html, consulted 7 March 2024

Enab Baladi, 'Russia Establishes Third Military Post on Borders of Occupied Golan Heights', *Enab Baladi*, 2 April 2024, https://english.enabbaladi.net/archives/2024/04/russia-establishes-third-military-post-on-borders-of-occupied-golan-heights/, consulted 6 April 2024

Entous, Adam, 'The Secret History of the Ukraine War', *The New York Times*, 29 March 2025, https://archive.ph/0oEnY#selection-3735.293-37, consulted 30 March 2025

Ernst, Iulian, 'Moldova Rejects Ukraine's Offer to Seize Transnistria', *bne News*, 28 April 2022, https://www.intellinews.com/moldova-rejects-ukraine-s-offer-to-seize-transnistria-242742/, consulted 1 December 2024

Euronews, 'Germany Seeks Arrest of Ukrainian National for Nord Stream Blasts, Reports Claim', *Euronews*, 14 August 2024, https://www.euronews.com/my-europe/2024/08/14/germany-issues-first-arrest-warrant-over-nord-stream-pipeline-blasts-reports, consulted 17 August 2024

Evans, Gareth, 'Biden: "I Don't Know" If Netanyahu Is Trying to Sway US Election', *BBC News*, 5 October 2024, https://www.bbc.co.uk/news/articles/cje3zl0dq2ko, consulted 6 October 2024

Fabian, Emanuel, 'IDF Strikes Syria After Rocket Attack on North; 8 Syrian Soldiers Said killed', *Times of Israel*, 25 October 2023, https://www.timesofisrael.com/idf-strikes-syria-after-rocket-attack-on-north-8-syrian-soldiers-said-killed/, consulted 16 April 2024

Facoun, Benoit, 'US Intelligence Points to Wagner Plot Against Key Western Ally in Africa', *Wall Street Journal*, February 23 2023, https://www.wsj.com/articles/u-s-intelligence-points-to-wagner-plot-against-key-western-ally-in-africa-29867547, consulted 30 December 2024

Farmer, Ben, 'UAE Using Wagner Fighters to Smuggle Weapons Into Sudan', *The Telegraph*, 14 September 2024, https://www.telegraph.co.uk/world-news/2024/09/14/uae-wagner-group-fighters-weapons-sudanese-civil-war/, consulted, 29 March 2025

FOX 9 Minneapolis-St Paul, 'President Trump Wants to Be Remembered as a "Peacemaker"', https://www.youtube.com/watch?v=PjY6sfWzykU, consulted 13 March 2025

France24, 'NATO Member Turkey Says, "Process Is Under Way" To Join BRICS Nations', *France24*, 3 September 2024, https://www.france24.com/en/asia-pacific/20240903-nato-member-turkey-seeks-to-join-brics-nations-says-process-is-under-way, consulted 3 December 2024

Galeotti, Mark, *Putin's Wars: From Chechnya to Ukraine* (Osprey Publishing, Oxford, 2022)

Ganzeveld, Annika, Moore, Johanna, Braverman, Alexandra, Moorman, Carolyn, Rezaei, Ben, Campa, Kelly, Carillo, Anthony and Carl, Nicholas, 'Iran Update, October 25, 2024', Institute for the Study of War, 25 October 2024, https://www.understandingwar.org/backgrounder/iran-update-october-25-2024, consulted 27 October 2024

Gardner, Frank and Rawnsley, Jessica, 'Two Hungarians Detained Over Alleged Spy Plot in Ukraine', *BBC News*, 9 May 2025, https://www.bbc.co.uk/news/articles/cy8dx16q3nzo, consulted 9 May 2025

Geissler, Dominique, Bar, Dominik, Prollochs, Nicolas and Feurriegel, Stefan, 'Russian Propaganda on Social Media During the 2022 Invasion of Ukraine', EPJ Data Science, 12:35 (2023), https://epjdatascience.springeropen.com

Greenall, Robert, 'Transnistria: Ukraine Denies Attempt on Moldova Separatist Leader', *BBC News*, 9 March 2023, https://www.bbc.co.uk/news/world-europe-64901605, consulted 1 December 2024

Guien, Thomas, 'DOCUMENT LCI – *L'Ukraine combat la Russie en Afrique: les dessous d'une opération longtemps secrète*', *TF1 Info*, 21 March 2024, https://www.tf1info.fr/international/video-document-lci-comment-l-ukraine-combat-la-russie-et-wagner-en-afrique-2290212.html, consulted 1 April 2024

Haynes, Deborah, 'UK Defence Secretary Ben Wallace's "We Are Not Amazon" Jibe at Ukraine a Real Warning About the Risk of War Fatigue', *Sky News*, 13 July 2023, https://news.sky.com/story/uk-defence-secretary-ben-wallaces-we-are-not-amazon-jibe-at-ukraine-a-real-warning-about-the-risk-of-war-fatigue-12920142, consulted 12 August 2024

Hill, Evan and Horton, Alex, 'Ukraine Planned Attacks on Russian Forces in Syria, Leaked Document Shows', *The Washington Post*, 20 April 2023, https://www.washingtonpost.com/national-security/2023/04/20/russia-ukraine-war-syria-attacks/, consulted 16 April 2025

Inessa S., '"Men in Dark Suits" Rule the US – Putin on Deep State', https://www.youtube.com/watch?v=XP3D1sUSuzg, consulted 19 September 2024

Karimli, Ilham, 'Azerbaijani, Kazakh Presidents Watch China-Azerbaijan Container Train Arrival', *Caspian News*, 13 March 2024, https://caspiannews.com/news-detail/azerbaijani-kazakh-presidents-watch-china-azerbaijan-container-train-arrival-2024-3-12-0/, consulted 21 March 2024

Khrebet, Alexander, 'Zelensky Discusses Russia-Backed Groups With Sudan's Leader During Unplanned Meeting', *Kyiv Independent*, 23 September 2023, https://kyivindependent.com/zelensky-discusses-russia-backed-groups-with-sudans-leader-after-reported-ukrainian-attack-on-wagner/, consulted 7 March 2024

Kolsto, P., 'The New Russian Diaspora – An Identity of Its Own? Possible Identity Trajectories for Russians in the Former Soviet Republic', *Ethnic and Racial Studies*, 19:3 (1999), pp.609–639

Kolsto, P., 'The New Russian Diaspora: Minority Protection in the Soviet Successor States', *Journal of Piece Research*, 30:2 (1993), pp.197–217

Kyiv Independent, 'Ukrainian Soldiers on Capturing North Korean POW', https://www.youtube.com/watch?v=mCjbEm63POo, consulted 10 March 2025

Kyiv Post, 'EXCLUSIVE: Ukrainian Drone Footage Shows 'Destruction of Russian Mercenaries' in Sudan', https://www.youtube.com/watch?v=ekPM08w0WYI, consulted 7 March 2024

Kyiv Post, 'Russia Sends Interpreters and Mercenaries From Africa to Support Troops in Syria', *Kyiv Post*, 3 December 2024, https://www.kyivpost.com/post/43219, consulted 30 December 2024

Lanktree, Graham and Weizman, Jakob, 'Trump's Trade War Pushes EU Toward Pacific Free Traders', *Politico*, 11 May 2025, https://www.politico.eu/article/donald-trump-trade-war-eu-pacific-free-traders/, consulted 12 May 2025

Lariosa, Aaron-Matthew, 'UPDATED: Chinese Spy Ships Stalk US, Philippine and French Warships in South China Sea', *US Naval Institute*, 29 April 2024, https://news.usni.org/2024/04/29/chinese-spy-ship-live-stalks-u-s-philippine-and-french-warships-in-south-china-sea-interrupts-live-firedrill#:~:text=U.S.%2C%20Philippine%2C%20and%20French%20amphibs,Manila's%20largest%20annual%20military%20exercise, consulted 6 May 2024

Lazaroff, Tovah, 'US Trying to Overthrow Netanyahu's Government, Senior Israeli Official Says', *Times of Israel*, 12 March 2024, https://www.jpost.com/israel-news/article-791654, consulted 7 April 2024

Liboreiro, Jorge, 'EU Pauses Retaliatory Tariffs Against US to "Give Negotiations a Chance"', *Euronews*, 10 April 2025, https://www.euronews.com/my-europe/2025/04/10/eu-pauses-retaliatory-tariffs-against-us-to-give-negotiations-a-chance, consulted 12 May 2025

Lillis, Katie B., 'Newly Declassified US Intel Claims Russia is Laundering Propaganda Through Unwitting Westerners', *CNN News*, 26 August 2023, https://edition.cnn.com/2023/08/25/politics/us-intel-russia-propaganda/index.html, consulted 12 August 2024

LiveNOW from FOX, 'FULL: President Trump meets with British PM Starmer', https://www.youtube.com/watch?v=-QEck-mlFoE, consulted 2 March 2025

London Business School, 'Have the West's Sanctions Against Russia Been Effective?', *London Business School*, 9 April 2024, https://www.london.edu/news/the-impact-of-sanctions-against-russia-has-been-far-slower-than-anticipated, consulted 7 April 2024

Lovett, Ian. 'Ukraine Is Now Fighting Russia in Sudan', *Wall Street Journal*, 6 March 2024, https://www.wsj.com/world/ukraine-is-now-fighting-russia-in-sudan-87caf1d8, consulted 5 December 2024

Luvis, Jaroslav, 'Trump Will Not Give a Penny to Ukraine – Hungary PM Orban', *BBC News*, 11 March 2024, https://www.bbc.co.uk/news/world-europe-68533351, consulted 8 August 2024

Mackinnon, Amy, 'Belarus Is Abducting Ukrainian Children in Plain Sight', *Foreign Policy*, 11 August 2023, https://foreignpolicy.com/2023/08/11/belarus-abducting-deporting-ukrainian-children-social-media-networks-kyiv-minsk-camps-russia-war-donbas/, consulted 13 August 2024

MEMO: Middle Eastern Monitor, 'Saudi Arabia Prevented US Using Its Territories Strike Houthis, Official Says', *MEMO: Middle Eastern Monitor*, 22 March 2024, https://www.middleeastmonitor.com/20240322-saudi-arabia-prevented-us-using-its-territories-strike-houthis-official-says/, consulted 24 March 2024

Middle East Eye, 'Piers Morgan Pressures Israeli Spokesperson on Civilian Deaths in Gaza', https://www.youtube.com/watch?v=6podLdiCgaU, consulted 8 August 2024

Middle East Eye, 'Syria: US-Backed SDF "Open" to Working With Syrian Troops to Fight Off Turkey Invasion', *Middle East Eye*, 5 June 2022, https://www.middleeasteye.net/news/syria-sdf-open-working-syrian-troops-fight-turkey-invasion, consulted 12 May 2024

Militarnyi, 'Details of the Defense Intelligence of Ukraine Operation in Sudan Have Been Reported', *Militarnyi*, 7 March 2024, https://mil.in.ua/en/news/details-of-the-defense-intelligence-of-ukraine-operation-in-sudan-have-been-reported/, consulted 7 March 2024

Naranjo, José and Gutiérrez, Óscar, 'The US Is Losing Its Battle in the Sahel as Chad Joins Niger in Demanding Withdrawal of Military Personnel', *EL Pais*, 29 April 2024, https://english.elpais.com/international/2024-04-29/the-us-is-losing-its-battle-in-the-sahel-as-chad-joins-niger-in-demanding-withdrawal-of-military-personnel.html, consulted 1 December 2024

NATO, 'NATO Intercepted Russian Military Aircraft Over 300 Times in 2023', https://www.nato.int/cps/en/natohq/news_221598.htm?selectedLocale=en, consulted 5 August 2024

NATO, 'Relations With Ukraine', https://www.nato.int/cps/en/natohq/topics_37750.htm, consulted 23 July 2024

The New York Times, 'Leaked Pentagon Documents Reveal Secrets About Friends and Foes', *The New York Times*, 8 April 2023, https://www.nytimes.com/explain/2023/russia-ukraine-war-documents-leak, consulted 20 July 2024

Notes From Poland, 'NATO Chief Rejects Polish Proposal to Shoot Down Russian Missiles Over Ukraine', *Notes From Poland*, 15 July 2024, https://notesfrompoland.com/2024/07/15/nato-chief-rejects-polish-proposal-to-shoot-down-russian-missiles-over-ukraine/, consulted 1 August 2024

Orlova, Alisa, 'Ukraine Commandos Tried to Liberate Zaporizhzhia Nuclear Plant 3 Times, Budanov Says', *Kyiv Post*, 9 October 2023, https://www.kyivpost.com/post/22499, consulted 17 April 2024

Pancevski, Bojan, 'A Drunken Evening, a Rented Yacht: The Real Story of the Nord Stream Pipeline Sabotage', *Wall Street Journal*, 14 August 2024, https://www.wsj.com/world/europe/nord-stream-pipeline-explosion-real-story-da24839c, consulted 17 August 2024

Parker, Jessica and Gozzi, Laura, 'Ukraine War: Germany Under Pressure to Explain Intercepted Phone Call', *BBC News*, 4 March 2024, https://www.bbc.co.uk/news/world-europe-68467329, consulted 5 August 2024

Radio Free Europe, 'Wagner Troops In Belarus "Want To Go West" Into Poland, Lukashenka Quips During Meeting With Putin', *Radio Free Europe*, 23 July 2023, https://www.rferl.org/a/putin-lukashenka-wager poland/32515408.html, consulted 17 August 2024

Raghavan, Sudarsan, al-Batati, Saleh and Faucon, Benoit. 'US Accuses China of Helping the Houthis Target Their Attacks', *Wall Street Journal*, 18 April 2025, https://www.wsj.com/world/middle-east/u-s-accuses-china-of-helping-the-houthis-target-their-attacks-e56264da, consulted 14 May 2025

Reuters, 'Russia Says Military Plane Exposed to Coalition F-16s Guidance Systems Over Syria, TASS Reports', *Reuters*, 20 July 2023, https://www.reuters.com/world/russia-says-military-plane-exposed-coalition-f-16s-guidance-systems-over-syria-2023-07-20/, consulted 11 May 2024

Reuters, 'Trump Limits Kellogg's Role to Ukraine Envoy After Russian complaints', *Reuters*, 15 March 2025, https://www.reuters.com/world/us/trump-limits-kelloggs-role-ukraine-envoy-after-russian-complaints-2025-03-15/, consulted 19 April 2025

Reuters, 'Ukraine Evacuates 138 Civilians From Sudan', *Reuters*, 25 April 2023, https://www.reuters.com/world/ukraine-evacuates-138-civilians-sudan-2023-04-25/, consulted 7 March 2024

Reuters, 'Ukrainian Operatives Aided Syrian Rebels With Drones, *The Washington Post* Reports', *Reuters*, 11 December 2024, https://www.reuters.com/world/ukrainian-operatives-aided-syrian-rebels-with-drones-washington-post-reports-2024-12-11/, consulted 11 December 2024

Reuters, 'US Secretary of State Nominee Blinken Says Turkey Not Acting Like an Ally', *Reuters*, 20 January 2021, https://www.reuters.com/business/aerospace-defense/us-secretary-state-nominee-blinken-says-turkey-not-acting-like-an-ally-2021-01-20/, consulted 11 May 2024

Reuters, 'Yemen's Houthis Chief: Operations With Islamic Resistance in Iraq Against Israel Will Intensify', *Reuters*, 6 June 2024, https://www.reuters.com/world/middle-east/yemens-houthis-chief-operations-with-islamic-resistance-iraq-against-israel-will-2024-06-06/, consulted 8 July 2024

Rickett, Oscar and Amin, Mohammed, 'Sudan War: Russia Hedges Bets By Aiding Both Sides in Conflict', *Middle East Eye*, 6 May 2024, https://www.middleeasteye.net/news/russia-sudan-war-saf-rsf-hedges-bets-both-sides-support, consulted 1 March 2025

Rommen, Rebecca and Spirlet, Thibault, 'US Buys 81 Soviet-Era Combat Aircraft From Russia's Ally Costing on Average Less Than $20,000 Each, Report Says', *Business Insider*, 29 April 2024, https://www.businessinsider.

com/us-buys-81-soviet-fighter-jets-from-russian-ally-20k-2024
4#:~:text=US%20buys%2081%20Soviet%2Dera,than%20%2420%2C000%20
each%2C%20report%20says&text=The%20US%20has%20purchased%20
81,engaging%20more%20with%20Western%20nations, consulted 20
August 2024

Rutai, Lili, 'Why Is Viktor Orban Keeping the 100-Year-Old Treaty of Trianon
Alive?', *Radio Free Europe*, April 24 2024, https://www.rferl.org/a/
hungary-treaty-of-trianon-orban-fidesz-ethnic-hungarians/32919124.html,
consulted 8 August 2024

Schipani, Andres, Miller, Christopher, Ivanova, Polina and Cook, Chris,
'Russians and Ukrainians Help Train Same Side in Sudan's War', *Financial
Times*, 17 September 2024, https://www.ft.com/content/e581fc02-ef80-
4a00-bdf1-1be4b5e0a916, consulted 1 March 2025

Scottish Sun, The, 'Scots Mercenary Fighting for Vladimir Putin in Ukraine
Unmasked as Former Tennent's Brewery Worker', https://www.youtube.
com/watch?v=c2fiQtzIgbM, consulted 29 November 2024

Sharma, Ritu, 'Against Azerbaijan as Russia Gets Bogged Down In Ukraine
War', *Eurasian Times*, 9 October 2023, https://www.eurasiantimes.com/
france-joins-india-to-arm-armenia-against-azerbaijan/, consulted 13
December 2024

Sky News, 'Russia's Invasion of Ukraine Mapped – What Happened on Day
Seven', *Sky News*, 2 March 2022, https://news.sky.com/story/russias-
invasion-of-ukraine-mapped-what-happened-on-day-seven-12555754,
consulted 1 December 2024

Special Operations Forces of the Armed Forces of Ukraine, 'North Korean
Troops Went on the Assault: SSO Destroyed 18 Fighters in Kurshchyna',
https://t.me/ukr_sof/1370, consulted 10 March 2025

Stone, Mark, 'Trump Envoy Steve Witkoff Says He Has Developed a
"Friendship" With Putin', *Sky News*, 21 February 2025, https://news.
sky.com/story/trump-envoy-steve-witkoff-says-he-has-developed-a-
friendship-with-putin-13313676, consulted 22 May 2025

Suciu, Peter, 'The US Military Just Bought 81 Russian Jets (MiG-29
Fighters and Su-24 Bombers)', *National Interest*, 29 April 2024, https://
nationalinterest.org/blog/buzz/us-military-just-bought-81-russian-jets-
mig-29-fighters-and-su-24-bombers-210806, consulted 20 August 2024

Thorpe, Nick. 'War of Words Over Ukrainian POWs Handed to Hungary',
BBC News, 20 June 2023, https://www.bbc.co.uk/news/world-
europe-65959146, consulted 8 August 2024

The Times and *The Sunday Times*, 'US Serviceman Fights for Russia in
Ukraine', https://www.youtube.com/watch?v=HjRLWSEFlTk, consulted
29 November 2024

Times of Israel, 'Erdoğan: Over 1,000 Hamas Members Being Treated
in Hospitals in Turkey', *Times of Israel*, 13 May 2024, https://www.
timesofisrael.com/liveblog_entry/erdogan-over-1000-hamas-members-
being-treated-in-hospitals-in-turkey/#:~:text=Turkish%20President%20

Tayyip%20Erdogan%20says%20that%20more%20than%201,000, consulted 1 October 2024

Times of Israel, 'Netanyahu Says IDF Found "State-of-the-Art" Russian Arms in Hezbollah Bases', *Times of Israel*, 16 October 2024, https://www.timesofisrael.com/liveblog_entry/netanyahu-says-idf-found-state-of-the-art-russian-arms-in-hezbollah-bases/, consulted 27 October 2024

Turak, Natasha, '"Drone Wall" Against Russia: Six NATO Countries Announce Border Defense Plan', *CNBC*, May 27 2024, https://www.cnbc.com/2024/05/27/russia-drone-wall-six-nato-countries-announce-border-defense-plan.html, consulted 1 August 2024

Vernon, Will, 'Russian War Deserter Reveals War Secrets of Guarding Nuclear Base', *BBC News*, 26 November 2024, https://www.bbc.co.uk/news/articles/c9dl2pv0yj0o, consulted 2 December 2024

Walsh, Aoife, 'Turkey Halts Trade With Israel Over "Humanitarian Tragedy" in Gaza', *BBC News*, 3 May 2024, https://www.bbc.co.uk/news/world-middle-east-68945380#:~:text=Turkey%20has%20suspended%20all%20trade%20with%20Israel%20over,countries%20was%20worth%20almost%20%247bn%20%28%C2%A35.6bn%29%20last%20year, consulted 1 October 2024

Zakharchenko, Kateryna, 'EXCLUSIVE: Ukraine's HUR Special Forces Target Russian Drone Base in Syria', *Kyiv Post*, 16 September 2024, https://www.kyivpost.com/post/39074, consulted 19 September 2024

Zakharchenko, Kateryna, 'EXCLUSIVE VIDEO: Ukrainian Special Forces and Syrian Rebels Decimate Russian Mercenaries in Syria', *Kyiv Post*, 3 June 2024, https://www.kyivpost.com/post/33695, consulted 4 June 2024

Zakharchenko, Kateryna, 'Khartoum Gave Weapons to Kyiv So Zelensky Sent Ukrainian Special Forces to Sudan', *Kyiv Post*, 6 March 2024, https://www.kyivpost.com/post/29106, consulted 7 March 2024

Zakharchenko, Kateryna, 'Russian Forces Suffer Major Losses in Syria, Commander Fired as Hundreds Go Missing', *Kyiv Post*, 1 December 2024, https://www.kyivpost.com/post/43128, consulted 6 December 2024

Articles

Birch, J., 'Border Disputes and Disputed Borders: Border Disputes and Disputed Borders in the Soviet Federal System', *Nationalities Papers*, 15:8 (1987), pp.43–70

Geissler, Dominique, Bar, Dominik, Prollochs, Nicolas and Feurriegel, Stefan, 'Russian Propaganda on Social Media During the 2022 Invasion of Ukraine', EPJ Data Science, 12:35 (2023), https://epjdatascience.springeropen.com

Kolsto, P., 'The New Russian Diaspora – An Identity of Its Own? Possible Identity Trajectories for Russians in the Former Soviet Republic', *Ethnic and Racial Studies*, 19:3 (1999), pp.609–639

Kolsto, P., 'The New Russian Diaspora: Minority Protection in the Soviet Successor States', *Journal of Piece Research*, 30:2 (1993), pp.197–217

Books

de Waal, Thomas, *Black Garden: Armenia and Azerbaijan Through Peace and War* (New York University Press, New York, US, 2013)

de Waal, Thomas, 'The Nagorny-Karabagh Conflict in Its Fourth Decade' in de Waal, Thomas and Twickel, Nikolaus von, and Emerson, Michael (ed.), *Beyond Frozen Conflict: Scenarios for the Separatist Disputes of Eastern Europe* (Rowman and Littlefield International, London, 2020)

Galeotti, Mark, *Putin's Wars: From Chechnya to Ukraine* (Osprey Publishing, Oxford, 2022)

Illustrative Material

The author has endeavoured to locate all copyright holders and provide proper acknowledgments for illustrative material included in this book that is not his/her own. However, if a credit to any copyrighter holder has been omitted, please make yourself known to the publisher so that this may be corrected in any reprint or future edition.

Image 1:

https://commons.wikimedia.org/wiki/File:War_in_Ukraine_(2022)_en.png

Image 2:

https://commons.wikimedia.org/wiki/File:Moscow_Annexation_Ceremony_(free_image).png

Image 3:

https://commons.wikimedia.org/wiki/File:Ukrainian_soldier_removing_the_Russian_flag_from_Apanasovka,_during_the_Kursk_offensive.jpg

Image 4:

https://commons.wikimedia.org/wiki/File:Kyrylo_budanov_in_bakhmut_2.jpeg

Image 5:

https://commons.wikimedia.org/wiki/File:Armenian_Prime_Minister-_%E2%80%9CWe_must_move_steadily_towards_peace_with_Azerbaijan%E2%80%9D_-_53271624418.jpg

Image 6:

https://commons.wikimedia.org/wiki/File:Vladimir_Putin_and_Cyril_Ramaphosa_(2023-06-17).jpg

Image 7:

https://commons.wikimedia.org/wiki/File:Russian_mercenaries_in_CAR.jpg

Image 8:

https://commons.wikimedia.org/wiki/File:Russian_airbase_in_Syria_-_panoramio_(8).jpg

Image 9:

https://commons.wikimedia.org/wiki/File:Hamas_gunmen_storming_kibbutz_in_southern_Israel.jpg

Image 10:

https://commons.wikimedia.org/wiki/File:CENTCOM_12_January_2024-2.jpg

Image 11:

https://commons.wikimedia.org/wiki/File:9_dotted_line.png

Image 12:

https://commons.wikimedia.org/wiki/File:Chang%27e_6_mockup_at_IAC_2024_02.jpg

Image 13:

https://commons.wikimedia.org/wiki/File:Former_President_Donald_Trump_paying_respect_to_Corey_Comperatore_(53887491621).jpg

Image 14:

https://commons.wikimedia.org/wiki/File:Trump_Loses_Self-Control_During_Meeting_With_Zelensky,_28.02.2025.jpg

Image 15:

https://commons.wikimedia.org/wiki/File:United_Nations_General_Assembly_resolution_ES-11-7_vote.svg

Newspapers
ABC News
bne News
Chosun
EL Pais
Enab Baladi
Eurasian Times

Euronews
Financial Times
Guardian, The
Kyiv Independent
Kyiv Post
MEMO: Middle Eastern Monitor
Middle East Eye
New York Times, The
OC News
Politico
Reuters
Scottish Sun, The
Sunday Times, The
Telegraph, The
Times of Israel
Times, The,
Wall Street Journal
Washington Post, The

Radio Programmes
Radio Free Europe

Television Programmes
ABC News
Al-Jazeera
Al-Monitor
BBC News
Caspian News
CNBC
CNN News
Fox News
France24
Sky News
TF1 Info

Websites
ABC News: https://www.abc.net.au
Al-Jazeera: https://www.aljazeera.com/news

Al-Monitor: https://www.al-monitor.com
ABC News: https://www.abc.net.au/news
BBC News: https://www.bbc.co.uk/news
BBC Verify: https://www.bbc.co.uk/news
bne News: https://www.intellinews.com
Business Insider: https://www.businessinsider.com
Caspian News: https://caspiannews.com
Chosun: https://www.chosun.com
CNBC: https://www.cnbc.com
CNN News: https://edition.cnn.com
Danish Defence: https://www.forsvaret.dk
EPJ Data Science: https://epjdatascience.springeropen.com
EL Pais: https://english.elpais.com
Eurasian Times, https://www.eurasiantimes.com/
Euronews: https://www.euronews.com
Financial Times: https://www.ft.com
France24: https://www.france24.com
Guardian, The: https://www.theguardian.com
Institute for the Study of War: https://www.understandingwar.org
Kyiv Independent: https://kyivindependent.com
Kyiv Post: https://www.kyivpost.com
MEMO: Middle Eastern Monitor: https://www.middleeastmonitor.com
Middle East Eye: https://www.middleeasteye.net
New York Times, The: https://www.nytimes.com
OC News: https://oc-media.org
Politico: https://www.politico.eu
Radio Free Europe: https://www.rferl.org
Reuters: https://www.reuters.com
Sky News: https://news.sky.com
Telegraph, The: https://www.telegraph.co.uk
TF1 Info: https://www.tf1info.fr
Times of Israel: https://www.timesofisrael.com
US Naval Institute: https://news.usni.org
Wall Street Journal: https://www.wsj.com
Washington Post, The: https://www.washingtonpost.com
White House: https://www.whitehouse.gov/briefing-room
Wikimedia Commons: https://commons.wikimedia.org
X (Twitter): https://x.com
YouTube: https://www.youtube.com

NOTES

Chapter One: The Shaping of a New Cold War

1   Kolsto, P., 'The New Russian Diaspora – An Identity of Its Own? Possible Identity Trajectories for Russians in the Former Soviet Republic', *Ethnic and Racial Studies*, 19:3, (1999), p.616

2   Ibid, p.618

3   Galeotti, Mark, *Putin's Wars: From Chechnya to Ukraine* (Osprey Publishing, Oxford, 2022), p.70

4   Kolsto, P., 'The New Russian Diaspora: Minority Protection in the Soviet Successor States', *Journal of Piece Research*, 30:2, (1993), p.200

5   Askew, Joshua, 'Disloyal Views: Lithuania Strips Russians of Residency Permits', 18 July 2023, https://www.euronews.com/2023/07/18/disloyal-views-lithuania-strips-russians-residency-permits, consulted 6 March 2024

6   Vernon, Will, 'Russian War Deserter Reveals War Secrets of Guarding Nuclear Base', *BBC News*, 26 November 2024, https://www.bbc.co.uk/news/articles/c9dl2pv0yj0o, consulted 2 December 2024

Chapter Two: The Ukrainian War

7   Bailey, Riley, Barros, George, Kagan, Frederick W., Stepanenko, Kateryna and Williams, Madison, 'Russian Offensive Campaign Assessment, December [20]24' https://understandingwar.org/backgrounder/russian-offensive-campaign-assessment-december-24, consulted 17 April 2024

8   Orlova, Alisa, 'Ukraine Commandos Tried to Liberate Zaporizhzhia Nuclear Plant 3 Times, Budanov Says', *Kyiv Post*, 9 October 2023, https://www.kyivpost.com/post/22499, consulted 17 April 2024

Chapter Three: Pax-Europa in Peril

9   Rutai, Lili, 'Why Is Viktor Orban Keeping The 100-Year-Old Treaty Of Trianon Alive?', *Radio Free Europe*, 24 April 2024, https://www.rferl.org/a/hungary-treaty-of-trianon-orban-fidesz-ethnic-hungarians/32919124.html, consulted 8 August 2024

10   Thorpe, Nick, 'War of Words Over Ukrainian POWs Handed to Hungary', *BBC News*, 20 June 2023, https://www.bbc.co.uk/news/world-europe-65959146, consulted 8 August 2024

11   Gardner, Frank and Rawnsley, Jessica, 'Two Hungarians Detained Over Alleged Spy Plot in Ukraine', *BBC News*, 9 May 2025, https://www.bbc.co.uk/news/articles/cy8dx16q3nzo, consulted 9 May 2025

12   Luvis, Jaroslav, 'Trump Will Not Give a Penny to Ukraine – Hungary PM Orban', *BBC News*, 11 March 2024, https://www.bbc.co.uk/news/world-europe-68533351, consulted 8 August 2024

13   London Business School, 'Have the West's Sanctions Against Russia Been Effective?', London Business School, 9 April 2024, https://www.london.edu/news/the-impact-of-sanctions-against-russia-has-been-far-slower-than-anticipated, consulted 7 April 2024

14   *BBC News*, 'Nord Stream 2: Trump Approves Sanctions on Russia Gas Pipeline', *BBC News*, 21 December 2019, https://www.bbc.co.uk/news/world-europe-50875935, consulted 10 July 2024

15   Borger, Julian, 'Divers Used Chartered Yacht to Sabotage Nord Stream Pipelines – Report', *The Guardian*, 10 March 2023, https://www.theguardian.com/world/2023/mar/10/divers-used-chartered-yacht-to-sabotage-nord-stream-pipelines-report, consulted 10 July 2024

16   Pancevski, Bojan, 'A Drunken Evening, A Rented Yacht: The Real Story of the Nord Stream Pipeline Sabotage', *Wall Street Journal*, 14 August 2024, https://www.wsj.com/world/europe/nord-stream-pipeline-explosion-real-story-da24839c, consulted 17 August 2024

17   *Euronews*, 'Germany Seeks Arrest of Ukrainian National for Nord Stream Blasts, Reports Claim', *Euronews*, 14 August 2024, https://www.euronews.com/my-europe/2024/08/14/germany-issues-first-arrest-warrant-over-nord-stream-pipeline-blasts-reports, consulted 17 August 2024

18   NATO, 'Relations With Ukraine' https://www.nato.int/cps/en/natohq/topics_37750.htm, consulted 23 July 2024

19   *Times of Israel*, 'Erdoğan: Over 1,000 Hamas Members Being Treated in Hospitals in Turkey', *Times of Israel*, 13 May 2024, https://www.timesofisrael.com/liveblog_entry/erdogan-over-1000-hamas-members-being-treated-in-hospitals-in-turkey/#:~:text=Turkish%20President%20Tayyip%20Erdogan%20says%20that%20more%20than%201,000, consulted 1 October 2024; Walsh, Aoife, 'Turkey Halts Trade With Israel Over "Humanitarian Tragedy" in Gaza', *BBC News*, 3 May 2024, https://www.bbc.co.uk/news/world-middle-east-68945380#:~:text=Turkey%20has%20suspended%20all%20trade%20with%20Israel%20over,countries%20was%20worth%20almost%20%247bn%20%28%C2%A35.6bn%29%20last%20year

20   *France24*, 'NATO Member Turkey Says "Process Is Under Way" To Join BRICS Nations', *France24*, 3 September 2024, https://www.

france24.com/en/asia-pacific/20240903-nato-member-turkey-seeks-to-join-brics-nations-says-process-is-under-way, consulted 3 December 2024

21 *Sky News*, 'Russia's invasion of Ukraine Mapped – What Happened on Day Seven', *Sky News*, 2 March 2022, https://news.sky.com/story/russias-invasion-of-ukraine-mapped-what-happened-on-day-seven-12555754, consulted 1 December 2024

22 Ernst, Iulian, 'Moldova Rejects Ukraine's Offer to Seize Transnistria', *bne News*, 28 April 2022, https://www.intellinews.com/moldova-rejects-ukraine-s-offer-to-seize-transnistria-242742/, consulted 2 December 2024

23 Greenall, Robert, 'Transnistria: Ukraine Denies Attempt on Moldova Separatist Leader', *BBC News*, 9 March 2023, https://www.bbc.co.uk/news/world-europe-64901605, consulted 1 December 2024

24 Turak, Natasha, '"Drone Wall" Against Russia: Six NATO Countries Announce Border Defense [*sic*] Plan', *CNBC*, 27 May 2024, https://www.cnbc.com/2024/05/27/russia-drone-wall-six-nato-countries-announce-border-defense-plan.html, consulted 1 August 2024

25 *Notes From Poland*, 'NATO Chief Rejects Polish Proposal to Shoot Down Russian Missiles Over Ukraine', *Notes From Poland*, 15 July 2024, https://notesfrompoland.com/2024/07/15/nato-chief-rejects-polish-proposal-to-shoot-down-russian-missiles-over-ukraine/, consulted 1 August 2024

26 Beale, Jonathan, 'Rogue Russian Pilot Tried to Shoot Down RAF Aircraft in 2022', *BBC News*, 19 September 2023, https://www.bbc.co.uk/news/uk-66798508, consulted 5 August 2024

27 NATO, 'NATO Intercepted Russian Military Aircraft Over 300 Times in 2023', https://www.nato.int/cps/en/natohq/news_221598.htm?selectedLocale=en, consulted 5 August 2024

28 Parker, Jessica and Gozzi, Laura, 'Ukraine War: Germany Under Pressure to Explain Intercepted Phone Call', *BBC News*, 4 March 2024, https://www.bbc.co.uk/news/world-europe-68467329, consulted 5 August 2024

29 Barnes, Joe and Rothwell, James, 'British Soldiers Helping Fire Ukrainian Missiles, Olaf Scholz Reveals', *The Telegraph*, 28 February 2024, https://www.telegraph.co.uk/world-news/2024/02/28/british-soldiers-help-ukraine-fire-missiles-olaf-scholz/, consulted 14 May 2025

30 Pelham, Lipika and Newton, Lou, 'Nato Allies Reject Emmanuel Macron Idea of Troops to Ukraine' https://www.bbc.co.uk/news/world-europe-68417223 consulted 05/08/2024

31 Entous, Adam, 'The Secret History of the Ukraine War', *The New York Times*, 29 March 2025, https://archive.ph/0oEnY#selection-3735.293-37, consulted 30 March 2025

32   *The New York Times*, 'Leaked Pentagon Documents Reveal Secrets About Friends and Foes', *The New York Times*, 8 April 2023, https://www.nytimes.com/explain/2023/russia-ukraine-war-documents-leak consulted 20 July 2024

33   Special Operations Forces of the Armed Forces of Ukraine, 'North Korean Troops Went on the Assault: SSO Destroyed 18 Fighters in Kurshchyna' https://t.me/ukr_sof/1370, consulted 10 March 2025

34   Jung Chul-hwan. 'Exclusive: Captured North Korean Soldiers Speak Out on Deployment to Russia', *Chosun*, 19 February 2025, https://www.chosun.com/english/north-korea-en/2025/02/19/2TUJ44HQBVGJNJF EA6XD2A4IPU/, consulted 10 March 2025

35   *Kyiv Independent*, 'Ukrainian Soldiers on Capturing North Korean POW' https://www.youtube.com/watch?v=mCjbEm63POo, consulted 10 March 2025

Chapter Four: The Significance of the Media and Propaganda During the Ukrainian War

36   Lukov, Yaroslav and Murphy, Matt, 'Mariupol: Hundreds of Besieged Ukrainian Soldiers Evacuated' https://www.bbc.co.uk/news/world-europe-61472025, consulted 12 August 2024

37   Haynes, Deborah, 'UK Defence Secretary Ben Wallace's "We Are Not Amazon" Jibe at Ukraine a Real Warning About the Risk of War Fatigue', *Sky News*, 13 July 2023, https://news.sky.com/story/uk-defence-secretary-ben-wallaces-we-are-not-amazon-jibe-at-ukraine-a-real-warning-about-the-risk-of-war-fatigue-12920142, consulted 12 August 2024

38   Lillis, Katie B., 'Newly Declassified US Intel Claims Russia is Laundering Propaganda Through Unwitting Westerners', *CNN News*, 26 August 2023, https://edition.cnn.com/2023/08/25/politics/us-intel-russia-propaganda/index.html, consulted 12 August 2024 and Barnes, Julian E., 'Russia Pushes Long-Term Influence Operations Aimed at the US and Europe', *The New York Times*, 25 August 2023, https://www.nytimes.com/2023/08/25/us/politics/russia-intelligence-propaganda.html, consulted 12 August 2024 and Geissler, Dominique Bar, Dominik, Prollochs, Nicolas and Feurriegel, Stefan, 'Russian Propaganda on Social Media During the 2022 Invasion of Ukraine', *EPJ Data Science*, 12:35 (2023), consulted 12 August 2024

Chapter Five: The CSTO: The Testament of Allies

39   Mackinnon, Amy, 'Belarus Is Abducting Ukrainian Children in Plain Sight', *Foreign Policy*, 11 August 2023, https://foreignpolicy.com/2023/08/11/belarus-abducting-deporting-ukrainian-children-social-media-networks-kyiv-minsk-camps-russia-war-donbas/, consulted 13 August 2024

40   *Radio Free Europe*, 'Wagner Troops In Belarus "Want To Go West" Into Poland, Lukashenka Quips During Meeting With Putin', *Radio Free Europe*, 23 July 2023, https://www.rferl.org/a/putin-lukashenka-wager-poland/32515408.html, consulted 17 August 2024

41   *Radio Free Europe*, 'Kazakh President Assures Germany His Country Follows Sanctions Regime Against Russia' https://www.rferl.org/a/kazakhstan-germany-sanctions-regime-russia/32614735.html, consulted 20 August 2024

42   Suciu, Peter, 'The US Military Just Bought 81 Russian Jets (MiG-29 Fighters and Su-24 Bombers)', *National Interest*, 29 April 2024, https://nationalinterest.org/blog/buzz/us-military-just-bought-81-russian-jets-mig-29-fighters-and-su-24-bombers-210806, consulted 20 August 2024; and Rommen, Rebecca and Spirlet, Thibault, 'US Buys 81 Soviet-Era Combat Aircraft From Russia's Ally Costing on Average Less Than $20,000 Each, Report Says', *Business Insider*, 29 April 2024, https://www.businessinsider.com/us-buys-81-soviet-fighter-jets-from-russian-ally-20k-2024 4#:~:text=US%20buys%2081%20Soviet%2Dera,than%20%2420%2C000%20each%2C%20report%20says&text=The%20US%20has%20purchased%2081,engaging%20more%20with%20Western%20nations, consulted 20 August 2024

43   de Waal, Thomas, *Black Garden: Armenia and Azerbaijan Through Peace and War* (New York University Press, New York, US, 2013), p.47

44   Birch, J., 'Border Disputes and Disputed Borders: Border Disputes and Disputed Borders in in the Soviet Federal System' Nationalities Papers, 15:8, (1987), p.51

45   de Waal, Thomas, *Black Garden*, p.39

46   *Reuters*, 'Armenia's PM: "We are not Russia's ally" in war against Ukraine' https://www.reuters.com/world/europe/armenias-pm-we-are-not-russias-ally-war-against-ukraine-2024-02-11/, consulted 21 March 2024

47   Sharma, Ritu, 'Against Azerbaijan as Russia Gets Bogged Down in Ukraine War', *Eurasian Times*, 9 October 2023, https://www.eurasiantimes.com/france-joins-india-to-arm-armenia-against-azerbaijan/, consulted 13 December 2024

48   Karimli, Ilham, 'Azerbaijani, Kazakh Presidents Watch China-Azerbaijan Container Train Arrival', *Caspian News*, 13 March 2024, https://caspiannews.com/news-detail/azerbaijani-kazakh-presidents-watch-china-azerbaijan-container-train-arrival-2024-3-12-0/, consulted 21 March 2024

49   https://understandingwar.org/research/russia-ukraine/russian-offensive-campaign-assessment_2-15/

50   Barseghyan, Arshaluys, 'Armenia Sending Three Citizens Accused of Organising Coup Attempt to Court', *OC News*, 27 February 2025, https://oc-media.org/armenia-sending-three-citizens-accused-of-organising-coup-attempt-to-court/, consulted 9 May 2025

51   Barseghyan, Arshaluys, 'Armenian Parliamentary Speaker Says Russia
     Is Waging "A Hybrid War" Against Armenia', *OC News*, 6 May 2025,
     https://oc-media.org/armenian-parliamentary-speaker-says-russia-is-
     waging-a-hybrid-war-against-armenia/, consulted 9 May 2025

52   Court, Elsa, 'Moscow Issues Protest Note to Yerevan After Armenian
     Delegation Visits Bucha', *Kyiv Independent*, 9 June 2024, https://
     kyivindependent.com/moscow-issues-protest-note-to-yerevan-after-
     armenian-delegation-visits-bucha/#:~:text=Russia's%20Foreign%20
     Ministry%20issued%20a,TASS%20reported%20on%20June%209,
     consulted 6 August 2024

53   de Waal, Thomas, 'The Nagorny-Karabagh Conflict in Its Fourth
     Decade' in de Waal, Thomas and Twickel, Nikolaus von, and Emerson,
     Michael (ed.), *Beyond Frozen Conflict: Scenarios for the Separatist Disputes
     of Eastern Europe* (Rowman and Littlefield International, London, 2020),
     pp.217–222

Chapter Six: The African Monopoly

54   Binley, Alex and Beale, Jonathan, '43,000 Troops Killed in War With
     Russia, Zelensky Says', *BBC News*, 8 December 2024, https://www.bbc.
     co.uk/news/articles/c5yv75nydy3o, consulted 18 December 2024

55   Camut, Nicolas, 'Russia Strikes Kyiv Amid Visit by African Leaders on
     Peace Mission', *Politico*, 16 June 2023, https://www.politico.eu/article/
     russia-strike-kyiv-africa-leader-visit-ukraine-war/, consulted 30 April
     2024

56   *ABC News*, 'Russia Destroys 13,000 Tonnes of Ukrainian Grain
     Destined for Egypt and Romania', *ABC News*, 23 August 2023, https://
     www.abc.net.au/news/2023-08-23/russia-attacks-ukraine-port-and-
     school/102768324, consulted 5 May 2024

57   Farmer, Ben, 'UAE Using Wagner Fighters to Smuggle Weapons Into
     Sudan', *The Telegraph*, 14 September 2024, https://www.telegraph.
     co.uk/world-news/2024/09/14/uae-wagner-group-fighters-weapons-
     sudanese-civil-war/, consulted 29 March 2025

58   *Reuters*, 'Ukraine Evacuates 138 Civilians From Sudan', *Reuters*, 25
     April 2023, https://www.reuters.com/world/ukraine-evacuates-138-
     civilians-sudan-2023-04-25/, consulted 7 March 2024

59   Zakharchenko, Kateryna, 'Khartoum Gave Weapons to Kyiv So
     Zelensky Sent Ukrainian Special Forces to Sudan', *Kyiv Post*, 6 March
     2024, https://www.kyivpost.com/post/29106 consulted 7 March 2024

60   Elbagir, Nima, Mezzofiore, Gianluca, Qiblawi, Tamara and Arvanitidis,
     Barbara, 'Exclusive: Evidence Emerges of Russia's Wagner Arming
     Militia Leader Battling Sudan's Army', *CNN News*, 21 April 2023,
     https://edition.cnn.com/2023/04/20/africa/wagner-sudan-russia-
     libya-intl/index.html, consulted 7 March 2024; Lovett, Ian, 'Ukraine

Is Now Fighting Russia in Sudan', *Wall Street Journal*, 6 March 2024, https://www.wsj.com/world/ukraine-is-now-fighting-russia-in-sudan-87caf1d8, consulted 5 December 2024

61   Zakharchenko, Kateryna, 'Khartoum Gave Weapons to Kyiv so Zelensky Sent Ukrainian Special Forces to Sudan', *Kyiv Post*, 6 March 2024, https://www.kyivpost.com/post/29106, consulted 7 March 2024

62   Butenko, Victoria, Elbagir, Nima, Mezzofiore, Gianluca, Qiblawi, Tamara, Goodwin, Allegra, Carey, Andrew, Munsi, Pallabi, Zene, Mahamat Tahir, Arvanitidis, Barbara and Platt, Alex, 'Exclusive: Ukraine's Special Services 'Likely' Behind Strikes on Wagner-Backed Forces in Sudan, a Ukrainian Military Source Says', *CNN News*, 20 September 2023, https://edition.cnn.com/2023/09/19/africa/ukraine-military-sudan-wagner-cmd-intl/index.html, consulted 7 March 2024

63   Khrebet, Alexander, 'Zelensky Discusses Russia-Backed Groups With Sudan's Leader During Unplanned Meeting', *Kyiv Independent*, 23 September 2023, https://kyivindependent.com/zelensky-discusses-russia-backed-groups-with-sudans-leader-after-reported-ukrainian-attack-on-wagner/, consulted 7 March 2024

64   *Clash Report*, 'Video footage confirms presence of Ukrainian special forces in Sudan. Ukrainian special forces conduct operations in Sudan against the Russian Wagner PMC and their local allies from the Rapid Support Forces (RSF), who tried to stage a *coup d'état* in April.', X (Twitter), 6 October 2023, https://x.com/clashreport/status/1710241167751671844?ref_src=twsrc%5Etfw%7Ctwcamp%5Etweetembed%7Ctwterm%5E1710241167751671844%7Ctwgr%5E536d6cb1ecf01b0d96aedcc0df4a0ac9fb960d12%7Ctwcon%5Es1_&ref_url=https%3A%2F%2Fwww.bellingcat.com%2Fnews%2F2023%2F10%2F07%2Fexamining-videos-of-suspected-ukrainian-riflemen-in-sudan%2F, consulted 7 March 2024

65   *Kyiv Post*, 'EXCLUSIVE: Ukrainian Drone Footage Shows 'Destruction of Russian Mercenaries' in Sudan', https://www.youtube.com/watch?v=ekPM08w0WYI, consulted 7 March 2024

66   Zakharchenko, Kateryna, 'Khartoum Gave Weapons to Kyiv So Zelensky Sent Ukrainian Special Forces to Sudan', *Kyiv Post*, 6 March 2024, https://www.kyivpost.com/post/29106, consulted 7 March 2024

67   Militarnyi, 'Details of the Defense Intelligence of Ukraine Operation in Sudan Have Been Reported', *Militarnyi*, 7 March 2024, https://mil.in.ua/en/news/details-of-the-defense-intelligence-of-ukraine-operation-in-sudan-have-been-reported/, consulted 7 March 2024

68   Thomas Guien, 'DOCUMENT LCI – *L'Ukraine combat la Russie en Afrique: les dessous d'une opération longtemps secrète*', *TFI Info*, 21 March 2024, https://www.tf1info.fr/international/video-document-lci-comment-l-ukraine-combat-la-russie-et-wagner-en-afrique-2290212.html, consulted 1 April 2024

69   Rickett, Oscar and Amin, Mohammed, 'Sudan War: Russia Hedges Bets by Aiding Both Sides in Conflict', *Middle East Eye*, May 6 2024, https://www.middleeasteye.net/news/russia-sudan-war-saf-rsf-hedges-bets-both-sides-support, consulted 1 March 2025

70   Schipani, Andres, Miller, Christopher, Ivanova, Polina and Cook, Chris, 'Russians and Ukrainians Help Train Same Side in Sudan's War', *Financial Times*, 17 September 2024, https://www.ft.com/content/e581fc02-ef80-4a00-bdf1-1be4b5e0a916, consulted 1 March 2025

71   *Al-Jazeera*, 'Niger Becomes Hotbed of Disinformation After July 26 Coup', *Al-Jazeera*, 18 August 2023, https://www.aljazeera.com/news/2023/8/18/niger-becomes-hotbed-of-disinformation-after-july-26-coup, consulted 25 March 2024

72   Benoit Facoun, 'US Intelligence Points to Wagner Plot Against Key Western Ally in Africa', *Wall Street Journal*, 23 February 2023, https://www.wsj.com/articles/u-s-intelligence-points-to-wagner-plot-against-key-western-ally-in-africa-29867547, consulted 30 December 2024

Chapter Seven: Syria: The Land of Proxy Wars

73   Naranjo, José and Gutiérrez, Óscar, 'The US Is Losing Its Battle in the Sahel as Chad Joins Niger in Demanding Withdrawal of Military Personnel', *EL Pais*, April 29 2024, https://english.elpais.com/international/2024-04-29/the-us-is-losing-its-battle-in-the-sahel-as-chad-joins-niger-in-demanding-withdrawal-of-military-personnel.html, consulted 1 December 2024

74   *BBC Verify* found the Ukrainian Main Directorate's photo evidence to be a fake, https://www.bbc.co.uk/news/articles/cq5xvl1111yo

75   Schogol, Jeff, 'Russian Fighter Jets Have Harassed US Forces in Syria Nearly 100 Times in 2 Months', https://taskandpurpose.com/news/russian-pilots-aggressive-us-aircraft-troops-syria/, consulted 11 May 2024

76   *Reuters*, 'Russia Says Military Plane Exposed to Coalition F-16s Guidance Systems Over Syria, TASS Reports', *Reuters*, 20 July 2023, https://www.reuters.com/world/russia-says-military-plane-exposed-coalition-f-16s-guidance-systems-over-syria-2023-07-20/, consulted 11 May 2024

77   *Al-Jazerra*, https://www.aljazeera.com/news/2023/7/15/us-to-send-f-16-fighter-jets-to-gulf-amid-iran-shipping-tensions

78   Hill, Evan and Horton, Alex, 'Ukraine Planned Attacks on Russian Forces in Syria, Leaked Document Shows', *The Washington Post*, 20 April 2023, https://www.washingtonpost.com/national-security/2023/04/20/russia-ukraine-war-syria-attacks/, consulted 16 April 2025

79   *Enab Baladi*, 'Russia Establishes Third Military Post on Borders of Occupied Golan Heights', *Enab Baladi*, 2 April 2024, https://english. enabbaladi.net/archives/2024/04/russia-establishes-third-military-post-on-borders-of-occupied-golan-heights/, consulted 6 April 2024

80   Zakharchenko, Kateryna, 'EXCLUSIVE VIDEO: Ukrainian Special Forces and Syrian Rebels Decimate Russian Mercenaries in Syria', *Kyiv Post*, 3 June 2024, https://www.kyivpost.com/post/33695, consulted 4 June 2024

81   *Times of Israel*, 'Zelensky Hails "Positive Trend" in Israel Ties After Intel Sharing on Iranian Drones', https://www.timesofisrael.com/zelensky-hails-positive-trend-in-israel-ties-after-intel-sharing-on-iranian-drones/, consulted 20 July 2024

82   Zakharchenko, Kateryna, 'EXCLUSIVE: Ukraine's HUR Special Forces Target Russian Drone Base in Syria', *Kyiv Post*, 16 September 2024, https://www.kyivpost.com/post/39074, consulted 19 September 2024

83   Zakharchenko, Kateryna, 'Russian Forces Suffer Major Losses in Syria, Commander Fired as Hundreds Go Missing', *Kyiv Post*, 1 December 2024, https://www.kyivpost.com/post/43128, consulted 6 December 2024

84   *Reuters*, 'Ukrainian Operatives Aided Syrian Rebels With Drones, *The Washington Post* Reports', *Reuters*, 11 December 2024, https://www. reuters.com/world/ukrainian-operatives-aided-syrian-rebels-with-drones-washington-post-reports-2024-12-11/, consulted 11 December 2024

85   *Reuters*, 'US Secretary of State Nominee Blinken Says Turkey Not Acting Like an Ally', *Reuters*, 20 January 2021, https://www.reuters.com/business/aerospace-defense/us-secretary-state-nominee-blinken-says-turkey-not-acting-like-an-ally-2021-01-20/, consulted 11 May 2024

86   *Middle East Eye*, 'Syria: US-Backed SDF "Open" to Working with Syrian Troops to Fight Off Turkey Invasion', *Middle East Eye*, 5 June 2022, https://www.middleeasteye.net/news/syria-sdf-open-working-syrian-troops-fight-turkey-invasion, consulted 12 May 2024

87   *Al-Monitor*, 'Pentagon Floats Plan for Its Syrian Kurd Allies to Partner With Assad Against ISIS', *Al-Monitor*, 26 January 2024, https://www. al-monitor.com/originals/2024/01/pentagon-floats-plan-its-syrian-kurd-allies-partner-assad-against-isis, consulted 15 April 2024

88   Fabian, Emanuel, 'IDF Strikes Syria After Rocket Attack on North; 8 Syrian Soldiers Said Killed', *Times of Israel*, 25 October 2023, https://www.timesofisrael.com/idf-strikes-syria-after-rocket-attack-on-north-8-syrian-soldiers-said-killed/, consulted 16 April 2024

89   *Kyiv Post*, 'Russia Sends Interpreters and Mercenaries From Africa to Support Troops in Syria', *Kyiv Post*, 3 December 2024, https://www. kyivpost.com/post/43219, consulted 30 December 2024

90   Bromfield, Adrain, 'US Prepared Syrian Rebel Group to Help Topple Bashar al-Assad', *The Telegraph*, 18 December 2024, https://web.archive. org/web/20241218220120/https://www.telegraph.co.uk/world-news/2024/12/18/us-prepared-syrian-rebel-group-to-help-topple-bashar-assad/, consulted 21 December 2024

Chapter Eight: Iran and the Axis of Resistance

91   *MEMO: Middle Eastern Monitor*, 'Saudi Arabia Prevented US Using Its Territories Strike Houthis, Official Says', *MEMO: Middle Eastern Monitor*, 22 March 2024, https://www.middleeastmonitor.com/20240322-saudi-arabia-prevented-us-using-its-territories-strike-houthis-official-says/, consulted 24 March 2024

92   Lazaroff, Tovah, 'US Trying to Overthrow Netanyahu's Government, Senior Israeli Official Says', *Times of Israel*, 12 March 2024, https://www. jpost.com/israel-news/article-791654, consulted 7 April 2024

93   *Reuters*, 'Yemen's Houthis Chief: Operations With Islamic Resistance in Iraq Against Israel Will intensify', *Reuters*, 6 June 2024, https://www. reuters.com/world/middle-east/yemens-houthis-chief-operations-with-islamic-resistance-iraq-against-israel-will-2024-06-06/, consulted 8 July 2024

94   Berman, Lazar, 'Egypt, Qatar: Strikes in Beirut and Tehran Harm Hostage Talks; Blinken: Ceasefire Vital', *Times of Israel*, 31 July 2024, https:// www.timesofisrael.com/egypt-qatar-strikes-in-beirut-and-tehran-harm-hostage-talks-blinken-ceasefire-vital/, consulted 31 July 2024

95   Evans, Gareth, 'Biden: "I Don't Know" If Netanyahu Is Trying to Sway US Election', *BBC News*, 5 October 2024, https://www.bbc.co.uk/news/articles/cje3zl0dq2ko, consulted 6 October 2024

96   *Times of Israel*, 'Netanyahu Says IDF Found "State-of-the-Art" Russian Arms in Hezbollah Bases', *Times of Israel*, 16 October 2024, https:// www.timesofisrael.com/liveblog_entry/netanyahu-says-idf-found-state-of-the-art-russian-arms-in-hezbollah-bases/, consulted 27 October 2024

97   Ganzeveld, Annika, Moore, Johanna, Braverman, Alexandra, Moorman, Carolyn, Rezaei, Ben, Campa, Kelly, Carillo, Anthony and Carl, Nicholas, 'Iran Update, October 25, 2024', *Institute for the Study of War*, 25 October 2025, https://www.understandingwar.org/backgrounder/iran-update-october-25-2024, consulted 27 October 2024

98   Bertrand, Natasha and Lilli, Katie Bo, 'Russia Pulled Back Weapons Shipment to Houthis Amid US and Saudi Pressure', *CNN News*, 2 August 2024, https://edition.cnn.com/2024/08/02/politics/russia-weapons-houthis-saudi-arabia/index.html, consulted 19 March 2025

99   *Al-Jazeera*, 'Freed Russian Arms Dealer Viktor Bout Back in Business: Report', *Al-Jazeera*, 7 October 2024, https://www.aljazeera.com/

news/2024/10/7/freed-russian-arms-dealer-viktor-bout-back-in-business-report, consulted 11October 2024

100   Raghavan, Sudarsan, al-Batati, Saleh and Faucon, Benoit, 'US Accuses China of Helping the Houthis Target Their Attacks', *Wall Street Journal*, 18 April 2025, https://www.wsj.com/world/middle-east/u-s-accuses-china-of-helping-the-houthis-target-their-attacks-e56264da, consulted 14 May 2025

Chapter Nine: Dramas in the Far East

101   Lariosa, Aaron-Matthew, 'UPDATED: Chinese Spy Ships Stalk US, Philippine and French Warships in South China Sea', US Naval Institute, 29 April 2024, https://news.usni.org/2024/04/29/chinese-spy-ship-live-stalks-u-s-philippine-and-french-warships-in-south-china-sea-interrupts-live-fire-drill#:~:text=U.S.%2C%20Philippine%2C%20and%20French%20amphibs,Manila's%20largest%20annual%20military%20exercise, consulted 6 May 2024

Chapter Ten: The United States in the Age of Conspiracy Theories and Political Extremism

102   Inessa, S., 'Men in Dark Suits Rule the US – Putin on Deep State' https://www.youtube.com/watch?v=XP3D1sUSuzg, consulted 19 September 2024

103   *Scottish Sun, The*, 'Scots Mercenary Fighting for Vladimir Putin in Ukraine Unmasked as Former Tennent's Brewery Worker' https://www.youtube.com/watch?v=c2fiQtzIgbM consulted 29/11/24; *Times, The* and *Sunday Times, The*, 'US Serviceman Fights for Russia in Ukraine', https://www.youtube.com/watch?v=HjRLWSEFlTk, consulted 29 November 2024

104   Biden, President Joe, 'Remarks by President Biden and President Zelenskyy of Ukraine in Joint Press Conference', https://www.whitehouse.gov/briefing-room/speeches-remarks/2023/12/13/remarks-by-president-biden-and-president-zelenskyy-of-ukraine-in-joint-press-conference-2/, consulted 27 September 2024

Chapter Eleven: Enter Trump

105   *Reuters*, 'Trump Limits Kellogg's Role to Ukraine Envoy After Russian Complaints', *Reuters*, 15 March 2025, https://www.reuters.com/world/us/trump-limits-kelloggs-role-ukraine-envoy-after-russian-complaints-2025-03-15/, consulted 19 April 2025

106   LiveNOW from FOX, 'FULL: President Trump Meets with British PM Starmer', https://www.youtube.com/watch?v=-QEck-mlFoE, consulted 2 March 2025

107 Carlson, Tucker, 'Tucker Carlson Live Tour Grand Finale With President Donald Trump LIVE in Glendale, AZ', https://www.youtube.com/watch?v=9J0cdq_0SPE, consulted 17 April 2025

108 Danish Defence, 'Comment on Danish media story about "Danish soldiers to Ukraine"', Danish Defence, 16 April 2025, https://www.forsvaret.dk/en/news/2025/comment-on-danish-media-story/, consulted 2 May 2025

109 Jorge Liboreiro, 'EU Pauses Retaliatory Tariffs against US to "Give Negotiations a Chance"', *Euronews*, 10 April 2025, https://www.euronews.com/my-europe/2025/04/10/eu-pauses-retaliatory-tariffs-against-us-to-give-negotiations-a-chance, consulted 12 May 2025; Lanktree, Graham and Weizman, Jakob, 'Trump's Trade War Pushes EU Toward Pacific Free Traders', *Politico*, 11 May 2025, https://www.politico.eu/article/donald-trump-trade-war-eu-pacific-free-traders/, consulted 12 May 2025

110 FOX 9 Minneapolis-St Paul, 'President Trump "Wants to Be Remembered as a "Peacemaker"', https://www.youtube.com/watch?v=PjY6sfWzykU, consulted 13 March 2025

111 Carlson, Tucker, 'Steve Witkoff's Critical Role in Negotiating Global Peace, and the Warmongers Trying to Stop Him', https://www.youtube.com/watch?v=acvu2LBumGo, consulted 22 March 2025

112 Stone, Mark, 'Trump Envoy Steve Witkoff Says He Has Developed a "Friendship" With Putin', *Sky News*, 21 February 2025, https://news.sky.com/story/trump-envoy-steve-witkoff-says-he-has-developed-a-friendship-with-putin-13313676, consulted 22 May 2025

113 Banco, Erin, Slattery, Gram and Pamuk, Humeyra, 'Trump Envoy's Embrace of Russian Demands Worries Republicans, US Allies', *Reuters*, 11 April 2025, https://www.reuters.com/world/trump-envoys-embrace-russian-demands-worries-republicans-us-allies-2025-04-11/, consulted 19 April 2025

114 Ahmadi, Ali Abbas, 'Trump Administration Withdraws From Russian War Crime Investigations', *BBC*, 19 March 2025, https://www.bbc.co.uk/news/articles/c0rzygdn8w2o, consulted 19 April 2025

INDEX